AF760931

A Place Called Teesside

Other titles published with Durham University:

J. Britnell
JEAN BOUCHET

Richard A. Chapman
PUBLIC POLICY
The North East of England

Roy Davies
SERVICE IN THE ROMAN ARMY
Edited by D. Breeze and V. Maxwell

Gary Ferguson
MIRRORING BELIEF
Marguerite de Navarre's Devotional Poetry

Peter Lewis
FIELDING'S BURLESQUE DRAMA

Christopher Lloyd
J.-K. HUYSMANS AND THE FIN-DE-SIECLE NOVEL

Ian Roberts
CRAFT, CLASS AND CONTROL
The Sociology of a Shipbuilding Community

J. R. Watson
AN INFINITE COMPLEXITY
Essays in Romanticism

A PLACE CALLED TEESSIDE:
A Locality in a Global Economy

HUW BEYNON, RAY HUDSON
and DAVID SADLER

Published by Edinburgh University Press for
THE UNIVERSITY OF DURHAM

© Huw Beynon, Ray Hudson and David Sadler, 1994

Edinburgh University Press Ltd
22, George Square, Edinburgh

Typeset in Linotron Palatino
by Koinonia Ltd, Bury, and
printed in Great Britain by Hartnoll's Ltd, Bodmin

A CIP record for this book is available from the British Library

ISBN 0 7486 0468 5

Contents

List of Tables and Figures

TABLES

FIGURES

Preface

The immediate origins of this book lie in research that we carried out between 1985 and 1987 as part of the UK Economic and Social Research Council's 'Changing Urban and Regional Systems' (CURS) initiative (grant no. D04250018). Our study of Teesside was one of seven studies of English localities, along with a national overview (see Cooke, 1989; for a restatement of the programme's original objectives, see Massey, 1991). Our interest in Teesside did not, however, begin with the ESRC initiative; nor did it end with it. We had, for some time, been studying the social processes relating to change in the coal, chemicals and steel industries in North-east England (for example, see Beynon *et. al.*, 1991; Hudson, 1989a; Sadler, 1992) and continue to do so within the context of industrial restructuring and the refashioning of old industrial regions within Europe. The ESRC project allowed us to examine, more fully, questions relating to the social construction of place and locality within one particular area in North-east England.

In 1985 Teesside seemed to offer a very appropriate area in which to explore some of the main concerns of the ESRC programme. The way in which it had been built as a place (economically, politically and socially) around the locally dominant chemicals and steel industries over a period of a century and a half offered one particularly clear illustration of relationships between global processes of accumulation and restructuring and local change. Teesside also offered an interesting location because of the way in which national state strategies and regional and subregional modernisation policies intersected there, particularly during the 1960s. Furthermore, modernisation lay at the heart of a powerful cross-class consensus based on the place that had already promoted the interests of the area for over half a century. In some respects at least social action was grounded in a shared attachment to place. Moreover, Teesside was not immune from the pressures of de-industrialisation in the 1970s and 1980s, which began to undermine the bases of the consensus formed around 'modernisation' and to raise questions as to how both the coalition and the place could adapt and react to changing circumstances. Viewed from both a short- and a long-term perspective, Teesside offered a clearly focused and potentially enlightening case of the linkages between processes of economic, political and social differentiation at local, national and global scales.

As our research progressed we reported our findings in a series of project *Working Papers* (see Beynon *et al.*, 1985, 1986; Hudson, 1986; Hudson and Sadler, 1985; Sadler, 1986; Townsend, 1986). We have drawn heavily on these in parts of this book and also in other publications deriving from this research (including Beynon, *et al.*, 1989, 1991; Beynon and Hudson, 1991, 1993; Hudson, 1989a, 1989b, 1990b; Sadler, 1990b).

As with all books, this one has involved more people than just its authors, so we wish to acknowledge the assistance given to us by others. Our work on the Middlesbrough Locality Project was carried out collaboratively with two other colleagues in Durham, Alan Townsend and Jim Lewis. In warmly acknowledging their contribution to the project (some of which we draw upon here), we do not necessarily implicate them in our interpretation of change on Teesside. Nevertheless, we hope they agree with most of it. We are also very grateful to Frank Coffield, who read the entire manuscript and made helpful comments – again we absolve him from any blame as to the use we made of them. Cleveland County Council provided financial support for earlier research on the steel industry, and members of Cleveland County Council's Research and Intelligence Unit provided valuable help and information at various times, as did the staff of the National On-Line Manpower Information System within the Department of Geography at Durham University. This is again gratefully acknowledged though again we absolve them from any responsibility for interpretations that we have put on information supplied. The interviews which we draw upon were largely conducted by the authors. Where this is not the case we have indicated the source and we are grateful to all those who assisted us in this way. Finally, but by no means least, we gratefully acknowledge the help of the secretarial and technical staff in the Department of Geography at Durham University; in particular of Joan Dresser, who is no doubt glad to see this particular project brought to an end.

Huw Beynon, Manchester
Ray Hudson, Durham
David Sadler, Durham

CHAPTER ONE

Teesside: In the North but not Of the North

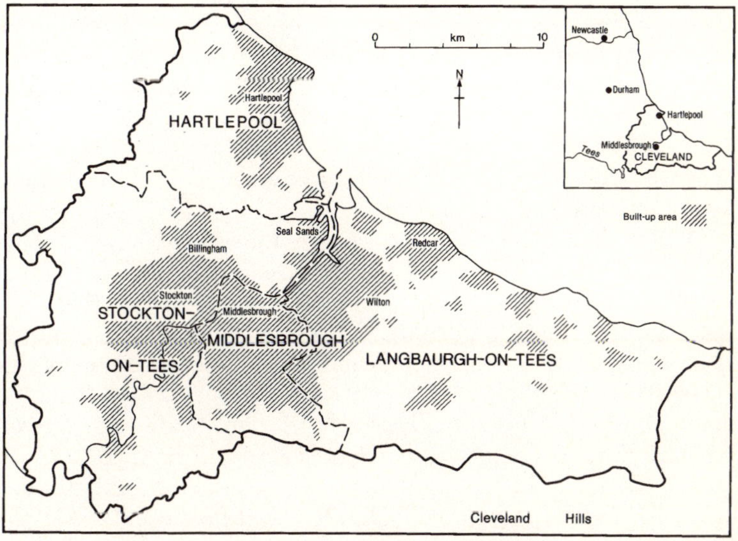

FIGURE 1.1: Location of Teesside.

1. INTRODUCTION

During the 1980s the economy of Teesside (see Figure 1.1)[1] was characterised by recession, job loss and unemployment. Teesside was by no means alone in suffering in this way but the impacts of industrial decline were felt particularly keenly there. As factories closed their gates for the last time, and those remaining open shed employment, a growing tide of redundancies threatened to emulate (if not quite surpass) the economic crisis of the last great recession in the 1920s and 1930s. Registered unemployment rates in Cleveland County at times exceeded 20 per cent – they were among the highest in the UK – and Teesside faced some of the most deep-rooted structural economic problems in the country, with particularly grave social consequences. Like many other areas affected by the ravages of domestic recession, international competitive pressure and national political strategy, Teesside became the focus of a sweeping array of policy responses. These ranged from the creative manipulation of unemployment statistics (and what were, to the individual inadequate, but in aggregate very considerable, state transfer payments to those still 'officially' unemployed), to measures such as retraining schemes and financial incentives for the creation of new businesses. The policy initiative with deepest symbolic significance, however, was the designation in 1987 of a new tier of non-elected administrative authority – an Urban Development Corporation (UDC) appointed by central government – charged with land reclamation and economic renewal. This was a further indication of the severity of the region's crisis, for Teesside acquired UDC status along with a limited number of other 'problem' areas. Significantly, too, the Teesside Development Corporation covered by far the largest deindustrialised land area of all UDCs.

Whilst the economic prognosis in the mid-1980s was bad enough in itself, it seemed even worse because of a marked contrast with previous highly optimistic forecasts. In the mid-1960s, Teesside had appeared to be set for a new period of rapid economic growth. To an extent, such development did take place, massively underpinned by government regional policy expenditures. During the 1970s the area around the Tees became one of Western Europe's biggest construction sites and claimed to be its most dynamic industrial centre. In 1977 gross domestic product (GDP) per caput in Cleveland County stood fourth in the league table of counties ranked by this measure (Cleveland County Council, 1988a). The contrast by the mid-1980s could not be more acute. Total employment had fallen by more than one-quarter; GDP per caput had declined sharply to stand below the UK average; Cleveland had slipped to seventeenth in the ranking of counties as manufacturing output collapsed. In the words of one of the local authorities, 'the dream had vanished' (Cleveland County Council, 1985a, p. 1).

At the same time and in its place a new vision of the future was emerging in Teesside. As in other parts of Mrs Thatcher's Britain, this involved permanent jobs for life being replaced by precarious jobs in a flexible labour market. For some, this was the bright new future; for others, it was a return to discredited and formerly discarded employment practices. This change of emphasis was reflected in academic and political debates on interpretations of the meaning of the 'flexibility of labour'. These ranged from

Utopian accounts of enriched employee satisfaction resulting from working in flexibly specialised, high-tech small firms to views of capital reimposing its managerial authority over labour in the cold climate of mass unemployment. It was the latter view which had most salience on Teesside in the 1980s.[2] The re-emergence of mass unemployment was particularly striking. In an area previously characterised by low unemployment and (for many men at least) secure and relatively well-paid jobs, high levels of unemployment (even by the national standards of the day) became almost endemic. Precarious forms of employment through 'off the cards' or casual work (in pubs, clubs and corner shops) was not a new phenomenon on Teesside. Nor was there anything particularly novel about part-time work and sub-contracting between companies. But what was changing, and dramatically so, was the overall extent and relative weight of these different forms of employment. In an area where the dominant chemical and steel employers had come to offer relatively high-waged jobs on contractual terms and conditions that were in many respects progressive from the point of view of labour, the changed labour market climate was both noticeable and resented.

In these ways the recent history of the Teesside area could be interpreted as one instance, severe but not particularly unusual, in a story of regional deindustrialisation in the context of Britain's decline as a major manufacturing power. Yet this is only one part of a fuller explanation of the serious socio-economic problems faced by the area in the 1980s. For Teesside's difficulties were most emphatically not those of a 'classic', 'depressed' or 'old' industrial region dependent on under-capitalised, technologically backward and uncompetitive companies and sectors. Indeed, nothing could be further from the truth: the steel and chemicals industries which formed the mainstay of the local economy received considerable financial investment and the dominant companies -British Steel and Imperial Chemical Industries (ICI) – were among the world leaders in their product ranges. As the County Council recognised and emphasised in 1983: 'the problems of Cleveland are *not* those of the caricature of a depressed area with low productivity, lack of competitiveness, poor industrial relations and a record of low levels of industrial investment' (Cleveland County Council, 1983a, para 1–11, emphasis in original). Whilst Teesside might be *in* the North, it was certainly not *of* the North, and it would be dangerous and wrong to regard it as somehow typical of some Northern malaise.

Such issues are important in their own right, pointing to the dangers inherent in stereotypes of national and regional industrial decline. They also raise other important questions: in particular, how is it that Teesside could have been so dependent and for so long upon such a limited range of industrial activities? What were the preconditions for, and implications of, its dominance by a narrow spectrum of economic interests? Part of the answer to these questions relates to the different and changing ways in which the area was always intimately connected with a global capitalist economy. This had a powerful and pervasive influence, shaping local economy and society. Another part of the answer is linked to the ways in which economic and social activity was secured and held together by different and shifting state policies. Even in a state-managed region, Teesside stands out as a locality in which state policies have taken a particularly decisive role. This is the case not only in relation to the restructuring of production but also in powerfully shaping the settings in which people live their lives.

2. PEOPLE IN PLACE

In the 1970s and 1980s social theorists became increasingly concerned with issues relating to space and place (see, for example, Massey, 1984). Politically, this related to a process whereby the closure and relocation of industrial plants had created localised economic and social crises in the traditional heartlands of industrial capitalism. 'Capital flight' became identified as a major problem for the integrity of places dependent upon industrial jobs (see Bluestone and Harrison, 1982). While in the 1950s and 1960s 'places' had appeared secure in the presence of continuing employment in established and expanding industries, by the 1970s things looked rather different. In the context of growing uncertainty, therefore, people began to ask questions about the future of industrial employment and the places that were dependent upon it. In assessing the character of employment and production, it is evident that in an earlier period of capitalist expansion (one during which labour movements were being formed) industrial capital was deeply embedded in particular places. Places became identified with particular industries – like coal, steel, shipyards etc. – and there was little sense or expectation that this would change. In this early phase, labour appeared more mobile than capital, as people migrated across oceans and continents to work in the new industries. Under contemporary conditions, however, these roles have been reversed, as capital has become increasingly global in scope, often leaving labour stranded in its wake. Of course, not all capitals are equally mobile, and not all working people are equally immobile, but in general this proposition now is a valid one. Locations that, for capital, are a (temporary) space for profitable production are for workers, their families and friends places in which to live; places in which they have considerable individual and collective cultural investment; places to which they are often deeply attached, and which may hold powerful emotional ties and socially endowed symbolic meanings for them. Particularly in the contemporary period, therefore, it may be helpful (terminologically and theoretically) to understand *spaces* as the domain of capital and *places* as the meaningful situations established by people, particularly workers, their families and friends.

Within 'places', people will have different orientations, commitments and understandings. In the 1950s and 1960s sociologists used the terms 'local' and 'cosmopolitan' as a way of differentiating between the orientations of groups who were emotionally and economically attached to one place, and those whose lives involved regular movement from one place to another (see Gouldner, 1967; Stacey, 1969). Similarly, it can be seen that different groups of workers (those with different skills, of different gender[3] or ethnic group) may perceive their attachment to places in very different ways. Nevertheless, for people with a local identity their town or village is not *just* (or, for many, *even*) a space in which to work for a wage.[4] It is a place where they have networks of friends, relatives and acquaintances, where they have learned about life and acquired a cultural frame of reference through which to interpret the social world around them; their place is where they are socialised as people rather than simply reproduced as bearers of the commodity labour power. As a result, people have often become profoundly attached to particular places, which come to have socially endowed and shared meanings which touch on all aspects of their lives, helping shape *who* they are by virtue of *where* they are. Often they are places to which people see themselves 'belonging' and where they have created political and social institutions to which they are attached. However, this process of 'belonging' itself requires analysis and empirical investigation (see Cohen, 1982).

If we move to the domain of space it is clear that we find capitals largely involved in a one-dimensional assessment of localities – these are understood in terms of their capacity to yield profits, and this is demonstrated in the countless questionnaires presented to local development corporations around the world. Driven by the competitive pressures that characterise capitalism, and the policies of national (and emergent supranational) states, investment and disinvestment decisions perpetually relate to a spatial dimension, and this can often pose a deep threat to the integrity of places. Such threats *may* well be contested but attachment to a place is not automatically translated into its defence in a simple mechanistic manner. Indeed, one could argue that grumbling disagreement with, or passive acceptance of, externally generated changes is at least as typical as an active opposition to them.

Unlike that of space, the evaluation of places is multidimensional. Certainly, for many people these locations must yield a monetary income to pay for at least part of the costs of living there and this entails successfully selling their labour power to capitals or, perhaps, to the state. Equally, senior plant or office management (however 'cosmopolitan' in outlook) will have an interest in a particular place, in staying there for a length of time and establishing links with the place and people within it. As one of them put it in the 1960s, when he heard that he was to be moved on: 'they should give you longer than two years in one place. If you've got a family they should give you longer than two years. I thought I'd settled for a bit here, it's not right' (Beynon, 1984, p. 106). In this sense, workers and managers, and their families, and capitals (those who employ them and those with whom they spend their wages) can share an interest in a particular location as a place to live and as a successful space for profitable production. This can provide the material basis for a shared commitment to a location which, in some circumstances, could underpin a sense of 'locality' and lead to locationally based political campaigns which transcend differences of class, race and gender as people come together to defend 'their locality'. This instrumental attachment to a given location as a source of wage income, therefore, can often link up with other attachments. Alone or in combinations they *may* lead workers and their families, sometimes in alliance with management groups (maybe interested in a 'buy out') or with small capitals that are tied to that location (such as those involved in retailing and the provision of personal services), to engage in competition with other places to keep existing jobs or gain new ones in an increasingly global place market. As a London taxi driver said to us in 1992: 'I know its been bad up north up your way and to be quite honest mate I don't give a shit. But it's happening down here now. Redundancies, recession. There's *no* money about. And that does bother me'.

Views like this one contribute to a process whereby the

working class can be seen simultaneously to form itself, divide itself and shape changing spatial divisions of labour. That working people have contributed to many campaigns which have been entirely localised and regressive is not in question. In the various steel closures in the 1980s this local parochialism was reflected both in the campaigns at the threatened plants and by the responses of workers in the plants that were to stay open. In the car and textile industries, workers threatened with the closure of their factory have often petitioned for the closure of another of the company's plants or for the restriction of imports from Japan or elsewhere. Management, aware of these tendencies, has often played an important part in orchestrating them. Equally, local campaigns can foster and represent a partial view of a locality and of the local interest. In the 1984–5 miners strike, for example, Scottish miners developed the demand of 'jobs for the boys' but not the girls.

However, attachment to place is grounded in a lot more than merely access to monetary wages, and as such political strategies to defend threatened places are not inevitably divisive or socially regressive: 'place-based' does not necessarily mean 'place-bound', as the strategies of local authorities such as the Greater London and Sheffield City Councils in the years of the early 1980s showed. Equally, the 1984–5 miners' strike in the UK simultaneously produced a campaign to defend jobs and colliery villages, to arrest the long-established decline in the use of coal as an energy resource and to challenge more generally the political economy of Thatcherism. While it undeniably contained parochial elements, in its practice it put miners in a position whereby they sought progressively to unite people in their different places (see Beynon, 1985). In doing so it posed questions not only of Thatcherism but also of the working-class mining culture that it sought to defend. This was most evident in relation to gender divisions and the role of women in civil society. The miners' support groups brought women out of the shadows in many pit villages and in their practice they challenged many of the assumptions involved in the 'jobs for the boys' slogan.

The failure of such campaigns to realise their political objectives raises important questions about spatial cleavages within the working class (and, in the case of the miners, within particular occupational groups). More importantly, it raises questions about asymmetries in power relations in society, and the structural limits which such campaigns came up against. Generally, relations between capital and labour are loaded in favour of capital; but this is only one aspect of power relations. National state strategies represent a force-field of their own and this too was made very clear during the British miners' dispute (see Beynon and McMylor, 1985).

In considering these local campaigns, some people have argued that 'local proactivity', and the establishment of new 'coalitions for growth' represent the best grounds for a progressive politics in the 1990s (see Cooke, 1989). However, the evidence for this is not encouraging to date. Place-based campaigns most typically do become place-bound and regularly pitch places against one another in a competitive struggle for jobs, investment and resources. In these ways they help to reproduce rather than challenge the allocative mechanisms of capitalism. Equally, where place-based campaigns have been progressive in intent they have often been unsuccessful in practice.

In the course of history, spatially uneven development has become a central political problem. This process, and the forms it takes (for example, inner-city problems, or regional problems) is important in itself, and it has taken place at different times in different states. It has nevertheless produced a series of problems that modern states have been compelled to address. This has to be seen as one element in the broader processes of social change, however, and in the range of activities undertaken by and in the form of the state itself. Such responses develop not in some mechanically functional sense, but as part of the *politics* of states retaining legitimacy for their own activities. There are a multitude of sources of pressure that may push for such policies; they cannot be derived abstractly from theoretical schemata but must be uncovered by empirical investigation. It is recognition of this that has ordered our investigation of Teesside.

THE STRUCTURE OF THE BOOK

The book offers an historical account of economy and society on Teesside, developing an interpretation of their changing character and form. Chapter 2 sketches out the processes and personalities that were decisive in the initial establishment of Teesside as a major centre of capitalist production. Chapter 3 concentrates upon the subsequent growth of what might be called Teesside's 'old' industrial economy, its iron and steel producing and processing activities and chemicals production, from the 1840s through to the mid-1960s. It traces in detail the evolution of Teesside, economically and socially, as it became one of the leading centres of fixed capital investment in heavy industry in Western Europe. Chapter

4 examines political developments on Teesside and the way in which a broadly based consensus, united by shared interests in the area, emerged and evolved a distinctive political programme for the area. Chapter 5 then identifies the ways in which the 'old' economy was swiftly and ruthlessly torn apart by international competitive pressures in the 1970s and 1980s. Deindustrialisation and mass unemployment combined to create a deep and broad-ranging crisis in the area. In Chapter 6 the implications of these changes in producing tensions within, and pressures for change in, established political institutions and the dominant consensus project of modernisation are revealed.

Chapter 7 focuses upon the conditions for, and consequences of, one set of responses to this situation in the 1980s. Employers in practically all sectors sought to take advantage of the existence of mass unemployment to impose dramatic changes in forms of work and production organisation. This search for flexibility in the emergent 'new' economy had important social implications and effects, just as did the growth and contraction of the 'old' economy. In fact, the decline of the latter was an important pre-condition for the growth of the former, and the points of inter-section between the two were particularly significant in the kind of social and economic changes which took place. Chapter 8 again picks up on the political aspects of change in more detail. It describes and analyses the ways in which a new consensus politics was reconstructed in the 1980s on Teesside, displaying both continuity with, and significant change from, the previous project. State policies were visibly shaped and influenced again by dominant, but now different, interests in the area. Finally, Chapter 9 draws together the strands of our argument and identifies some of the theoretical and political issues which remain to be addressed.

NOTES

1. In general terms, Teesside refers to the towns on both banks of the Tees, from Hartlepool and Billingham in the north to Stockton in the west, round to Middlesbrough and the built-up area which has coalesced along the south bank of the river, as portrayed in Figure 1.1. The picture has been somewhat complicated by several rounds of local government reorganisation (see note 3 to Chapter 3, pp. 54–5), with the County of Cleveland and its four constituent boroughs coming into existence only in 1974 (see Figure 1.1). Whilst Cleveland represents a reasonably well-defined economic unit (albeit with some disparities – the Hartlepool labour market, for instance, remains to some degree self-contained) – it is one with which few people who live locally identify in anything other than a formal sense.
2. During the 1980s, there was a growing intellectual debate about the

extent to which 'flexibility' was coming to characterise relations between companies and those between capital and labour, both within the labour market and the workplace. Moreover, there were sharply differing views as to the meaning and significance of 'flexibility' and the analytical levels at which concepts of 'flexibility' could be most appropriately applied. For some (following Atkinson, 1985), 'flexibility' was a concept to be applied at the level of the individual firm. For others (such as Storper and Scott, 1989) the focus was upon flexible production systems, typically composed of small interlinked firms spatially agglomerated in one place, whilst there were those for whom the central issue was an alleged transition from a Fordist to a flexible mode of capital accumulation (for instance, Harvey, 1989). It is not our purpose to review this debate here (though see Hudson, 1989b; Gertler, 1992) but rather to focus upon those issues from it that are of particular relevance to the sorts of changes in labour markets and terms and conditions of work characteristic of Teesside in the 1980s. In particular, we examine the extent to which different employers pursued a flexible deployment of labour. Even within this restricted context, there is considerable disagreement in the literature as to the extent of various forms of flexibility (such as financial, functional or numerical); the degree to which flexibility, at least as experienced by workers, was novel; and the desirability of any moves towards further flexibility.

3. There may well be systematic gender differences in this regard, arising from the ties of domestic labour confining women to the home. Such differences, which in any case are far from uniform between places, may be narrowing, at least in part because of changes in the gender division of waged labour.
4. We have discussed the issues summarised in this section at greater length elsewhere (see Beynon and Hudson, 1991, 1993; Hudson, 1990a).

CHAPTER TWO

The Making of a Place

1. INTRODUCTION

The growth of Teesside in the nineteenth century was truly remarkable – and indeed was seen in these terms by contemporary commentators, even in the context of that era of unprecedented industrial and urban growth. Within a few years, areas that were formerly green fields on the banks of the Tees were incorporated into a major centre of industrial production, of global significance in a burgeoning capitalist economy. At the same time, but more slowly and uncertainly, the booming conurbation ceased to be simply a space for profitable production and gradually became a place in which people lived out their lives, developing attachments both to people and place in the process.

2. TEESSIDE IN THE GLOBAL ECONOMY: CONSTRUCTING A SPACE FOR PRODUCTION

A distinguishing feature of Teesside is the extent to which it was (and remains) a product of nineteenth century industrial expansion. There were small market towns such as Stockton-on-Tees and Yarm in the area before the onset of industrialisation, but Middlesbrough, the heart of industrial Teesside, wholly owed its existence to the emergence and consolidation of capitalist relations of production. At the start of the nineteenth century Middlesbrough was a tiny hamlet on a bleak expanse of salt marsh alongside the river Tees. Then, in 1829, one Joseph Pease and his partners bought a five hundred acre estate by the river for £30,000. Subsequently, they extended the Stockton and Darlington Railway to the new town, and it rapidly became a thriving port, exporting Durham coal to the London market. In 1831 Middlesbrough had a population of just 154; at the next census, in 1841, this had risen to over 5,000. In that year iron-making began in the town, after one of Pease's colleagues had convinced Henry Bolckow and John Vaughan to open a new foundry and rolling mill located on six acres of their new estate (which they had

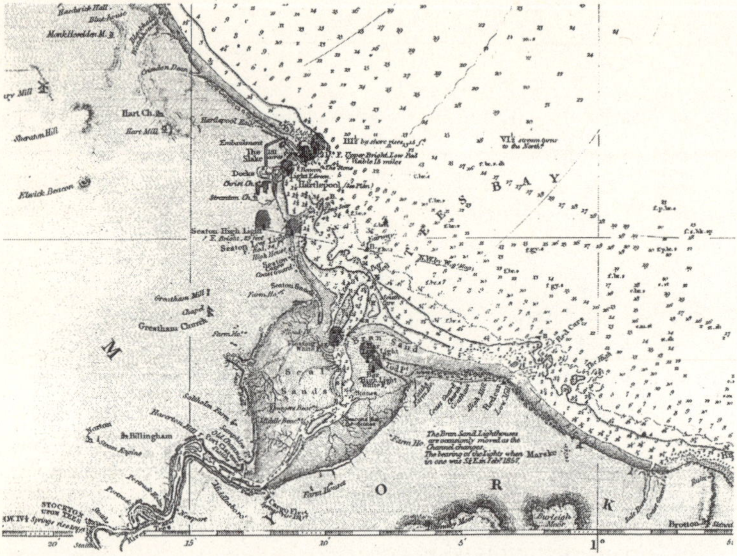

FIGURE 2.1: Teesside before reclamation, 1832.

purchased from Pease) using supplies of Durham coal, Weardale limestone and Scottish pig iron. It also represented a decisive landmark in the history of Teesside. The long-term future of the iron and steel industry remained uncertain, however, until a guaranteed supply of all raw materials was secured. In 1846, in response to fluctuations in the price of pig iron, Bolckow and Vaughan built their own blast furnace at Witton Park in south-west Durham. The iron ore seams within the Durham coal measures soon proved to be inadequate, however, and ore supplies had to be transported from the North Yorkshire moors. This entailed extra transport costs, so now a search for iron-bearing strata concentrated on areas closer to Middlesbrough. In 1850 extensive reserves of relatively rich iron ore were proved in the Eston hills, just south of the town. These added to locally accessible reserves of coal and excellent rail and sea communications to make Middlesbrough an exceptionally well-located site for iron production.

Bolckow and Vaughan moved rapidly to exploit this new-found potential, constructing blast furnaces at Middlesbrough in 1851. Other smaller producers soon followed their example. The firm of Bell Brothers (founded in 1844) secured access to iron-bearing strata at Skelton on the condition that it constructed a works at Port Clarence, on the north bank of the Tees. This was to enable the West Hartlepool Railway Company (in which the landowner held shares) to derive revenue from transporting the ore. In ways like these capitalist production emerged as a powerful force. It was shaped by the emergence of national unions and the influence of key individuals operating within networks of personal relationships.

In this way much of Teesside was constructed from scratch from the mid-nineteenth century onwards in direct response to the requirements of capitalist interests for profitable production. Much of the area physically did not exist before the onset of this period, owing its origins to land reclamation driven by the booming demand for land and access to the sea (see Figure 2.1). Elsewhere on Teesside, as metal-using engineering and shipbuilding industries grew around the steel works, old market towns such as Stockton were transformed and new industrial towns were created as the area became a major industrial conurbation. At the time of the 1901 census the population of Middlesbrough had increased to over 90,000.

This expansion involved major fixed capital investment in iron and steel plants, shipyards and engineering works, port facilities and housing. It also affected ongoing personal relationships which were regulated through the establishment and reproduction of distinctive paternalist forms of wage relations. The labour force on Teesside was recruited through migration (from the North of England and from Ireland) and these workers were introduced to forms of employment which borrowed from the bonded arrangements which applied on the Durham coalfield (see Beynon and Austrin, 1993a). The companies built houses (as tied cottages) for their workers. As part of these arrangements the place of women was very much in the home, and this particular form of gender relations was established within households in Middlesbrough. In all this, the interests of private capital were pre-eminent. They drove the construction process, materially and socially, as capitalists helped to create, and then strove to satisfy, the structural constraints imposed by the law of value. In this way the policies of the emergent local authorities became subservient to and shaped by the interests of private capital. Labour was not passive, but it was in a very weak position in relation to capital in shaping the emergence of the social relations of Teesside. As institutions of organised labour gradually emerged, the balance between capital and labour (mediated increasingly through the state) altered a little; but the dominance and prioritisation of capitalist interests (especially in the key manufacturing sectors) were never seriously threatened.

From the very earliest days, Teesside as an industrial centre was intimately bound up with the shifting fortunes of a global economic system. During the late nineteenth century, it was among the most important manufacturing complexes, not just in the UK but in the world. Such a situation was not, of course, to last indefinitely. As the century wore on, the UK's economic and military global pre-eminence was increasingly challenged by the ascendance of other national states. None the less, around the turn of the century mechanical engineering and shipbuilding were still in a strong position, with guaranteed access to UK and international markets. Equally, expansion of chemicals production on the north bank of the Tees at Billingham after 1918 by Brunner-Mond also reinforced the international orientation of Teesside's industrial base, especially after the company became part of the newly-formed Imperial Chemical Industries (ICI) in 1926. The very name of the new company conjured images of an imperial market secured and guaranteed if necessary by ultimate force and military power.

In spite of its strengths, the history of the area was far from one of smoothly sustained industrial growth. In the nineteenth century cyclical crises threatened profitability and led to agreed cuts in wages (one expression of the dominant liberal ideology of the time). During the great depression of the 1920s and 1930s the area was badly hit, shipbuilding being especially affected by collapsing demand. In the autumn of 1933, as part of his celebrated journey through England, the author J. B. Priestley visited Stockton. From a bridge over the river, Priestley (1934, p. 343) could see:

> the shipyards and slips, the sheds that are beginning to tumble down, the big chimneys that have stopped smoking, the unmoving cranes, and one small ship where once there were dozens. The other men who are standing on this bridge – they have just shuffled up from the Labour Exchange – used to work in those yards and sheds, as riveters and platers and fitters, used to be good men of their hands, but are now, as you can quickly see, not good men of their hands any longer, but are depressed and defeated fellows, sagging and slouching and going grey even in their very cheeks.

What was particularly significant about his account was the comparison which could be drawn with the environmental dereliction and mass unemployment of large parts of Teesside in a later recession of the 1980s; and with the causes of decline. For he was

TABLE 2.1: Employment in Teesside, 1947.

	Employment (1000s)	Percentage of total
Iron- and steel-making	24.2	19.0
Mechanical engineering	13.5	10.7
Shipbuilding	7.1	5.5
Chemicals	17.8	14.0
Light engineering	6.1	4.8
Administration, services	25.5	20.1
Construction	11.2	8.9
Total all employment	127.1	

Source: TIDB, 1948, 56–60.

adamant that the demise of ship-building at Stockton-on-Tees was one undesirable consequence of an *international* crisis (pp. 344–5):

> the world, as we know only too well, entered a period of extreme disorganisation: currencies wobbled, trade declined, tariffs went up, quotas were established, coffee and wheat were burned, fruit was dumped into the sea, and half the bounty of the earth was wasted while half the people of the earth drew nearer and nearer to starvation. In this era of rapidly declining trade, very few ships were wanted; it was not long before good vessels were lying up idle in every estuary.

This meant that (p. 345):

> For such a place as Stockton, the game was up. Such new industries as we have had went south. Stockton and the rest, miles from London, and with soaring rates, were useless as centres for new enterprises. They were left to rot. And that would perhaps not have mattered very much, for the bricks and mortar of these towns are not sacred, if it were not for one fact. These places left to rot have people living in them. Some of these people are rotting too.

Rearmament in the late 1930s, the war economy and post-war reconstruction proved to be the salvation (if only temporarily) for much of Teesside's manufacturing capacity (Table 2.1). This interlude of prosperity merely postponed the necessity for more profound policy changes in an attempt to cope with implications of the area's changing location within the international economy. Teesside, an area which once led the world as an engine house of accumulation, was on the way to becoming just another cog in the machinery of the global capitalist system of production and exchange – but this is to anticipate the story.

3. BEYOND THE WORKPLACE: CONSTRUCTING THE SOCIAL RELATIONS OF AN EMERGENT PLACE

Whilst the area's position in the international economy unquestionably changed (and dramatically so) over the first century of its development, capitalist relations of production continued to play a decisive role in structuring the social composition of Teesside. In the early years – the 1850s and 1860s – the growing town of Middlesbrough was overwhelmingly dominated by a small group of men with close family and marriage ties. The rapidly-expanding economy centred on their mutual interdependence and their recruitment of, and control over, substantial labour forces, themselves characterised by marked social and technical divisions of labour. The contract system of labour recruitment meant that the Ironmasters, the dominant figures in the town, dealt directly only with skilled workers, who in turn employed the majority of the labour force and fixed wage rates. Wages were regulated by the principle of sliding scales, so that they were cut by agreement at times of reduced demand. As steel displaced iron production, a marked technical and social division of labour continued. The open-hearth steel furnaces, for example, were operated by teams of first, second, third and fourth hands, and progression to first-hand smelter – if it came at all – was long and arduous, often taking a full working life. Seniority, discipline and experience ordered social relations in the workplace. Despite (very real) shared hazards, a clear hierarchy existed within the manual labour force. This was based upon experience rather than a skill obtained through an apprenticeship system. The dominance of the 'first hand' over the work teams, however, had a further significance for it had a marked effect on the emergent character of trades unionism. Additionally, the workforce was fragmented by the operation of a shift pattern, allied to continuous production. The needs of the iron and steel companies ordered time in the area, not just in the works but also beyond them in the household and in the community. In these and other ways the character of the industry left its impression upon local social and cultural life.

Acceptance of the system of sliding scales for the determination of wages was symptomatic of a broader view which propounded a harmony of interests between capital and labour. Such beliefs

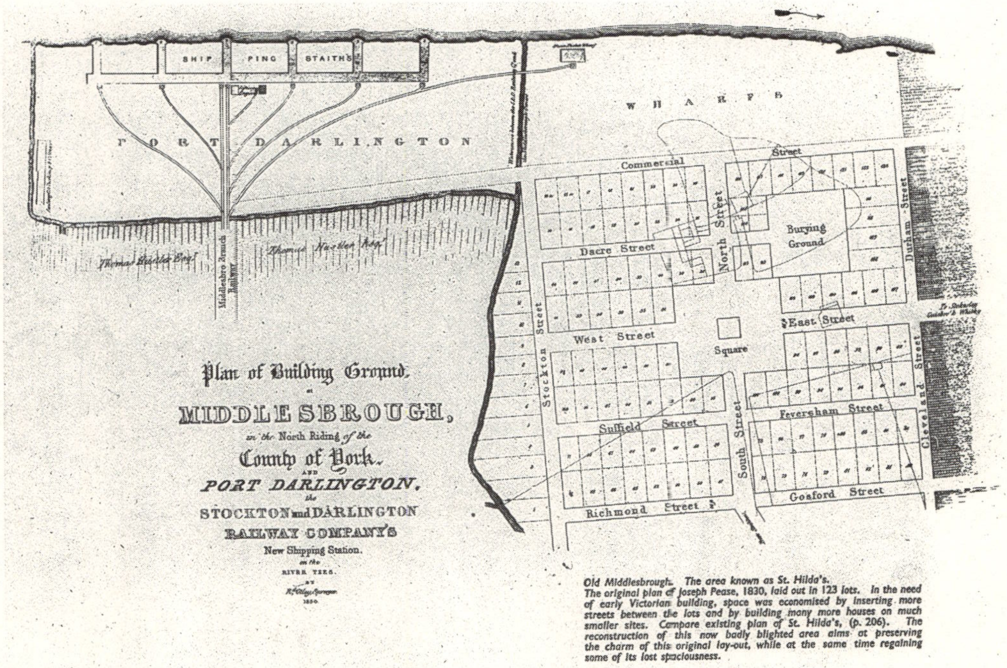

FIGURE 2.2: Plan of building ground at Middlesbrough, 1830.

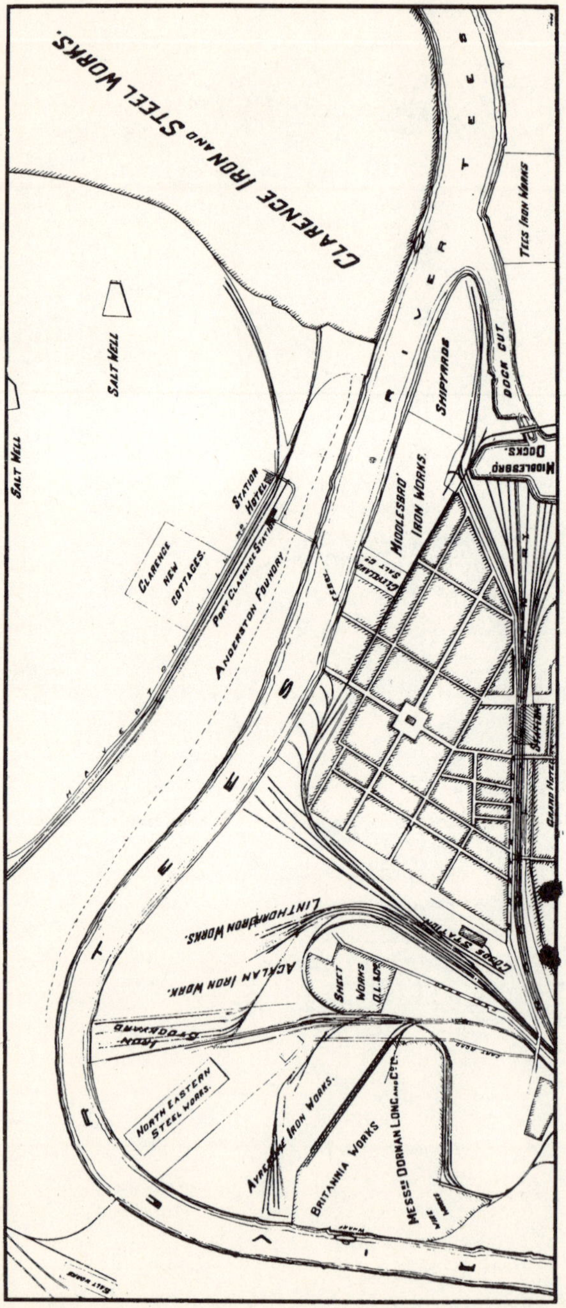

FIGURE 2.3: Plan of Middlesbrough and the Ironmasters District, 1901.

shaped the early trades union organisations which emerged, both locally and nationally. The Amalgamated Malleable Ironworkers Association was founded in 1862, and the National Amalgamated Association of Ironworkers in 1868. They merged to form the Associated Iron and Steel Workers of Great Britain in 1887. These institutions participated in a range of formal and informal procedures for the settlement of disputes and the avoidance of conflict. The Board of Conciliation for the Manufactured Iron Trade of the North of England was established in 1869 and was still active in the 1920s (see Bowen, 1976). In this way the early division of labour in the industry (heavily influenced by the employers) played a significant role, both materially and socially, in shaping developments on Teesside.

The region carried the imprint of nineteenth-century capitalist industrialisation in other ways. Pease's original Middlesbrough estate developed at first around a central grid plan, with a square and four main streets, designed to ease the emergence of a new community (see Figures 2.2 and 2.3). Such was the pace of growth, though, that any further attempt at regulation and planned expansion ended in failure. This frantic growth had a more than local significance. On a visit to the town in 1862, W. E. Gladstone referred to it as 'an infant Hercules'. One survey of Victorian England commented on its expansion as follows (Briggs, 1963, p. 241):

> within the reign of Queen Victoria, Middlesbrough grew from a tiny rural community to a very large town of [around] one hundred thousand people. There were cities outside Britain, in the United States or Australia, which grew from nothing even faster during the nineteenth century, but there was no other English town.

A wholly new built environment sprang up on Teesside around the iron-and-steel producing and using industries, as the expanding works drew in large numbers of migrant workers. Writing in 1907 Lady Bell, wife of one of the Ironmasters, described the consequences of the frantic expansion (Bell, 1985, pp. 2–3):

> there springs, and too rapidly, into existence a community of a preordained inevitable kind, the members of which must live near their work. They must therefore have houses built as quickly as possible; the houses must be cheap, must be as big as the workman wants, and no bigger; and as they are built, there arise, hastily erected, instantly occupied, the rows and rows of little brown streets of the aspect that in

> some place or another is familiar to all of us. A town arising in this way cannot wait to consider anything else than time and space; and none of either must be wasted on what is merely agreeable to the eye, or even on what is merely sanitary. There can be no question under these conditions of building model cottages, or of laying out a district into ideal settlements. As one owner after another starts ironworks in the growing place, there is a fresh inrush of workmen, and day by day the little houses spring hurriedly into existence, until at last we find ourselves in the middle of a town. It is, unhappily, for the most part a side issue for the workman whether he and his family are going to live under healthy conditions. The main object of his life is to be at work: that is the one absolute necessity.

Some forty years later, the social relationships of housing production in nineteenth century Middlesbrough were dissected with a sharper analytic insight by Glass (1948, p. 9):

> The system of ownership in Middlesbrough has certainly contributed to the bad housing conditions obtaining. The land was largely owned by the 'Owners of the Middlesbrough Estate Ltd' [originally set up by Pease to establish the town]. They have sold their land piece-meal for development on the smallest scale, continuously buying up more land on the outskirts, for the purpose of parcelling and selling as before. Few people administer their own property and rent collection is in the hand of not more than a dozen principal agents. These act for various small property owning trusts. None of the trusts provide sinking funds for the replacement of obsolete houses. They appear to regard the brick structure of their houses as everlasting. They have no direct contact with their tenants and do not concern themselves with their living conditions.

This graphically describes the pervasive influence of the dominant local capitalist interests on the form of housing provision and urban expansion in Middlesbrough. For them, this was simply one more source of revenues. The quality of the living conditions that resulted for their tenants was not an issue of concern.

The legacy of this kind of development, predicated on the 'absolute necessity' of wage labour, was still evident to Glass even in the early post-1945 years. She saw Middlesbrough as

> the very prototype of a town born and reared during the past century ... it has grown around coke ovens and blast furnaces. The founders of the great combines have been its

> Lords of the Manor. The scenery is marred by weird and giant industrial structures. The sky is obscured by the twin bursts of flame and smoke which emanate from industrial processes.

Such a description pointed accurately and graphically to the town's lack of a feudal history and its total dependence upon capitalist social relations.

The particular kind of industrialisation which took place in Middlesbrough and, more generally, in the Teesside area during the nineteenth century also had distinctive consequences for the construction of gender relations within households. The dominance of male-centred extractive and heavy manufacturing employment was accompanied by a near-total lack of waged employment opportunities for women. These economic arrangements reinforced a conception of gender relations, which was dramatically constrained even by the standards of the day. This was observed quite acutely by Lady Bell (1985, p. 178):

> The position of the women of the working classes in Middlesbrough is different from that which they occupy in the other big manufacturing towns, for the reason that what is practically the only large industry in the town, the iron trade, offers absolutely no field for women in any part of it. There are not, as in most manufacturing towns, large factories; there is therefore no organized women's labour. The women have no independent existence of their own. They mostly marry very young; the conditions of the town point to their doing so. It is one of the few in the kingdom in which from the constant influx of men in search of work, and not of women, the males outnumber the females.

Whilst it would be wrong to read gender relations directly from employment structure and class relations, the kind of industries established on Teesside relied upon the employment of large numbers of men in work that was arduous and dangerous. This had an important influence upon the structuring of gender relations in this and subsequent periods.

Further impacts of industrialisation were expressed in Teesside's physical environment. The 'twin bursts of flame and smoke' which were still evident in the mid-twentieth century, and indeed the less visible but potentially more insidious emissions from both steel and chemical plants which persisted beyond then, had extremely serious long-term consequences for health and were symptomatic of other more general problems (see Phillimore and Morris, 1991). The original township of Middlesbrough – located in what was once marshland – was on a site wholly unsuited to large-scale settlement, being especially prone to flooding and damp. The constant stream of pollution from iron and steel works was an additional hazard. At the start of the twentieth century it was described in this way (Bell, 1985, p. 30):

> besides the fumes and the gases, every breath of wind at the ironworks carries dust with it, whirling through the air in a wind, dropping through it in a calm, covering the ground, filling the cabins, settling on the clothes of those who are within reach, filling their eyes and their mouths, covering their hands and their faces. The calcined ironstone sends forth red dust, the smoke from the chimneys and furnaces is deposited in white dust, the smoke from the steel rolling mills falls in black dust: and, most constant difficulty of all, the gases escaping from the furnaces are charged with a fine, impalpable brownish dust, which is shed everywhere, on everything.

This particular problem was long-lasting both in its source and its consequences. From 1935 to 1939 Middlesbrough had the second highest infant mortality rate of all County Boroughs in the UK (Glass, 1948, p. 52).

The area's early development, then, left a grim environmental legacy and particular forms of wage and gender relations which had wide-ranging consequences for many aspects of social life. They produced on Teesside a classic polarisation between capital and labour and would perhaps appear at first sight to present many of the preconditions for radical working-class organisation to emerge and prosper. However, this was never the case. In part, this reflected the influence of the paternalist forms of political representation which developed locally and the pervasiveness of the employers' patronage and prejudice. It was also influenced by the geography of the construction of its built environment. Glass (1948, p. 14), for instance, said of Middlesbrough that it was 'predominantly a working-class town, but its working-class settlements are too dispersed to admit of close social relationships between them'. Almost thirty years later Gladstone (1976, p. 39) wrote of Teesside that it was

> an industrial area: no more, no less. The majority of its population are employed in industry and its shape has been largely determined by industry's needs … Teesside grew up in separate parts and the parts have failed to cohere. There is a fierce spirit of separatism preventing them from doing so.

This social and spatial composition and patterning of the area –

almost in a series of distinctive company towns – was a further reflection of the paternalism of the staple employers. The influence of the dominant employers had political consequences which were, if not deterministic, certainly determinate in this process of constructing Teesside.

4. CONCLUDING COMMENTS

Teesside's development was, from the outset, deeply marked by the ways in which it was inserted into international divisions of labour. This had a profound effect upon the material and social construction of the area, as a space for capital and as a place for people. Teesside was built as a series of discrete settlements, company towns, characterised by paternalistic capital:labour relations and patriarchical gender relations. As capital was invested in new industries and an associated built environment, labour was provided via a process of immigration which the dominant employers regulated to meet their needs. This was one expression of the links between Teesside and a wider economy, symbolic of the way in which it was open to broader political and economic influences from its very beginnings as a space and as a place. Its sensitivity to fluctuations in the international economy were revealed particularly sharply in the 1920s and 1930s.

CHAPTER THREE

Constructing the Old Industrial Economy: Iron, Steel and Chemicals on Teesside from the 1840s to the 1960s

1. INTRODUCTION

Many major centres of industrialisation in Western Europe and North America initially developed around iron and steel. Other industries, either supplying essential raw materials such as coking coal and iron ore, or fashioning finished products such as railways and ships, grew up alongside the blast furnaces and steel mills, often within large conglomerates tied with a complex web of personal and financial linkages. Iron and steel manufacture quite literally helped to shape many of the industrial heartlands of the late nineteenth century. They were characterised by a built environment which was designed to satisfy a booming demand for labour, and especially by high-density terraced housing within walking distance of the works.

The early development of Middlesbrough epitomised these characteristics of the Industrial Revolution. Its phenomenal growth in the second half of the nineteenth century was led by the dynamism of the iron, steel, engineering and shipbuilding industries. Then, from the start of the twentieth century onwards, a second decisive set of industrial groupings emerged on Teesside and began to command a position of similar pre-eminence. The chemicals industry, led by ICI, constructed a new range of equally vast undertakings – on both banks of the Tees – so that by the middle of the twentieth century the Teesside area was among the most heavily industrialized regions of Western Europe.

2. THE DEVELOPMENT OF A MAJOR IRON AND STEEL MANUFACTURING COMPLEX, 1841–1967

Following the opening of the first iron works in Middlesbrough in 1841, pig iron and iron ore production expanded very rapidly through the 1850s and 1860s. Output of iron ore from the North Riding of Yorkshire (effectively, the area to the south of the river Tees) rose steadily from 0.7 million tonnes in 1854 to 6.1 million tonnes in 1875, while pig iron output grew from 0.1 million tonnes

TABLE 3.1: Number of blast furnaces, Yorkshire North Riding and Durham (Teesside only), 1860 and 1871.

Name of works	Owners	Number of furnaces 1860	1871
Yorkshire North Riding			
Ayresome	Gjers Mills	–	4
Beck Hole	Whitby Iron Co.	2	–
Cargo Fleet	Swan Coates	–	4
Carlton	Industrial Iron and Coal	–	2
Clay Lane	Clay Lane Iron Co.	3	–
Clay Lane Eston	Thomas Vaughan	–	6
South Bank	Thomas Vaughan	–	9
South Bank	B. Samuelson	3	–
Cleveland	Bolckow Vaughan	4	–
Eston	Bolckow Vaughan	5	
Middlesbrough	Bolckow Vaughan	3	15
Witton Park	Bolckow Vaughan	–	
Glaisdale	George Wilson	–	3
Grosmont	Chas. & Thos. Bagnall	–	2
Lackenby	Lackenby Iron Co.	–	2
Linthorpe	Lloyd & Co.	–	6
Newport	B. Samuelson	–	7
Normanby	Jones Dunning	2	3
Ormesby	Cochrane & Co.	4	3
Tees	Gilkes Wilson Pease	5	5
Teesside	Hopkins Gilkes	2	4
Total		33	75
Durham (Teesside only)			
Acklam	Stevenson Jaques	–	4
Clarence	Bell Brothers	5	8
Stockton	Holdsworth, Bennington Byers & Co.	3	–
Thornaby	W. Whitwell	3	3
Witton Park	Bolckow Vaughan	4	–
Total		15	15
Grand Total		48	90

Source: derived from North (1975), pp. 222–3.

in 1855 to 1.2 million tonnes twenty years later. Technical advances and bigger blast furnaces meant that output per furnace increased; but even so the number of blast furnaces in the North Riding of Yorkshire rose dramatically, from 33 in 1860 to 75 in 1871, as demand for iron boomed. Over this period 15 furnaces in County Durham were also constructed on the north bank of the Tees. By 1871 some 90 blast furnaces ringed the riverside (see Table 3.1) and Teesside produced nearly one-third of the country's iron output, as the whole area was transformed into a giant iron and then steel works. As a result, Teesside became a place deeply marked by the influence of dangerous, dirty, male-dominated employment. Conditions at the iron works were described by Lady Bell as follows (1985, pp. 39–40):

> When the moment comes to open the furnace for the next casting ... a hole is drilled through the bottom of the 'hearth' in the solid piece of clay with which the furnace was closed the last time it was tapped. This is done by a great iron bar, held by three men, being thrust again and again against the clay, clearing away the loose rubbish and beginning to make the hole, against which it is then held in position by two men, while two others deal alternate blows on it with big hammers ... When [the] moment has come, the bar, with a mighty effort, is withdrawn, and the blazing stream rushes out in foaming and leaping red-hot waves through the opening, into the deep main channel prepared for it. The heat to those standing on the bank of that molten river is almost unbearable, the glare hardly to be endured. The onlooker is half blinded, half choked, as the flood rushes fiercely past him.

Throughout the latter decades of the nineteenth century further technical developments led to steel displacing puddled iron as the main product. The slow process of puddling to remove impurities in pig iron had a limited life after 1856 when Henry Bessemer proved that a blast of air through the metal would achieve the same result much more rapidly. The Siemens-Martin open hearth furnace, developed in the following decade, represented another advance in steel-making technology. Cleveland ore was initially unsuitable for these processes, since it was phosphoric in character and the then-contemporary technology could be used only with acidic ores. Consequently, the first steel produced on Teesside, around 1875, was produced by Bolckow Vaughan in a Bessemer plant but using haematite ore from Spain. Four years later it was demonstrated that a basic slag could absorb the phosphorous from the local ore provided that the converters were lined with a basic material such as dolomite. The technical problem of using Cleveland ore in steel-making had been overcome.

Subsequently, the pace of the switch to steel-making varied between companies on Teesside. Bell Brothers specialised in producing iron plates, bars and angles for the shipbuilding industry, buoyant products in the 1870s. In contrast Bolckow Vaughan gradually expanded steel production as did Dorman Long, established in 1875 by Arthur Dorman and Albert de Lande Long. Initially, they aimed to make iron bars and angles for the shipbuilding industry, then iron girders, but rapidly saw the advantages of steel for this particular product and replaced half of the 122 puddling furnaces at the Britannia works with seven open hearth steel furnaces. Dorman Long, too, initially used imported ore but then switched to Cleveland ore and the basic open hearth process.

Throughout this period of frenetic growth (and subsequently) markets for Teesside's iron and steel were secured by equally spectacular expansion in the area's shipbuilding and engineering industries. A complex and closely interlinked industrial structure emerged. By 1843 Bolckow and Vaughan had already begun downstream integration of their activities, starting an engineering works to construct marine engines. Other major engineering companies were formed in this period: Teesside Bridge and Engineering in 1850, Head Wrightson (later to become the dominant engineering firm and, at one point, among the three biggest employers in the area) in 1866, and Cleveland Bridge and Engineering in 1877. Most of these were associated via ownership ties and key individuals with the major iron and steel producers. Furthermore, the steel companies diversified their own activities. Dorman Long established a separate Bridge and Constructional works at its Britannia site in the 1890s, for example. Similarly, the shipbuilding industry – also closely connected to the iron and steel producers – switched from wood to iron (the first iron ship on the Tees was built in 1854) and then steel. By the end of the nineteenth century six major Teesside shipbuilders had emerged and the area accounted for over one-tenth of world merchant shipping production. The north east region as a whole launched almost half of the world's merchant shipping tonnage in this period. This diversification of activity and enlargement of the region's manufacturing base – albeit still centred on a limited range of activities – was crucial to continued economic dynamism. As North put it (1975, p. 33):

> when the iron and steel firms on Teesside were threatened by the growth of competition in other parts of the world, it was the design and production of highly sophisticated engineering products such as engines, bridges, iron, steel and chemical plants which helped to maintain a continuing overseas market for iron and steel.

The emergence of a vertically integrated manufacturing complex, in which specialist knowledge, research and development and product innovation played key roles, was therefore crucial to Teesside's dominant role within the international division of labour as a profitable space for production.

Around the turn of the century there were several significant mergers in the iron and steel industry. This centralisation of capital partly reflected the increasing scale of production but it was also partly in response to a downturn in the shipbuilding industry – another indication of the interdependence between steel manufacturing and processing activities. In 1899 Dorman Long took over Bell Brothers, a major acquisition given that it employed some 6,000 men, double the workforce of Dorman Long. Bell Brothers' specialisation in iron production guaranteed inputs to Dorman Long's expanding steel capacity. Four years later Dorman Long bought the Acklam works of the North Eastern Steel Company, giving it an additional steel capacity of 0.45 million tonnes annually. Further, in 1898, South Durham Steel and Iron was established by William Gray and Christopher Furness (who was also active in the shipbuilding industry and in Parliament as a Conservative MP) to take over four existing iron and steel companies, one of which owned a site at Cargo Fleet on Teesside. By the start of the twentieth century these processes of merger and take-over meant that three major steel producers had emerged on Teesside: Bolckow Vaughan, Dorman Long and South Durham Steel and Iron.

The national economic slump after the end of the First World War was felt very strongly on Teesside. During the 1920s exports fell and imports rose because of unfavourable exchange rates, while home demand shrank, causing increasingly acute problems of over-capacity. The responses to this crisis involved a further centralisation within the steel industry and continued diversification. Bolckow Vaughan was in considerable financial difficulty, having built a large new steel plant during the war. In 1929 two of the three big producers, Dorman Long and Bolckow Vaughan, merged – the last major reorganisation of the ownership structure of the Teesside steel industry in private hands (see Figure 3.1).

1841	Bolckow Vaughan's first iron works opened in Middlesbrough
1844	Bell Brothers founded
1875	Dorman Long established
1898	South Durham Steel and Iron created to take over four existing iron and steel companies
1899	Dorman Long took over Bell Brothers
1929	Dorman Long and Bolckow Vaughan merged
1967	Dorman Long and South Durham Steel and Iron agreed tentative merger proposals, then became part of the nationalised British Steel Corporation
1988	British Steel privatised

FIGURE 3.1: Evolution of ownership structure in the Teesside iron and steel industry.

After this take-over, Dorman Long employed some 33,000 men and had an annual steel capacity of 1.5 million tonnes. During the same period it also acquired further engineering companies. After winning the prestigious Sydney Harbour Bridge contract in 1914, a separate Bridge Department was created. To this was added the structural engineering firm of Redpath Brown, acquired by Bolckow Vaughan shortly before its merger with Dorman Long, and Teesside Bridge and Engineering Works, taken over in 1930.

Dorman Long was clearly the dominant iron and steel producer on Teesside from the 1930s onwards, although it, too, struggled to cope with recession. Nationally, as protectionist sentiment grew in trade policies, a tariff was imposed on imported steel in 1932 in order to protect domestic producers. The Clarence steel works, Grangetown blast furnaces and Carlton iron works closed during the depths of the depression and new investment was concentrated on larger production units. The first of these was a new battery of coke ovens, opened in 1936 at Cleveland, followed by a new mill to produce light sections and bars. The rolling of plate was concentrated at Redcar and that of heavy sections at Britannia. Port Clarence became a centre for the recovery of coke oven by-products, principally tar. By this date, too, higher-grade imported ore was increasing in significance, favouring locations closer to the mouth of the Tees. Two-thirds of Dorman Long's iron production came from blast furnaces east of Middlesbrough in 1939 compared to one-half in 1919, the first indication of what was to be a long-term trend. The Tees estuary was crucial as a gateway to the world, a means of integrating the iron and steel industry into a changing global economic environment. As one survey of the industry commented in 1938: 'even today, when local supplies of ore are nearing exhaustion, the region can maintain its predominance, because of the ease with which foreign ores can be imported to the works situated along the river bank' (Gleave, 1938, p 454). In this way, and via continuous technological advance as a route to competitive advantage, Teesside steel companies continued to adapt and survive.

In this period Dorman Long was at the centre of a complex web of activities within not just Teesside but the North-east of England generally, and increasingly elsewhere in the UK as well. Dorman Long was an archetypal example of the 'coal combines' which consolidated their control over a variety of branches of production during the inter-war period. The company directly owned eight pits in County Durham, employing 9,000 men with an annual output of 4 million tonnes. Two of its directors were on the board of Horden Collieries, which operated four pits employing a further 5,000. In turn, one of the directors of Horden Collieries was on the board of Wearmouth Coal Company, employing a further 3,000 men. Dorman Long's mineral holdings within North east England (see Figure 3.2) were a clear expression of the strength of the inter-connections between branches of production – still directed and orchestrated by a few key individuals – within the region. Nor were the coal interests of Dorman Long confined to County Durham. The company also had a joint interest in Pearson and Dorman Long which owned two pits in the Kent coalfield employing 4,600 men and producing 1.5 million tonnes of coal annually. A contemporary survey (Labour Research Department, 1939, p. 6) concluded that 'it would be difficult to find a closer link between coal, by-products and all branches of the iron and steel industry than is represented by this well-knit Durham combine'.

After the Second World War the development of the two leading Teesside steel companies was initially conditioned by political uncertainty. The coal industry was nationalised in 1947 and the mineral holdings of Dorman Long and its satellite companies were acquired by the newly formed National Coal Board. The steel industry was also taken into public ownership in 1951 but was then denationalised later the same year when a Conservative Government replaced Labour (for details see McEachern, 1979,

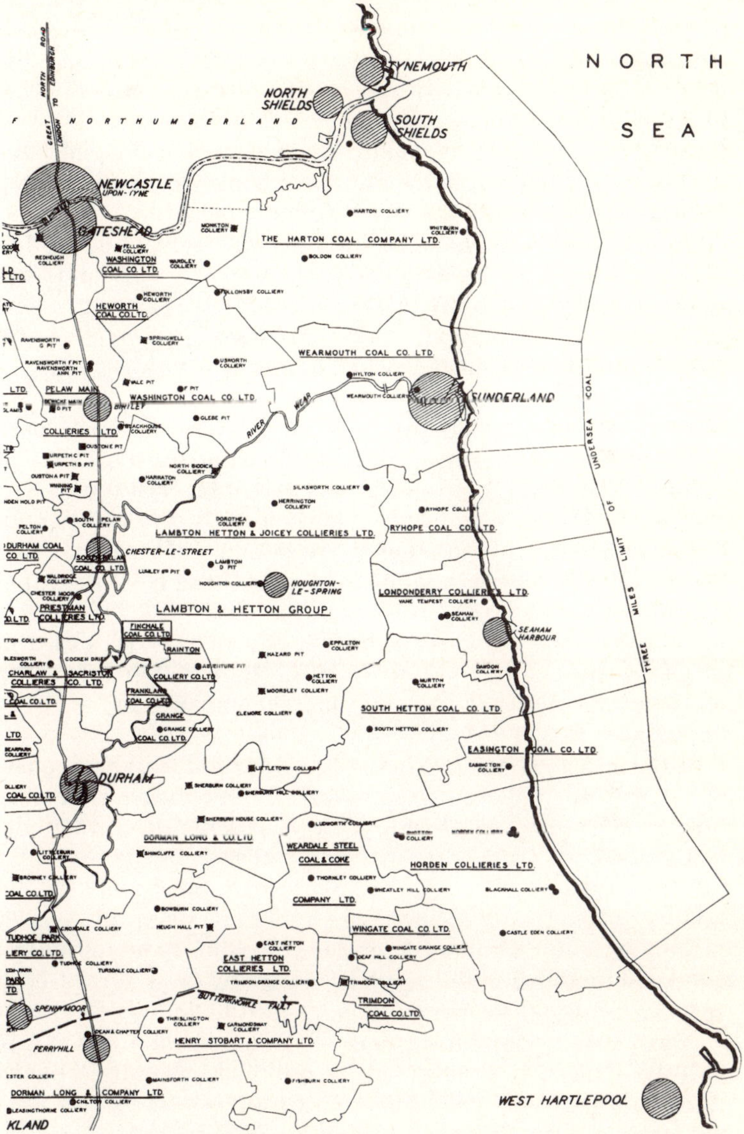

FIGURE 3.2: Dorman Long's mineral holdings in North-east England, 1947.

1980; Ross,1965). A consequence of the uncertainty that this engendered was that it was not until the mid-1950s that new investment plans were put into operation. In 1955 South Durham Steel and Iron opened a new mill at Stockton, capable of rolling pipes up to 40 inches in diameter. Two years later the Iron and Steel Board, established by central government to regulate the industry under private ownership, gave formal approval to the company's plan to establish a steel works on a new site, the South Works in Hartlepool. Intended to raise output of heavy plate, this was completed in 1962. In the same year a new beam mill started operation at the Cargo Fleet works south of the river.

Dorman Long also proceeded with development plans. During 1956 and 1957 two batteries of coke ovens at South Bank came into production, along with two blast furnaces at Clay Lane and a new ore wharf at the Cleveland works. Additional steel-making and rolling capacity was installed at Lackenby, a new site east of Middlesbrough, including a medium section mill (1957), a universal beam mill (1958) and a rod mill (1959). A third blast furnace was opened at Clay Lane in 1962. Much of this was replacement investment so that older capacity, for example, blast furnaces at Cleveland and a steel plant at Acklam, closed during this period. The new sea terminal represented a recognition of the impending exhaustion of local ores and the increasing benefits of importing foreign ore with a higher iron content in terms of lowering production cost. The last Cleveland mine, North Skelton, closed in 1964. One effect of the run-down and cessation of iron ore mining was to create localised pools of unemployment to the south of Teesside.

By the mid-1960s the two major Teesside producers had undertaken extensive replacement investments, but their profitability during the preceding decade was generally lower than the national average (Table 3.2). In 1966 Dorman Long produced 1.5 million tonnes of steel, and South Durham Steel and Iron 1.3 million tonnes. The following year – under pressure from signs of impending nationalisation to produce plans for reorganisation – Dorman Long and South Durham Steel and Iron agreed on a tentative proposal to merge, along with the Scunthorpe-based Stewarts and Lloyds, to form a major plate, pipe and tubes group. However, this was pre-empted by the renationalisation of the fourteen largest steel producers in 1967 to form the British Steel Corporation (BSC). Faced with heightened international competition – especially from Japan – it was evident that a major reappraisal and reorganisation of the UK steel industry was essential, not least because of the implications of the price of steel for the international competitiveness of steel consuming industries located within the UK. With profit margins diminishing rapidly in the bulk steel industry, the particular form of public ownership

TABLE 3.2: Comparative ratios of profit to capital employment of three major North-east steel producers, 1958–67 (%).[1]

	Consett Iron	Dorman Long	South Durham Steel and Iron	Mean for 14 companies nationalised in 1967
1958	9.1	10.1	23.7	17.3
1959	4.7[2]	8.6	17.8	15.7
1960	9.5	11.8	12.8	18.8
1961	9.8	11.0	6.0	12.4
1962	−0.1	5.9	0.2	6.6
1963	−1.9	6.4	1.6	4.8
1964	1.6	7.0	5.7	7.3
1965	8.4	5.8	6.9	6.7
1966	4.9	0.2	4.4	3.8
1967	0.7	–	–	1.9

Notes:

1. The company figures are calculated from annual reports using the definition adopted in BSC's *Annual Report* 1968, to enable comparison with the table presented therein and reproduced here. Profit is defined as gross profit after depreciation but before interest and taxation, other than interest on bank overdrafts. Capital employed comprises share capital, reserves and long–term borrowings, and relates to the start of the financial year (i.e. the end of the previous financial year).
2. A six-month accounting period, with the profit figure doubled to calculate a comparable profit ratio statistic.

Sources: Consett Iron, *Annual Reports*, 1958–67.
Dorman Long, *Annual Reports*, 1958–67.
South Durham Steel and Iron, *Annual Reports*, 1958–67.
BSC, *Annual Report*, 1968.

adopted (leaving the more profitable, lower volume special-steel producers mainly in the private sector) meant that this second attempt at nationalisation was to be longer lasting and more far-reaching in its impact. It was a political compromise, a nationalisation *in* not *of* the industry, and the policies of the newly nationalised BSC were to have particularly dramatic and, ultimately, traumatic consequences on Teesside.

3. EXPANSION IN CHEMICALS PRODUCTION ON TEESSIDE FROM 1918 TO THE MID-1960s

Whilst expansion in steel production created a centre of major national and international importance, the chemicals industry achieved a position of similar dominance within Teesside and of greater significance to the international economy. It expanded dramatically around several locations on the Tees estuary from 1918 onwards. The natural advantages of a coastal location, the availability of vast areas of suitable land and the possibility of constructing wholly new labour forces proved to be decisive locational attractions. Two sites of major international significance were created: Billingham on the north bank of the Tees, from 1918 onwards; and Wilton on the south bank, after 1945.

Despite some (limited) attempts at extracting alkali from natural salt deposits in the nineteenth century,[1] it was many years before the chemicals industry really flourished on Teesside. Almost from the start, this twentieth-century development hinged upon guaranteed access to an international market and centred on the sophisticated manœuvring within that arena by one major company, ICI, although it took several years for ICI to emerge as the dominant actor. For the immediate trigger to chemicals production on Teesside was a perceived threat to nitrate supplies (essential for the manufacture of explosives) posed by the German blockade of the sea routes to South America during the First World War. In response to this, central government initiated work in 1918 on a plant to produce synthetic ammonia by the Haber – Bosch process. Billingham offered a large, accessible, flat site and adequate supplies of water, local raw materials and electricity (from the recently completed power station of the Newcastle Electric Supply Company) as well as labour. The ending of hostilities resulted in a cessation of direct state involvement. The still-undeveloped site was taken over by a subsidiary company of Brunner–Mond in 1920, which completed the development. Considerable technical difficulties had to be overcome in producing ammonia at high pressure and a temperature of 500°C with the then contemporary technology. The first ammonia and sulphate of ammonia were none the less produced at the end of 1923. By 1924 production had increased to 30 tonnes per day.

The major expansion of Billingham, though, was a direct consequence of the merger, in 1926, of Brunner–Mond with three other British companies to form Imperial Chemical Industries (ICI). ICI attempted to emulate the integrated complexes of the German chemical industry, selling to the vast market offered by the British Empire for various chemicals products, such as fertilisers (see Reader, 1970, pp. 451–66). The formation of ICI led to a tripling of new ammonia capacity already under construction at Billingham. This was accompanied by a diversification of production (although

TABLE 3.3: Production of chemicals at Billingham, 1929–45 (tonnes).

	1929	1939	Peak war year
Ammonia	103,000	140,000	178,000 (1943)
Anhydrite		447,000	700,000 (1945)
Sulphate of ammonia	327,000	243,000	372,000 (1943)
'Nitro–chalk'		77,000	148,000 (1944)
Concentrated complete fertilisers		99,000	118,000 (1945)
Sulphuric acid		66,000	73,000 (1945)

Source: Semmens (1970), p. 333.

still largely of inorganic chemicals) into the manufacture of cement and sulphuric acid (the latter based on anhydrite deposits, extraction of which began in 1928), as well as the first compound fertilisers based on nitrogen and phosphate.

During the 1930s output was somewhat reduced at Billingham as demand fell, but one response to this was a search for new products and further diversification of production into a plant to hydrogenate coal and creosote to petrol. The build-up to the Second World War and the demands of the wartime economy led to both an increased demand for existing products from Billingham as well as the further development of new ones (for example, iso-octane and victane for aviation fuel). Thus, new production levels were attained in the war years (Table 3.3). By 1945 ICI had developed a diverse and complex web of both national and international linkages (Figures 3.3 and 3.4) and, within this, Billingham was the largest single chemicals production complex in the world, producing a wide range of products based on sulphuric acid, nitrates, petroleum (from creosote) and calor gas.

The development of production at Billingham in the post-war period cannot be understood without reference to the major new works at Wilton, with a considerable interchange of products between the two sites, as the outputs of one became inputs to the other and vice versa. While some new products were introduced, however, Billingham continued to concentrate on existing inorganic chemicals production. In the later years of the 1940s and 1950s there was considerable demand for commodities produced at Billingham. Consequently, employment levels remained stable at around 13,000. Towards the end of the 1950s and beginning of the 1960s, though, international competitive pressures intensified. In response to this, a decisive set of changes was set in motion

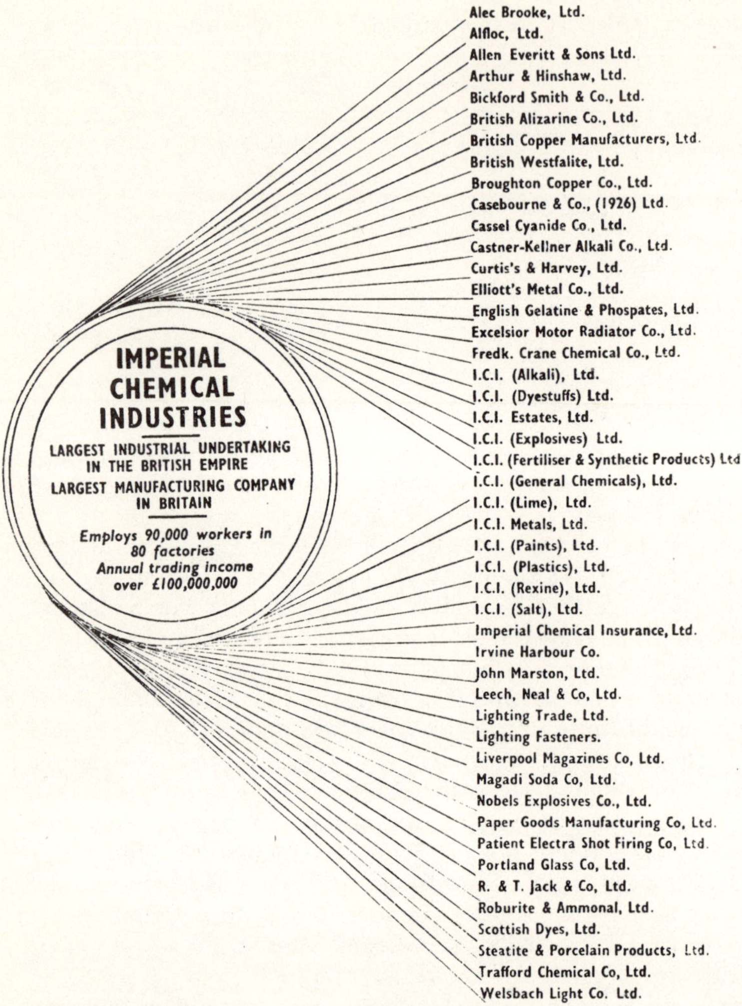

FIGURE 3.3: ICI's national connections, 1945.

from 1962 involving major investment and technological changes in ammonia production, accompanied by considerable increases in labour productivity and the loss of several thousand jobs.

There were in fact two technical changes in ammonia production. The first involved introduction of the steam-reforming process, which displaced the coke-based process as the starting point for producing synthetic gas for ammonia production. The coke ovens and associated plant (which dated back in part to the

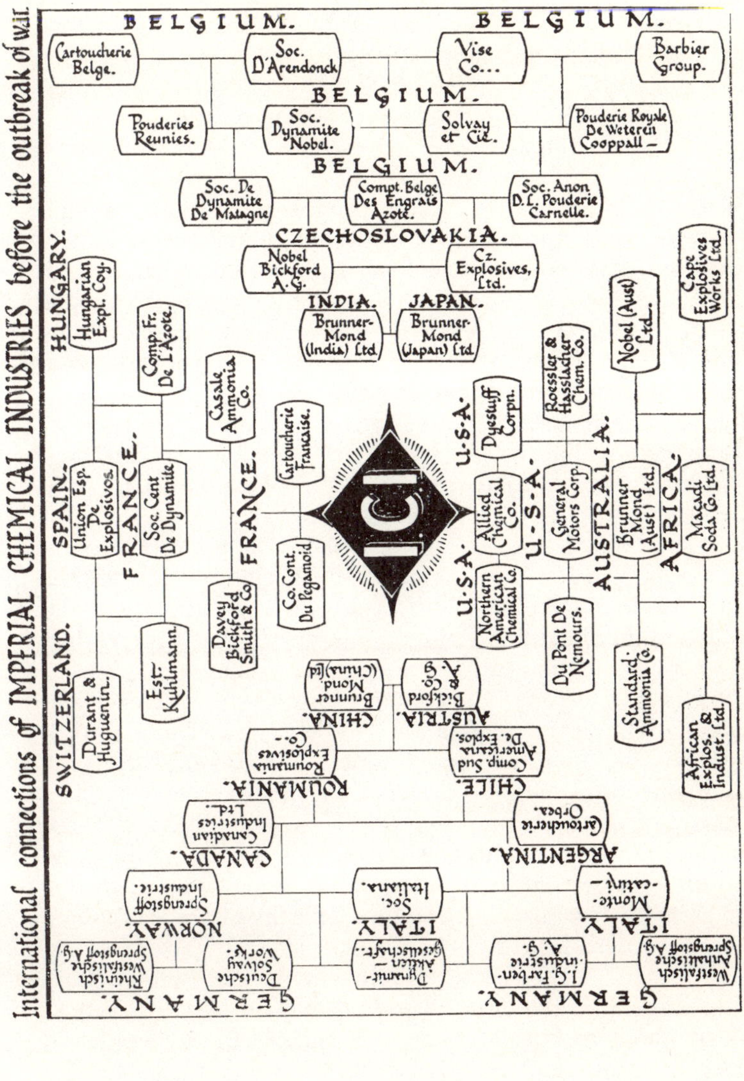

FIGURE 3.4: ICI's international connections, 1945.

1930s) were all replaced by four steam-reforming units. These improved Billingham's competitive position in two ways. They utilised naphtha, a cheaper feedstock than coal; and they required much less labour – each reformer could be operated by seven people per shift compared with sixty per shift on the plants which they replaced.

However, in themselves these technological changes could not guarantee that commodities produced at Billingham remained competitive with those produced in larger ammonia plants utilising natural gas as feedstock in other parts of the world. Three new ammonia plants were therefore constructed, each capable of producing over 40 tonnes of ammonia an hour, increasing annual capacity by over 300,000 tonnes to give a total in excess of 1 million tonnes by the late 1960s. The introduction of these larger units cut production costs by half. The labour time per employee necessarily required to produce 1 tonne of ammonia was cut dramatically, from 11.6 to 0.3 hours.

A further major technological breakthrough was achieved in 1966, when, as a result of research and development by ICI, the world's first commercial low-pressure methanol plant entered production at Billingham. This considerably reduced unit production costs, but required sulphur-free feedstock (such as naphtha or North Sea gas) because the copper catalyst which it used was sensitive to minor traces of sulphur in the synthesis gas. To deal with this requirement two oil refineries, with an annual capacity of 5 million tonnes, were developed at an adjoining site by Phillips Imperial Petroleum (a joint venture by ICI and Phillips). These primarily produced naphtha as a feedstock for both Billingham and Wilton. Associated with these refineries ICI developed two large aromatics plants with an annual capacity of 900,000 tonnes, largely to provide feedstocks for its other plants on Teesside.

In these and other ways, the Billingham plant became more closely integrated into a complex production system on both banks of the Tees (although, as we shall see, the ICI works on Teesside were also increasingly becoming just one part of a major national and international production system). The Wilton site – specialising in organic chemicals – grew strongly after 1945 to more than rival Billingham in size and significance. The location had a number of positive attributes for ICI, apart from the obvious proximity to Billingham (the two sites were rapidly linked by a ten-mile pipeline under the Tees). Its 2,000 acres of flat land were sufficient for planned developments, water supplies were locally available and port facilities existed. With government approval came deemed planning permission so that ICI could avoid the usual planning procedures. In short, Wilton was an ideal site (see Reader, 1975, pp. 391–412).

Developments at Wilton proceeded in stages. The first consisted of ten complementary and interrelated plants, centred on No. 1 Olefine, a cracker with an annual capacity of 30,000 tonnes, used to produce ethylene from light oil distillate (which, until the development of the North Tees refinery in the 1960s, was imported from Grangemouth and Thameshaven). The cracker also produced various other products: petrol; a mixture of butane and butylene; propylene; and a mixture of hydrogen and ammonia. With the exception of ethylene, used at Wilton in the production of polythene, ethylene oxide and ethylene glycol, all of these products were sent to Billingham via the pipeline link. At Billingham propylene was converted to acetone and methylmethacrylate and returned to Wilton for use in the 'Perspex' plant. Other products brought from Billingham to Wilton via the pipeline included brine, used in chlorine and caustic soda production and, in turn, in the production of ethylene oxide. A further input from Billingham was methanol, used in the formaldehyde plant and in turn in the production of phenol/formaldehyde and urea/formaldehyde.

Subsequently, further plants were added to manufacture both existing products and also capacity to manufacture new ones. Stage II of Wilton's development added the first 'Terylene' plant, Stage III saw the addition of a butadiene plant, extracting this from the cracker output and then converting it into a range of materials in the 'Bukaton' plant. In Stage IV a nylon plant was added, using benzene brought in by rail tanker from various UK sources and ammonia from Heysham and Billingham.

By the end of the 1950s a major petrochemicals complex was emerging at Wilton. Output had increased from 5,000 tonnes of products in 1950 to 346,000 in 1957. Over 500 of the 2,000 acres had been developed at a total fixed capital cost (to the end of 1958) of £58 million (see House and Fullerton, 1960). Paralleling this growth in fixed capital, there was quite considerable employment growth both in chemicals production and construction. By 1958 some 6,000 were employed by ICI at Wilton in production whilst a further 3,000 worked for ICI and private contractors on ongoing construction activities. With the continued development of the interlinked plants at Wilton and Billingham and the associated refinery, ICI created a chemicals complex on Teesside of considerable international significance.

The 1950s, then, represented an era of booming capital investment on Teesside, led by ICI at its Wilton works but also encompassing major replacement of older plant in other industries like steel, shipbuilding and engineering. The whole area seemed, to the eyes of industrialists at least, to be participating in this growth process. In many senses a strongly self-fulfilling prophecy was emerging, wherein continued expansion would lead inevitably to continued prosperity. This growth ethic was eagerly embraced by local government, which did all in its power to facilitate the plans of companies like Dorman Long and ICI and to ease the problems of labour supply and housing in the area at a time of strong national economic growth. It was also supported by national governments anxious to see expansion in selected 'key' industrial sectors. It became a dogma which was to prove particularly pervasive and influential in the 1960s.

4. TRADES UNIONS IN THE CHEMICALS INDUSTRY AND LABOUR RELATIONS AT ICI: COMPANY UNIONISM AND ITS IMPACTS ON TEESSIDE

In the nineteenth century the most remarkable characteristic of employment in the chemicals industry was its sheer physical hardship and damage to health. Twelve-hour shifts, seven days a week, without meal breaks, were mandatory. Protective clothing was unknown. Industrial diseases such as chrome ulcerations, dermatitis, poisoning, cyanosis and respiratory problems were common. Under these conditions chemical works were largely regarded as a source of employment only in the last resort. Production technology was such that there were few maintenance craftsmen and a mass of labourers, often employed on a casual or sub-contract basis. The chemical works were regarded as fit for only a temporary stay. Partly as a consequence of this and partly because the industry was relatively new trade unionism developed relatively late. Of twelve chemical companies examined by the 1882 Royal Commission on Labour, three claimed no history whatsoever of union presence at their works (see Edwards, 1946; Gill *et al.*, 1978).

There was, then, relatively little impetus to trades union growth within the industry itself. Instead, the push came from trades unions with bases of membership strength elsewhere, and from the government's concern for national industrial agreements after the First World War. The first peacetime national negotiating body, the Chemical Trade Joint Industrial Council, was not organised until 1918. Among the unions represented were the Dock

Wharf, Riverside and General Workers' Union; the National Union of General Workers; the Workers' Union; and the National Amalgamated Union of Labour.

From its formation in 1926 ICI proceeded actively to promote and take advantage of low levels of unionisation. Its conscious policy was to seek to ally workers with the company, incorporating them through a series of company bodies. A three-tier system of participation (Works Councils, Division Councils and a Central Council) was initiated in the first few years. Works Council agendas strictly excluded wages and conditions. As the market leader, the company was able to concede wages and conditions in advance of comparable firms and industries. It could head off pressures towards militant unionisation without actively discouraging collective bargaining in principle. The Chief Labour Officer, Lloyd Roberts, stated the company's philosophy when he wrote in 1928 that

> There is a fundamental antagonism between the company's policy and that of the unions ... their whole effort is directed towards allying ICI workers with workers generally whereas the company's policy continually tends to ally the workers with the company. (Quoted in Reader, 1975, p. 64.)

Visiting Rome, Henry Mond, the company's Labour Director, endorsed the Mussolini regime. He found Fascist labour policy, with its notion of corporate industrial endeavour unhampered by conflict between capital and labour, particularly appealing (Gill, *et al.*, 1978, pp. 83–4). In 1936 the company took its policy a stage further when it broke from the Chemical Employers' Federation and began to negotiate independently of the other main companies.

Drawing on the paternalist traditions of the area, ICI developed an internal labour market during this period, often recruiting generations of the same family from residential areas surrounding the works. Nowhere was this more apparent than at Billingham. ICI also developed very clear policies towards the local labour market, mirroring the role played by the iron and steel companies in other parts of Teesside during the later nineteenth century. The company had an all-embracing influence over life outside as well as inside the workplace. In 1922 Billingham was a village green with forty houses, a pub and a church. Between the wars ICI built 2,330 houses at Billingham, which was transformed from a hamlet into a one-industry company town. Sickness benefit schemes were set up as part of the Works Council activities. As the works expanded, labour was drawn from the Durham coalfield and from industries in recession. This intra-regional labour migration in the inter-war years was indicative of the linkages between chemical production on Teesside and the Durham coalfield. Whereas the steel companies on Teesside sought coking coal from south-east Durham, ICI sought labour power. One manager recalled how

> There was a lot of very good labour in the Durham coal fields which flocked down to Teesside. They were a very good workforce. We didn't have any union trouble. They were thankful they'd got a job on the surface with fairly reasonable conditions. (Quoted in Pettigrew, 1985, p. 126.)

This labour surplus in surrounding areas and the reference to limited 'union trouble', were particularly significant in the context of ICI's own distinctive labour relations policy. Like the iron and steel employers in the previous century, ICI sought to develop a particular kind of attitude towards industrial relations which allied its workers with ICI's corporate goals and objectives. This resonated clearly with the earlier ideology of consensus and accommodation between capital and labour on Teesside, and was especially influential in the development of Billingham.

After 1945 the company paid further attention to its stance on labour relations. Maintenance of an adequate labour force and stable industrial relations were particularly important to ICI at its new Wilton complex, as well as at Billingham. Company paternalism had so constricted the development of trade unionism that less than half of the manual workforce were union members. On the other hand, the emergent post-war political consensus produced pressure for nationalisation from the small but strident Chemical Workers Union. Its Assistant General Secretary wrote in 1946:

> State control, if it is to be of practical value in the chemical trade, must develop into the nationalisation of the ICI, otherwise the ICI will dictate the nation's industrial policy not merely as it affects chemicals, but actually the country's whole economic policy. (Cited in Edwards, 1946, p. 83.)

Certainly, ICI had a vast range of national and international connections (see Figures. 3.3 and 3.4). In 1947 negotiations between ICI and the trades unions resulted in the introduction of a new negotiating procedure for eighteen signatory unions. ICI further undertook to bring to the notice of its employees a company recommendation in favour of trades union membership but would not agree to compulsory union membership. In return the trades unions recognised the Works Councils, which they had opposed during the inter-war period as an inadequate substitute for genuine collective bargaining (see Gill *et al.*, 1978, pp. 86–8).

In practice, ICI continued to develop its personnel management techniques, culminating in the introduction of MUPS (Manpower Utilisation and Payment Structure) in 1965 and its successor, WSA (Weekly Staff Agreement) in 1969. These were sophisticated work measurement schemes aimed at tightening management control over the labour process in return for incentive payments on a series of widely differentiated scales (see Roeber, 1975). They met with considerable opposition, not least on the Wilton site. In this period marked differences in the character of the workforce at the two ICI Teesside sites were apparent. Wilton presented a sharp contrast to the company town of Billingham. It grew in the 1950s, at a time of relative trades union strength and drew in workers from all parts of the area – partly because of state policy (see Chapter 4). One ICI manager was later to remark how 'Billingham is ICI, the place is ICI. Wilton isn't ICI. Wilton is a farming village' (quoted in Pettigrew, 1985, p. 223).

In practical terms what management wanted from MUPS and WSA was the elimination of all restrictive practices, a general increase in job flexibility, an increase in commitment to the job; and tied in with the resulting increase in productivity, a reduction in manning levels. Managers knew that this could not be achieved on command. It would require a mixture of attractive financial rewards, a more co-operative management style, and the appearance of greater shop floor control. A number of features of the two-year process whereby the new agreement was tested, re-thought, negotiated and finally implemented stand out.

First is the resources, effort and attention given by ICI to the centrally devised and organised *training* of every level of its management in the practical – and often theoretical – psychology of defusing and diffusing conflict, dealing with real and potential opposition, and getting what it wanted in a manner which appeared democratic and satisfactory to its opponents. Stewards from different sites described how they were 'completely thrown by it'.

Secondly, there is the degree of control which the Central Personnel Department (CPD) built up at least over the management of the different sites, and through this acquired an understanding of the psychology of the workforce, enabling the CPD to formulate and implement a long-term strategy. For the WSA was no fly-by-night productivity deal. It was an attempt permanently to halt the creeping strength which workers had been building on the shop floor and to lay the basis for a continuing responsiveness to new productivity requirements and technology. The sophistication of the CPD's approach is illustrated by its ability to retreat in order to advance: the first agreement (MUPS) failed, mainly because of opposition from craftsmen at Wilton, but management was able to orchestrate a fairly orderly retreat, to learn from the lessons of failure, to destroy, via victimisation, the opposition and implement a new scheme to achieve fundamentally the same objectives as the original scheme.

Thirdly, and crucial to this success, was the building up of a good relationship with the national negotiating officers of the signatory unions. This was very important, for example, in ultimately controlling opposition at Wilton. This, however, could not be relied on indefinitely. It worked in the 1960s and early 1970s when ICI's approach was new and the trades union leaders, like Len Edmundson at the AUEW, were of a generation formed by the struggle for basic trades union rights. To them ICI seemed progressive; they, the negotiators, got the impression that they were winning – they 'won' a 100 per cent closed shop, for example. The situation subsequently changed as trades unionists gained experience of this new brand of corporate management. While some negotiators saw it as part of their job to co-operate with 'progressive' managements, others were of a more independent bent, having themselves, like John Miller of the TGWU, been leading members of militant combine committees. Evidently, then, some of ICI's control over its workforce depends on the innovativeness of its management techniques, combined with the limited experience of sections of the trades union leadership and the greenness of some of its workforce (a feature of the workforce which is not accidental). On the one hand, ICI in its company towns tries to keep a monopoly of the labour market and therefore restrict trades union experience and pressure. On the other hand, it invariably locates its new plants in greenfield/green labour sites like Severnside in Somerset – but increasingly completely outside the UK. Stewards are aware of the tendency for militant trade unionism to be nipped in the bud before participants know what has happened to them.

A further source of management control is the fragmented nature of the workforce compared with the co-ordinated, centralised nature of management (see especially Nichols and Beynon, 1977). The vulnerability this creates is reflected in the shop stewards' ignorance about what is going on, or what the feeling is, in other shifts, plants, sites, divisions or unions. It is also reflected in management having far more knowledge than the national officers about whether a claim, or offer, will get support. And, as one activist put it: 'when management know your strength better than you, half the battle is lost'.

The battle at Wilton against MUPS and WSA was lost after management recognised the weaknesses on its own side. In 1968 John Harvey-Jones was appointed deputy chairman of the Heavy Organic Chemicals Division with overall responsibility for the Wilton site. The Wilton site management committee, with representation from the five divisions with works on the site, was strengthened. A more collaborative form of site management became the order of the day. A leading shop steward, Paddy Tombe, was fired in 1969 and management stood firm against a protest strike. John Harvey-Jones later remembered how he aimed to try to 'rebalance the power between management and shop stewards. We solved it really by taking and winning a number of quite small strikes, culminating by firing the leader of the shop stewards committee' (quoted in Pettigrew, 1985, 232). And in 1970 individual unions were allowed to go on to WSA, breaking an earlier insistence that the whole site 'went on' simultaneously. At Wilton the general workers accepted WSA and the craft unions were forced to follow in 1971 by a growing disparity in pay rates.

ICI's special labour relations strategy, then, presented considerable difficulties for trades unionists actively organising in its works. One attempt to counter these problems was via an interworks combine committee of union activists (see also Hales, 1980). Throughout the 1960s leadership of the combine committee was based primarily at Wilton. The influence of the wider union organisation, especially the AUEW district committee, strengthened the militancy of the ICI stewards considerably, especially in their struggle against MUPS. A major problem for the combine committee was the uneven development of industrial relations and trades unionism between different ICI sites.[2]

In general terms, the strength of support for the combine committee has always been in inverse proportion to support for the consultative system. Where the consultative system has taken root it has been difficult to get even the most rudimentary elements of an independent plant organisation off the ground. Most trades unionists see the importance of some degree of unity, even if it is just keeping in touch and knowing what is going on. In the first stages of a plant- or a combine-wide organisation these basic factors are important in bringing people together. At ICI, however, the *company* brought people together, at the company's expense, on the company's beer, and in the company's comfortable surroundings. Consequently, only trades unionists who have been to some degree critical of the company's system and understand the specific importance of independent unity, saw much point in meeting together as a union body. Trades unions' unity in ICI, whether at a plant or a company level, therefore requires a much more sophisticated, more political level of consciousness than in companies where management lacks such effective strategies of incorporation.

This oppositional significance attached to unity and these more complex conditions for unity, as well as the centralised nature of management's strategy, were reflected in the character of combine committee discussions and in the content of the newspaper that it produced in the late 1970s, *Chemco News*. The ICI combine would discuss the strategic and ideological significance of the company's latest move; as well as, of course, discussing campaigns around the next wage claim. At ICI the case for independent trades unionism had to be argued. The combine newspaper was very explicit, therefore, about the workings of capitalism; it had to be, in order to put the case for independent trades unionism. In 1979 the third issue of *Chemco News*, for example,considered the decision to invest at Wilhelmshaven:

> Whatever way we as employees of ICI look at the situation, we have suffered because of the decision to build the German plant, the way that decision was made and the way it is being built. There is more trouble in store. The decision is an indication of the future of ICI as an employer based in the UK; and the use of contractors to design and build the plant is yet another nail in the coffin for ICI's in house engineering staff.

This pressure to take a directly and politically oppositional stance to management, combined with the weakness of many of the site organisations, posed problems for the growth of the combine committee. Stewards who supported the principle of combine committees, nevertheless, felt that the ICI combine committee was just an ideas group, a talking shop not an organisation with muscle. Looking at it from a trades union point of view, they did not think it worth attending – though they were not usually hostile. This approach was especially characteristic of the shop stewards at Wilton. For them it was confirmed by the experience of the combine committee strike in 1975. This strike was connected with the wage claim. At the combine committee meeting there was full support for strike action. Wilton struck and the site stopped. But nothing came of the strike call elsewhere. The Wilton stewards felt let down, and rethought their commitment to the combine. They set high conditions on their membership. As a senior steward put it: 'We'll join a strong and genuine combine; that means a combine committee whose decisions are meaningful, whose decisions can be backed up with action.' This identified the nub of the problem for the combine. As an unofficial body, it found difficulty in backing its decisions with action. In many cases trades unionists who attended ICI combine meetings were individuals who decided themselves to come with informal backing and contributions to their costs from a section of their branch. They were still fighting hard for trades unionism, let alone for the combine committee, to be taken seriously. It was this reality which saw the committee turning towards propaganda – via *Chemco News* – and communication as its main role.

This inability to lead or initiate company-wide action was not unique. All combine committees experienced such problems and at ICI it was the major flaw in an earlier phase of the committee's development in the early 1960s. According to Alf Waddington, a leading AUEW steward at Northwich, attendance at those early combine committee meetings was large – 50–60, sometimes more – much larger than later meetings: 'But as far as policy was concerned we never came out with anything very clear, partly because we knew we could not get the backing on the sites.'

The combine committee's main strength was not so much in initiating and leading action, but in *generalising* and *supporting* action, initiated at a particular site. This was the case with the campaign for a £3 extra shift allowance in 1978. This campaign started in mid-Cheshire, spread through the combine committee network and finally won, with considerable credit due to the combine committee:

> People could see it really meant something; whenever they want to know what's going on elsewhere in the company, stewards come to see me because of the combine committee. As far as information and support from within the company is concerned they've come to rely far more on the combine than the officials. (Alf Waddington)

The increase in shift allowance was a victory which benefited the process workers. It meant nothing to the craft workers except, as they saw it, a reduction in differentials. And this raised another major problem for the combine committee; the traditional divisions between craft and process workers in ICI. The consultative system retarded the growth of even minimum negotiating unity at shop floor level. But the problem extended more deeply. The division of labour within ICI set process workers and craft workers apart. Continuous production and continental shifts meant that process workers lived a completely different life from the craft workers, who had only a single day shift. Even when they were at work at the same time they were unlikely to develop shared concerns. For the craft workers move from job to job, as different sections of the plant require maintenance. In addition to this division of labour were the financial divisions, whose effects on relations between general and craft workers were reinforced by the WSA. With the WSA, craftsmen were on the top two grades, unable to move any further. The process workers, however, could move up. Moving up, in fact, was the only way of increasing earnings between wage claims. Consequently, process workers seemed to be at an advantage and craft workers seemed to be stuck. The combine committee's policy on wages has been for 'across the board' claims, thereby tending to identify it with the general workers and alienate the craft workers. The history of the committee had been plagued with the problem of seeming to be identified with one or other of the two groups. In the early days, in the 1960s, it was seen mainly as a craft combine. The later combine consciously tried to avoid this sectarianism, with some success, especially with staff workers. It tried to do this by concentrating on issues that effected everyone, such as investment, redundancy, consultation and so on, though not evading the wages issue. *Chemco News* was important in conveying the image of a multi-interest combine which discussed the views and concerns of all ICI workers.

The only other vehicle for trades union unity at ICI is the national negotiating procedure. A crucial issue for the combine committee was its relationship with the national negotiators. One direction in which it could have gone is indicated by the early Ford combine committee. This pressured for lay representation on the National Joint Negotiating Committee, won it and, after some initial successes, faded as an independent body. The ICI combine committee fought to make the negotiators more accountable, through lay representation and some form of more adequate reporting back and mandating than was provided by either the AUEW advisory group or the TGWU trade group. But there were important differences between ICI and Ford which gave the ICI combine committee a greater independence from the national officials. First, the Ford combine committee was a semi-official body in that it was made up of convenors and senior stewards and was organised around the annual wage claim. In this sense it was little more than an extension of the existing trades union structures; though at times it acted independently of them. It was relatively easy to incorporate. In ICI, on the other hand, because of the incorporated nature of trades unionism in the company, the combine committee had come together on a more oppositional, ideological basis. It had support among the national officers, one or two of whom saw it as an important means of strengthening their own negotiating position. On wages and allowances it acted in this way, although mainly of its own accord, without any real help from sympathetic officials. But on the issue of the consultation system and other aspects of ICI strategy, it has taken very much more independent positions than the officials. The officials are to some extent part of the web by which ICI has incorporated 'its' trades unions.

5. THE CHALLENGE OF THE 1960S: MODERNISATION OF THE OLD INDUSTRIAL ECONOMY AND OPTIMISM ON TEESSIDE

In 1962, in response to a relatively sharp increase in unemployment within the North-east (to rates of 5–6 per cent), the Conservative Government appointed Lord Hailsham as Minister with special responsibility for the region. The concentration of past economic growth on Teesside assumed special importance, as a strategy for the North-east was published the following year in a White Paper (HMSO, 1963). Teesside was designated as a key part of a growth zone, supposedly capable of absorbing workers from declining industries like coal-mining and playing the lead in the 'modernisation' of the North-east economy. The Hailsham programme also made several suggestions as to what the content of modernisation policies on Teesside should be. These included the provision of more land for the steel and chemicals industries, the construction of new industrial estates, and the development of new road systems to improve links between industrial and residential areas. It also suggested that the area required a comprehensive urban planning framework to provide guidelines for implementing modernisation policies and to manage the growth which it was assumed would occur.

Work began on the *Teesside Survey and Plan* (with national government encouragement) in 1964. A steering committee was established in an attempt to resolve the conflicting interests of various local authorities. Completion of the plan in 1968 coincided with wholesale local government reorganisation.[3] None the less, *Teesplan* was an important landmark in the evolution of state policies for the area generally, and for the steel and chemicals industries there in particular.

Teesplan represented a clear expression of contemporary

optimism over the prospect of managed expansion. Modernising and strengthening the region's economy so as to absorb a significant population increase was a central concern. Three major policy objectives followed from this (see HMSO, 1969): the maintenance of Teesside as a port complex of national importance and provision for the locational requirements of the chemicals and steel industries; the diversification of the economy by attracting labour-intensive industries, both in manufacturing and the service sector; and the promotion of Middlesbrough as a sub-regional commercial and service centre. Particular stress was placed upon meeting the requirements of the capital-intensive chemicals and steel producers, though it was widely recognised that there would be major rationalisation programmes within them. Expansion of capacity and output would be accompanied by, at best, gently falling employment. This prioritisation reflected the continuing powerful representation of chemicals and steel interests in local government, and a recognition of the strategic national importance of these industries on Teesside, leading to a considerable commitment of resources to support their restructuring programmes. The *quid pro quo* for this, however, was a political commitment to provide alternative employment in manufacturing and services.

One central element in the expansion programme of steel and chemicals companies, and in local authority support for further envisaged growth in these sectors, was the provision of adequate flat land. Chemicals and steel accounted for about half of the industrial land on Teesside, some 6,000 acres, equivalent to about one-eighth of the entire Teesside area (Teesside County Borough Council, 1973, p. 29). Even so, there were growing demands for more land to be allocated to these uses. Changes in technical conditions of production in both industries allied to growing reliance upon imported raw materials (as production and trade in them were increasingly internationalised) produced pressures for a downstream relocation to large, flat sites with access to the deepwater channel of the river Tees. Expected future employment densities in these industries were very low, so that employment reductions due to rationalisation were expected to be accompanied by the amount of land demanded by these industries increasing. Both BSC and ICI had extensive holdings of undeveloped land to cater for their own future planned expansion. As a legacy of pre-nationalisation plans by Dorman Long, BSC held 1,500 acres on the south bank of the Tees at Bran Sands; while ICI had 900 acres of undeveloped land on its huge Wilton site. There was,

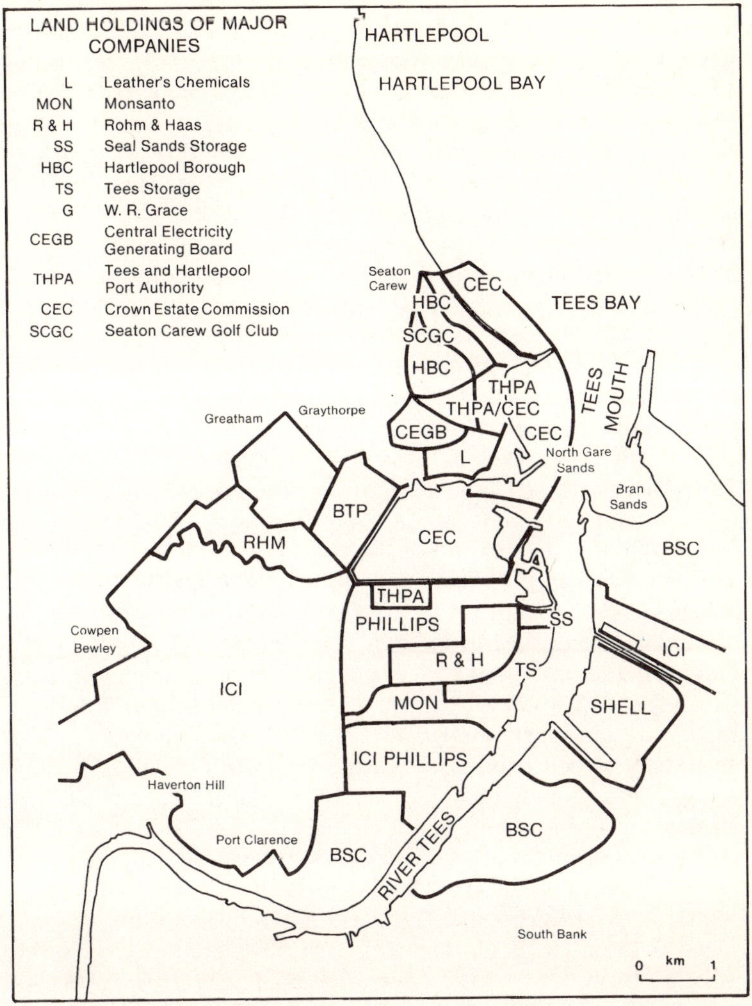

FIGURE 3.5: Land holdings of major companies on Teesside, late 1970s.

however, a marked shortage of suitable sites for other chemicals companies that might want to locate on Teesside (Figure 3.5). This was especially so as a large, flat and stable site between Hartlepool and the Tees estuary became, rather controversially in the context of decline in the North-east coalfield, the location of a major new nuclear power station in the late 1960s (Crossman, 1977, p. 162).

It was in this context that proposals to reclaim another huge area of land at Seal Sands on the northern side of the estuary gained powerful and widespread support, especially after publication of the Regional Ports Survey (NEPC, 1969). This recommended that the Tees alone of the Northern Region's ports should be the focus of major development. It also suggested that the Tees become a prototype for a new central government plan to develop selected port areas into major industrial complexes via the Maritime Industrial Development Area Scheme (MIDAS). The MIDAS areas were to link major new port facilities with complexes of bulk processing and associated industries. The Tees was selected as the best UK site for such developments because of its existing port facilities, European connections and the availability of vast areas of flat land adjacent to the river. Although the MIDAS proposals were abandoned, part of their legacy was that they helped to shape views as to the most appropriate development strategy for Teesside. Its industrial port complex continued to evolve along the lines mapped out by MIDAS, for reasons that were related more to national than to local needs.

The 1960s was, therefore, a period of great optimism on and for Teesside. Already a major focus of economic growth in the North-east, it seemed destined for a long boom period. It clearly occupied a central place both in the production strategies of major chemicals and steel companies, and in the regional and national modernisation programmes of the state. Industries such as chemicals and steel, which produced inputs for a large swathe of other manufacturing activities, were vital to the emergent national strategy of transforming manufacturing in the UK into an internationally competitive sector. Teesside was specifically identified as a key location in the Hailsham White Paper proposals to modernise the North-east. The area thus came to occupy a unique niche at the intersection of national and regional modernisation policies during the 1960s. In response to this, the structure of local government there was altered so as to be better able to cope with formulating and implementing policies complementary and appropriate to the requirements of central government and the big corporations on whose decisions the implementation of modernisation policies ultimately depended. The alliance between major chemicals and steel companies, trades unions and local authorities, many of whose members were employed by these companies, was an extremely powerful one. It cut across class boundaries in a vigorous promotion of one concept of what Teesside's future ought to be. Consequently, local authority land use and infrastructure provision policies tended to be geared to the requirements of the major chemicals, oil and steel companies, and to those of commercial and financial capitals seeking lucrative city-centre sites. They usually evolved in this way without obvious pressure being directly exerted by these capitalist interests themselves. Modernisation - at least for a time until some of its limitations became apparent – was a truly hegemonic project.

6. CONCLUDING COMMENTS

Whilst the Teesside area had an abundance of natural resources which facilitated the emergence of capitalist industrialisation, one prerequisite which it did not possess was a ready supply of labour. This was to be a central concern for the steel and chemicals companies from their earliest days, and in part explains the emphasis attached by them to the construction of company housing, company towns and, in due course, company trades unions. Massive immigration from the countryside in the nineteenth century helped to fashion Middlesbrough as an evolving steel town. Wholesale moves from the Durham coalfield in the 1920s and 1930s similarly helped to create Billingham as an ICI town and filled the works with ICI employees. Through a selective provision of housing, roads, schools and other amenities, the steel and chemicals companies developed a built environment and social climate ideally suited to the reproduction of acquiescent and tractable labour forces. There was, quite deliberately, little opportunity created for waged employment other than in chemicals, steel and related industries. Partly because of this, the companies which led the development of the area exerted a particularly pervasive influence which extended beyond the relations of the workplace far into those of civil society.

After 1945 the area's economy boomed, led by investment at ICI's Wilton complex but matched also by developments in other sectors. In the 1940s and 1950s, the success of developments at ICI Wilton depended upon tacit political opposition to the establishment of competing, male-employing industries, as it built up another substantial labour force. More and more, the provision of necessary working-class housing and related infrastructure was not simply orchestrated through, but was directly provided by, the state. This period of economic growth and growing state involvement in managing growth culminated with the region acquiring a distinctive role in the context of 1960s-style national and local economic policy. It was to be a focal point within a growth zone, capable of leading the modernisation of the North-east regional economy. This entailed the continuing prioritisation of steel and chemicals companies' interests, with a promise of planned diversification and service sector growth to offset some of the worst effects of continued dependence upon these two industries. These processes are explored at greater length in the next chapter.

NOTES

1. For a number of reasons, this largely depended upon companies not involved in the iron and steel trade, although during the 1880s both Bolckow Vaughan and Bell Brothers were involved in salt extraction. By comparison with major deposits in Cheshire, though, Tees salt was deposited at greater depth, covered by water-bearing strata and did not produce a natural brine, making it difficult to work. Partly in consequence, the iron and steel companies on Teesside never really diversified into alkali production in anything other than an experimental fashion (see North, 1975, pp. 37–9; Warren 1980, p. 41).
2. At Huddersfield, too, the influence of the district union organisation has been important. The AUEW resigned from the consultative system, although some people felt it could be used. At Doncaster (another stronghold of the combine committee) the ICI consultative system never developed deep roots. This site, along with two others in the Fibre division, was part of British Nylon Spinners. They had their own negotiating procedure and the shop stewards had had considerable experience of building an independent organisation, an embryonic combine committee, before they came into ICI. Moving along the spectrum, at Northwich, the situation was more polarised. A 'company town', with little interference from a strong district union, and with a workforce predominantly from ICI families, management had more of its own way – but not entirely its own way. In the 1970s one of the TGWU branches resigned from the consultative system: 'I thought that with the new system, involving the shop stewards, we might get somewhere, but all the time it was management saying no, no, no – never put as bluntly as that mind.' That is how the secretary of this TGWU branch at Northwich saw it. He was surprised at the support given to the decision to resign. A 2:1 majority. He did not realise that the frustration was so widely felt. There are other signs of this frustration beneath the surface – even at some of the sites where the shop floor organisation had never known anything other than ICI's consultative system. Some of these feelings came to the surface at a delegate conference called by the national officials in 1977. The meeting was called as a result of pressure from the members for the unions to develop a policy in relation to the consultative system. The national officers allowed four combine members to attend so that the highly critical view could be heard. 'Considering our numbers our contributions were very well received. We really had an impact. I think we said what a lot of delegates were coming to feel. One of the national officers put in a plug for us too. A very good meeting for the combine', commented the chairman of the combine committee.
3. These involved the creation of Teesside County Borough, although this was soon overtaken by more general change in the structure of local government. The Royal Commission on Local Government argued for an expanded Teesside local government area but, not

surprisingly, this provoked fierce resistance from existing local authorities who would lose out as a result. After considerable conflict (especially between urban and rural authorities) and much debate, a compromise was successfully sought and the new County of Cleveland was created in 1974, made up of four constituent Boroughs: Hartlepool, Langbaurgh, Middlesbrough and Stockton. As well as a Teesside Structure Plan, preparation began on Structure Plans for Hartlepool, East Cleveland and West Cleveland. Despite the complexity of the changes that resulted from this reorganisation of local government and despite, or because of, changes in party political control over local government on Teesside in this period, there was a marked continuity in overall planning and policy objectives. This was reflected in the similarity between *Teesplan* and the subsequent Structure Plans. Both major political parties shared a powerful commitment to modernisation policies.

CHAPTER FOUR

Political Processes: The Emergence of an Old Politics of Labour and Policies for Modernisation

1. INTRODUCTION

A distinguishing characteristic of the Teesside area is the extent to which it has been fashioned by the designs and accidents of political strategy, and the distinctiveness of these political interventions in the constitution of the place. Much of this is again related to, though not reducible to, the kind of economic growth which took place there from the mid-nineteenth century. The seemingly accommodative consensus between capital and labour on Teesside had an influence which lasted well into the twentieth century. State planning for reconstruction in the years after 1945 was coloured by such notions. When Teesside came subsequently to be the focus of a major regional growth zone and modernisation policy in the 1960s, it seemed almost as if its historical destiny was being fulfilled.

2. THE POLITICAL CONSTRUCTION AND STATE REGULATION OF TEESSIDE

The paternalist forms of capitalist wage relations encouraged by the early Ironmasters were intimately connected with their effective control of local politics. In the early years of growth, especially the 1850s and 1860s, the basis of local economic and political life resided in the hands of a small, closely related group of men. Of these, Henry Bolckow was the most outstanding: becoming Middlesbrough's first mayor, when it was incorporated in 1853; its first President of the Chamber of Commerce, when that was formed in 1863; and the first Member of Parliament, when it became a parliamentary constituency in 1868. In these years, too, the Town Council was dominated by the iron producers. Its membership comprised ten Ironmasters and seven shopkeepers in 1872. As the town grew, so it became increasingly difficult for one group of families to control all aspects of its existence, and the composition of the Town Council shifted accordingly; but the overall political influence of the leading employers and the relatively muted development of independent trades unionism and political representation of labour interests remained (see especially Briggs, 1963). It was not until 1924, for instance, that Teesside elected its first Labour Member of Parliament in Middlesbrough East.

Indeed, Middlesbrough in many ways exemplified the broader party political history of the area. For on Teesside the Labour Party as a political institution, and labourism as a form of political ideology and practice, neither carried the same meanings nor achieved the same degree of hegemonic dominance as they did over other parts of North-east England (for example, see Beynon and Austrin, 1993a, b; Bulmer, 1978, pp. 91–142). Whereas other parts of the North-east solidly elected Labour councillors and Members of Parliament, Teesside's electoral and party political history has been much more volatile. This volatility both reflected and was a formative influence upon a labourist culture that espoused a markedly moderate form of politics and remained deeply influenced by the legacies of paternalism and acquiescent company trades unionism.

For many decades, party politics on Teesside remained a contest between Conservatives and Liberals. Both local and national elections were dominated by competition between, and occasionally within, these two parties, with local landowners often prominent among the former and the emergent industrial bourgeoisie among both, but especially the latter. As the Labour Party (and its predecessors) emerged at national level, it remained largely anonymous within electoral contests on Teesside. In part, this reflected the impacts of paternalistic capital : labour relations on forms of party politics. But the presence of occasional Liberal/Labour candidates simply seemed to emphasise the ways in which representation of working-class interests and popular demands was sporadically incorporated into the existing political institutions and structures of the area. Middlesbrough East, a constituency dominated by the workforces of the chemicals and steel industries, remained Labour but it was very unusual within Teesside in doing so. Hartlepool, for example, returned Conservative Members of Parliament in all four General Elections between 1924 and 1935; Stockton and Cleveland returned Conservatives in three of the four. Harold Macmillan's experiences as Stockton's MP were to have a decisive formative influence on his vision of 'One Nation' Conservatism and this in turn was to have important ramifications for Teesside in the grand era of cross-party consensus 'modernisation policies' that so dominated the area in the 1960s.

It was not, then, until the 1945 General Election and Labour's sweeping national victory that Teesside began to take on the appearance of a Labour Party stronghold, and some constituencies regularly returned Labour Members of Parliament for the next forty years. However, others were much more volatile. The electors of Middlesbrough West returned Conservative Members in 1951, 1955, 1959 and 1970; those of Cleveland a Conservative in 1962. At local government level, there was greater variability of party political dominance and control. This partly reflected well-established differences between inner urban areas dominated by heavy industry and more peripheral agricultural and/or middle-class residential areas, such as Guisborough. Another of these places, Yarm, had, in the words of one of its residents, become '... a dormitory town for those who own the industries of Teesside', characterised by its 'entrenched Conservatism' (quoted in Lumb, 1976, p. 78). Variability at local level is neatly illustrated by the outcomes of the first two elections to the newly formed Teesside County Borough Council: in 1967 the Conservatives won a majority of 56 of the 104 seats, but in 1970 Labour gained control by winning 57. Such changes in party political control, in the middle of a period that represents the high-point of cross-party consensus formed around the theme of 'modernising Teesside', are suggestive of the moderate character of both Conservative and Labour politics there. Again, the accommodative legacy of paternalist industrial relations on the character and content of party politics is clear. Whilst Conservative politics bore the progressive mark of Macmillan's 'One Nation' vision, those of Labour bore the more sinister mark of deference: Labour politicians informed people of what was happening whilst people deferred to the judgement and wisdom of their councillors (see Lynch, 1976, p. 14). In this sense, the role of the Labour Party was one of social control, stifling dissent from those within it and silencing grass-roots criticisms which challenged the dominant vision of the benefits of Teesside modernised. If such criticisms could not be silenced, then those who articulated them were to be encouraged to form organisations that could then be manipulated and used as channels through which to promote dominant party views (see Lynch, 1976, p. 57). As long as modernisation policies seemed to be successfully implemented, then this approach to politics was just about sustainable. Once they failed to deliver, however, they would come under increasing strain.

One consequence of Labour's increased prominence and dominance within the formal sphere of politics on Teesside from 1945 was that some attempt was at last being made to rein in the worst abuses of industrial monopoly over Teesside's political agenda. The Town and Country Planning Acts of 1944 and 1947 gave local authorities new powers of land purchase and a responsibility to prepare for the redevelopment of towns and cities. These Acts were intended to set a legislative framework within which local authorities could plan land use patterns and regulate the undesirable effects of various activities on people's living conditions. How far such national aspirations could be translated into practice in areas such as Teesside remained an open question. Planning in practice involved local authorities indicating their needs as to desired land use patterns while lacking the powers and resources necessary to ensure that these developed as they would wish. Middlesbrough County Borough Council was one of the first local authorities to explore the opportunity seemingly offered by the new legislation. It commissioned a consultant town planner, Max Lock, who prepared the mammoth *Middlesbrough Survey and Plan* – ten reports accompanied by 240 maps and diagrams. This was, in his own words, 'a comprehensive survey or diagnosis of the town's ills' created after interviewing 'many hundreds of the citizens of the town' (Lock, 1945). It outlined planning proposals for the following thirty years. Very much a product of its time, it reflected its origins in the post-war settlement and the first tentative days of the welfare state. It also incorporated – often implicitly – a clear recognition of the political agenda which was responsible for some of the worst socio-economic difficulties of the area. As one member of the planning team put it (Glass, 1948, p. 187):

> not only are Middlesbrough's problems all inter-twined, but they also derive from one common cause: nineteenth century *laissez-faire*. Uncontrolled development has caused all the cumulative maladjustments; it has continually widened the social cleavages within the town. It cannot be allowed to persist.

Lock's survey and plan contained a clear-sighted recognition of the economic and political processes that had shaped Middlesbrough's trajectory of uneven development, although many of its proposals represented little more than a fine-tuning of existing regulatory mechanisms. There were clearly limits to the extent to which local 'planning' could act on causative processes and constrain the pursuit of private interests. In developing a Middlesbrough plan, there were also other, powerful forces at work in this period which led to a different emphasis in state policies and national political priorities, which were once again grounded in and prioritised the needs of heavy manufacturing industry. Even during the 1930s local industrial interests had been concerned to re-establish some of the basic preconditions for profitable production. Their tacit acceptance of the necessity for some kind of national political involvement in industrial location laid the basis for a new, more interventionist phase of state policies, heavily geared towards the interests of certain fractions of manufacturing capital.

Despite claims by the Teesside Industrial Development Board (TIDB) – formed in 1945 to represent a cross-section of local industrial opinion and incorporating some representatives of organised labour – that diversification of the local economy was essential to minimise the impacts of cyclical fluctuation (see TIDB, 1948), the objectives of national economic planning and the strategies of key manufacturing companies quickly overlapped. Expansion of ICI's new Wilton complex, for example, was given a high priority. There was a deliberate political decision to exclude *alternative* employers which might compete with ICI for what was, in this area at this time, relatively scarce male labour. In 1949 an Interim Outline Plan for the North East Development Area was prepared for the Ministry of Town and Country Planning. Whilst this document proved to be so sensitive that it was never formally published, it came to inform much local and national government planning in the early post-war years. One of its conclusions was that 'the development of such a large unit as Wilton on Teesside, the one area where labour is in short supply, must entail some influx of population if its labour requirements are to be fully met' (Pepler and MacFarlane, 1949, p. 100). And given the high national profile of the chemicals industry, it recommended that: 'it would be unwise to prejudice the redeployment of Cleveland labour in heavy chemicals by offering it alternative male employment' (ibid., p. 76). Such a prescription was by no means unique to Teesside. Large parts of the Durham coalfield saw a similar exclusion of alternative male employing industries as a result of objections from the National Coal Board (see Hudson, 1989a). On Teesside, as in much of County Durham, the consequences of these strategic decisions – in particular the limited extent of industrial diversification – were far-reaching. So, too, were the ways in which the emergence of the Labour Party on to the political stage on Teesside went hand in hand with its incorporation, along with that of the main trades unions in chemicals and steel, into a consensual view as to appropriate policies for the area.

3. FROM THE INTER-WAR YEARS TO THE 1960S: THE CREATION OF CONSENSUS OVER INDUSTRIAL EXPANSION, MODERNISATION AND STATE INTERVENTION

The political foundations for the consensual image of growth and harmony on Teesside lay in the legacy of paternalist labour relations and regulated working practices in its traditional heavy industries. These were finally resolved in the context of discussions in the 1960s and profoundly shaped the character of formal Labour Party politics. On this basis, a variety of other political structures, institutions and relationships, was constructed. These were built around the aim of winning and maintaining support for the construction and/or restoration of conditions which made Teesside an attractive investment proposition for certain types of manufacturing industry. In this way, or so the argument went, working-class needs for jobs and the incomes that they provided would be met. Thus companies and their workers shared common interests. Attaining such objectives came increasingly to depend upon the content and form of state policy and access to political power.

In one form of response to the deep economic crisis of the 1930s, several organisations were established in the North-east region to investigate ways and means of encouraging the growth of new sources of employment and restoring the dynamism of the old economy (see Hudson, 1989a). The Tees District Development Board was established in 1931, encompassing representatives of local government, the Tees Conservancy Commission, the London and North East Railway Company, the Cleveland and Durham Electric Power Company, and Teesside Chamber of Commerce. Similar development boards were established in Sunderland and on Tyneside. In 1935 the North East Development Board was created under the chairmanship of Lord Ridley – a powerful capitalist voice within the region – in an attempt to broaden the basis of support for what was then just the merest outline of a regional development policy. This rapidly expanded to include representatives of the Durham Miners' Association, and so of the Durham County Council which the Association dominated in terms of membership. In this way formerly fierce critics of such a cross-class approach – for example, miners' leader William Lawther – were incorporated into the emerging regionalist approach. Thus the obstacles to bringing in trades unions with a more moderate political tradition, such as those in chemicals and steel on Teesside, were removed. An alliance of interests was created, led by key industrialists, which came to the tentative conclusion that some kind of state intervention in the location of industry was necessary if the region's economy was to recover from depression.

Rearmament (which helped to boost demand for the goods of the region's traditional heavy industries) deflected attention away from such issues for a time, but the experience of a command economy during wartime further strengthened the resolve of those who argued for new forms of state policy. There was, at this time, little alternative available to most capitalist interests since they were, by and large, still heavily regionally based. In 1943 a revised grouping of industrial interests and union representatives met (again under the chairmanship of Lord Ridley) as the Northern Industrial Group, to consider the problems that could arise in the transition to a peacetime economy. This foresaw quite a broad role for state involvement to ensure both stability in the heavy industries and some diversification within the economy. In this way, the idea that there was a role for the state – in one form or another – to intervene in and guide the path of development came to be accepted within regions such as the North-east and in places such as Teesside. A state-managed peacetime economy, in which they held key controlling positions as in the war economy, was, therefore, by no means unattractive to major industrial capitalists.

This emergent tradition of territorial alliance was carried forward by the Teesside Industrial Development Board, founded in 1945. This was a cross-party and cross-class political institution for the promotion of economic development on Teesside. Its membership encompassed representatives of local government, employers' organisations such as the Teesside Chamber of Commerce, and trades unions such as the Iron and Steel Trades Confederation and the Confederation of Shipbuilding and Engineering Unions. It produced a frank (if restricted in circulation) survey of economic prospects for the area in the early post-war period (TIDB, 1948), and a special report on housing (TIDB, 1949). Housing was a particular priority issue for many employers on Teesside, anxious to retain existing skilled workers and rebuild workforces dissipated by the war effort. There was a 20 per cent turnover of labour on Teesside during 1948 alone. The survey pointed to the re-emergence of growth conditions in the area – particularly inspired by the massive new ICI development at Wilton – and the need to recruit an extra 5,000 men to the industrial labour force over the period 1949–51, entailing inward migration. It was in such an environment of fears of crippling labour shortages and a potential strengthening of workers' bargaining position in the labour market that further, alternative development within Teesside was tacitly discouraged (see Pepler and MacFarlane, 1949).

For local government, housing a new labour force was a particularly sensitive issue, for it clashed in part with efforts to reconstruct housing for existing residents (especially acute after wartime destruction but also a much more long-standing problem). For Labour politicians at this time, public sector provision of decent working class housing was a long-established goal. The election of a Labour national government raised the prospect of significantly strengthening the first tentative steps taken in this direction in the inter-war years (for example, see Centre for Environmental Studies, 1985). For their part industrialists argued (TIDB, 1949, p. 9) that it was no longer practicable to adopt the response of building company housing (most recently practised by ICI at Billingham):

> Much has been said about the ability of industry to look after itself but after all industry is the goose which lays the golden egg and it is always well to take utmost care of the goose otherwise she may cease to lay. Industry in these days is finding it difficult to finance its own affairs without adding the burden of house purchasing or house building.

Clearly, housing provision was now seen as a cost of production to be socialised, with responsibility for it transferred to the state. Aware of the potential conflict of interests, yet seeking to promote the potential for growth on Teesside, the TIDB (1948, p. 9) put forward its view – and, by implication, that of the major employers – as follows:

> Teesside clearly needs a greater share of such building labour and materials as the nation can afford if it is to contribute towards the solving of national and regional economic recovery, in the way in which the present opportunity offers. Extra allocations of houses should be issued by the Ministry of Health specifically earmarked for occupation by the nominees of industry and the electorate told the circumstances under which the construction of houses has been authorised.

Such issues were to tax some local authorities quite directly, creating tensions between a desire to increase public sector housing provision but not to be seen, overtly at least, to favour company interests in allocation policies. For example, the housing shortage was felt acutely by ICI at its Wilton complex and by the relevant local government body, Eston Urban District Council.[1] Eston UDC was anxious to accommodate the company's expansion plans, seeing the lucrative bonus of additional revenue from rates. It faced a problem, however, outlined in a letter from the Ministry of Health's housing division, that 'it would not be in keeping with Section 85 (2) of the 1936 Housing Act for the council to enter into an undertaking with ICI' for the provision of council houses specifically for ICI workers. In order to circumvent this difficulty, an alternative formula was evolved, which complied with the letter, if not spirit, of the law while seeking to guarantee that the company's need for workers' housing would be met. It was outlined in a letter from Mr Potter of ICI Wilton to Mr Gofton of Eston in 1947:

> We appreciate the fact that your Council are not permitted to enter into a binding agreement to let these homes to our employees, and that the arrangements in this connection must therefore rest on the basis of a 'Gentleman's Agreement' between the Council and the Company. If you will let me know when the first of the houses are nearing completion I will arrange to supply you with a list of our employees in the order of priority in which we would like the tenancies allocating.

The nature of the agreement was emphasised again in a letter from Gofton to the council's accountant, Mr Simpson: 'we must, of course, always avoid saying that the houses are actually reserved for ICI'.

In 1957 the Teesside Industrial Development Board convened a special conference amidst fears that a housing deficit might lead to local labour shortages[2]. Its president, Mr Simmerson, commented that 'the activities of many of the large and important concerns on Teesside were being restricted and their developments curtailed because of the lack of skilled labour due, in part, to the shortage of housing accommodation'. The area had seen a substantial post-war house-building programme, strongly backed by national government (see Figure 4.1). Companies like Smith's Dock, ICI and Dorman Long paid tribute to the efforts made on their behalf by local government, but argued forcefully that still more housing was required. Partnership to serve the needs of industrial expansion was a key theme, one emphasised by Mr. Simmerson in his closing address. 'The greatest possible progress', he argued, ' was likely to be made out of the closest and continued co-operation between industrialists who needed houses and the local authorities'. Such close co-operation continued during the major public sector housing expansions that formed part of the 1960s apex of modernisation policies.

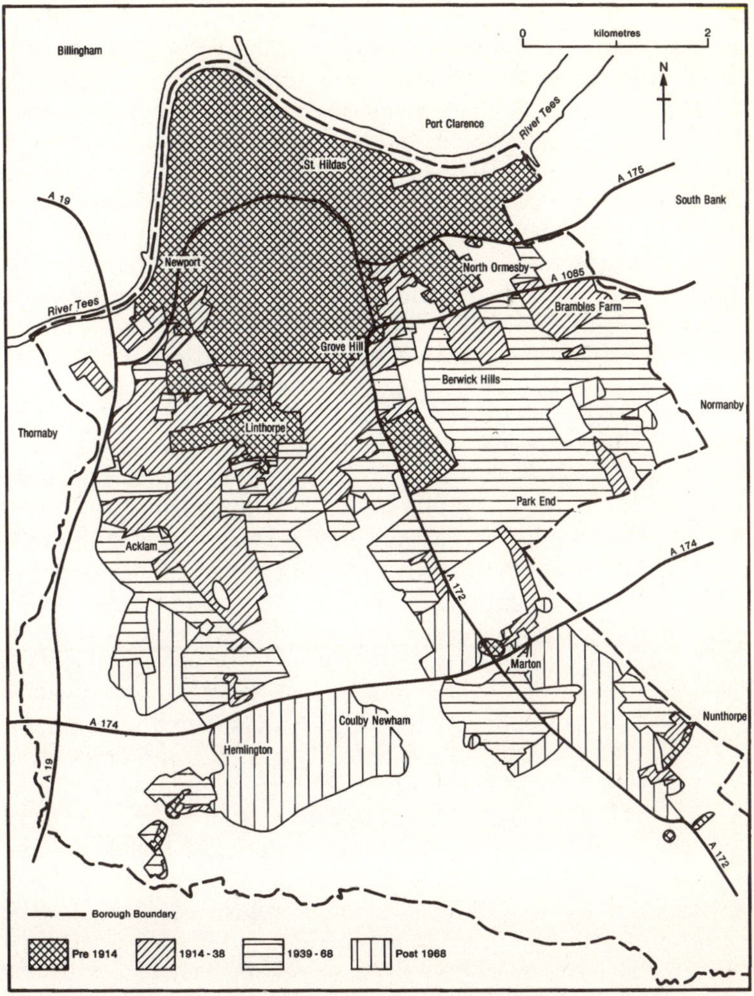

FIGURE 4.1: The growth of housing in Middlesbrough.

In this, and in other ways, the spirit of corporate patronage lived on in Teesside after 1945. Despite the mounting evidence of previous abuses, the new Labour-controlled authority operated with a very strong assumption of shared interest between itself and local manufacturing industry.

As such, local government policies on housing provision and allocation were influenced by corporate demands for labour. In other spheres, too, the pervasive influence of the major local industries was very evident. Substantial numbers of local Labour councillors were employed by the major industrial concerns who were sympathetic to time taken off work on council business. In their turn, councillors were nervous about adopting policies which were anything but subservient to the interests of their employer and to jobs in their constituencies. Radical challenges to the power of these companies were controlled by the Labour Party, which by this time had emerged as a classic political machine. As such, questions about issues such as the environmental impacts of ICI's developments at Billingham in the 1950s were quickly smothered and nullified within the structure of Labour politics because of the threat they might pose to jobs.

This failure to offer a strong opposition to industrial interests was not simply a question of political will; it was more a question of power. The subservient position of councillors as workers was taken over to the political realm, and this reaction was added to by the framework of national legislation within which local government operated. This became only too apparent as the chemicals and steel companies explored the extent to which their activities were in practice regulated by the 1947 Town and Country Planning Act. Their concern was to define the limits set by the new legislative framework, a process that had profound implications for environmental pollution and living conditions over much of Teesside. One example of this process with particularly important long-term considerations concerned Dorman Long's proposal to redevelop the blast furnace and coke oven complex at its Cleveland Works, in the heart of the built-up area on the south bank of the river and a major source of environmental pollution.[3] The company secretary wrote in 1952 to the Clerk of Eston Urban District Council, Mr T. M. Baker, that it was 'necessary for it to be determined how far (if at all) the carrying out of these operations would constitute or involve development of the land within the meaning of the [1947] Act', and enquiring whether planning permission was required. In his reply Baker informed the company that in the council's opinion, such permission was required. But the powers available to Eston to oppose Dorman Long's proposals were to prove strictly limited.

At a meeting between the two parties in October, local councillors 'drew attention to the present nuisance existing as a result of the emission of smoke and solid matter'. Despite reassurances from Dorman Long, they grew increasingly agitated at the consequences of an expansion of coke-making in this densely populated area. The council wrote to the National Smoke Abatement

Society and the Inspector of Alkali and Chemical Works, requesting advice and support. The local Medical Officer of Health commented that 'the most important point is that these coke ovens should be placed as far as possible away from human habitation'.

Eventually, permission was granted, under pressure from an appeal by Dorman Long to the Ministry of Housing and Local Government. It was issued subject to a clause that the company took 'all practicable precautions to prevent the emission from the new plant of gas, smoke, dirt, grit, or other offensive or objectionable matter'. Such a condition was of limited value, however, since in Baker's own words it was 'little more than requiring the company to observe the requirements of the existing law'. As a letter from the secretary of the Teesside Smoke Abatement Society made clear, 'compliance with the condition, or indeed existing legislation, does not prevent atmospheric pollution'. The Ministry clause merely required Dorman Long to take all practicable precautions, rather than *effective* anti-pollution measures. The powers open to local government to contain the environmental impact of this new development had been quite inadequate; one more source of pollution survived to create a range of health problems.

In this context, as in others, the work of Max Lock and his team for Middlesbrough County Borough Council was a significant exception to a more general trend. Conceived at the time of the 1944 Town and Country Planning Act, the *Middlesbrough Survey and Plan* (see Lock, 1945), was a clear illustration of both the vision of an alternative perspective on land use planning, which went beyond land use *per se* to explore notions of integrated social planning, and of the limits placed upon such an approach by the political influence of a particular set of capitalist interests. The plan was noteworthy both for its far-sighted prescription and the short-lived nature of its impact.

The *Middlesbrough Survey and Plan* began with a clear recognition of the severity of the town's social problems. It contained a sad catalogue of neglect of the housing stock in Middlesbrough's older districts. The background papers on housing described St Hilda's Ward as 'in a condition of extreme dilapidation'.[4] In recommending wholesale clearance of the area, the papers pointed out that 'some houses in St. Hilda's Ward are standing yet which were condemned by the Medical Officer of Health before the 1914–18 war'. The whole tenor of the *Survey and Plan* was very much bound up with the social reformist spirit of the latter years of, and immediate aftermath to, the Second World War. It was informed by a belief that the state could and should intervene to improve people's living conditions. Designed for the people, some 22,000 residents attended an extensive exhibition before it was formally adopted. Its more detailed, unpublished working documents demonstrated concern for a new kind of consultation and participation in the planning process. On housing, for example, it had this to say:

> Our sociologists believe that an effort should be made to move groups of people together. If public meetings could be held before clearance takes place, it should not be too difficult to find out which people from one neighbourhood would like to move together to a new one, and which clubs or other institutions would suitably go with them'.[5]

It assumed that through indicative planning and the appropriate processes of consultation, a degree of social engineering was both feasible and desirable. In an address to the council in 1945, Max Lock gave voice to such sentiments as follows (Lock, 1945, pp. 19–20):

> It was 115 years ago that Middlesbrough started to build with a 'clean slate', and it was the almost aggressive faith of Joseph Pease that conceived and implemented his project of 1830... It may be that you are now showing yourselves as great pioneers in the field of town planning as were the Middlesbrough Ironmasters in the mid-nineteenth century in the field of industry.

Much of this pioneering approach lay in a recognition of the significance of neighbourhood units and communities; of the *social* bases of the town grounded in the *social* relations of civil society rather than those of the workplace. Glass (1948, pp. 14–15) eloquently expressed this point of view in terms which encompassed a concern for planning so as to ensure both physical and social reconstruction:

> Industry used to be the focus and the very *raison d'être* of Middlesbrough. But industry has become huge and economically unstable, depersonalised and dispersed ... so the sovereignty of industry has been challenged. It still dominates Middlesbrough but it is no longer the magnet which draws the whole town together. There is no such magnet at present ... In terms of its social relationships, Middlesbrough now lacks a focus.

This analysis was significant, not least because later events were to demonstrate that though the 'sovereignty of industry' may have been challenged, industry still decisively ordered the political and social fabric of the town and, indeed, of the greater Teesside area. Whilst the direct influence of the Victorian era was less visible, the interests of heavy industry still dominated many aspects of local social and political life, mediated with increasing sophistication through the various channels of the state. In a sense, perhaps, Glass envisaged such a possibility when she concluded in the following, more cautionary, terms. The plan, she wrote (1948, p. 188):

> may appear to be utopian ... But although the plan may be ahead of the times and may not be fully implemented, it does provide a framework for reconstruction and new development. At the very least, its proposals are a measure of our shortcomings.

Even as the reformist optimism of immediate post-war years briefly flickered and then faded, the supremacy of key industrial interests in determining the political agenda was hastily reasserted. What was good for them was good for Teesside.

Growth, then, was the watchword and policies had to be devised to ensure that it continued. When cyclical recession in the national economy impacted heavily on Teesside's economy in 1962, and local unemployment rates began to rise from 1–2 per cent to 5–6 per cent, the local growth coalition was vociferous in its championing of new policies to restore the growth path. The outcome served to consolidate the main themes of an emergent political agenda. A local government conference held on Teesside in early 1963 called for designation of the region as a Development Area, to help attract new industries via building advance factories and the expansion of public works. The Hailsham Programme for the North East (HMSO, 1963) subsequently emphasised the continued expansion and further transformation of Teesside as part of a growth zone, capable of absorbing workers from declining industries elsewhere in the North-east. It was welcomed, by and large, especially on Teesside. It was something of a landmark in the evolution of state policies and in the political influence of the representatives of key industrial sectors such as those on Teesside. This message was reinforced by the *National Plan* (HMSO, 1965), which emphasised modernisation of the economy through selective expansion of key sectors (including those which dominated on Teesside). In this way, prioritisation of growth on the political agenda in and for Teesside was reaffirmed and reinforced.

Hailsham's strategy was produced as quickly as it was and received the grudging support that it did (from a region dominated by the Labour Party for a policy of the Conservative Government) largely because it was little more than a collation and modification of already existing local authority objectives. John

Gillis, chief planning officer of Cleveland County Council in the 1980s, put it like this: 'To a large extent the Hailsham proposals were a recognition of what was already happening. It was a strategy produced from the bits and pieces already there, rather than a national strategy.' The local authority role was seen as one of *enabling* growth, of *allowing* – indeed being *obliged* to enable and allow – investment to flood into Teesside. Gillis again:

> In the 1960s local authorities saw themselves as the facilitators of development. Teesside was a unique location, with large areas of flat land for capital intensive industry. The new era of economic development was taking place here. It was an obligation on the area for it to take place here.

In so doing, local government was responding to the needs of the national economy and to the demands of industry, both directly and indirectly. In addition to the provision of infrastructure necessary for production, companies were to receive considerable assistance with the provision of a built environment to ensure the maintenance and reproduction of labour power via enhanced public sector provision of houses, hospitals and schools. To quote Bryan Hanson, leader of Cleveland County Council in the late 1980s and an active politician in the 1960s: 'All we were doing in the 1960s was running like hell to keep up with everything. Education was always a problem. You opened a new school and it was always two classrooms short.'

Growth was the objective and forecasts were prepared to that end. Plans were drawn up which assumed that growth would occur as forecast. One of the most important of these policy statements was the *Teesside Survey and Plan*, foreshadowed by Hailsham and completed in 1968. The *Teesside Survey and Plan* was one of a new generation of sub-regional land use and transportation plans aimed at creating the preconditions for sustained economic growth. Its rhetoric captures well the spirit of the times (HMSO, 1969, p. 3):

> Teesside, born in the Industrial Revolution, offers to the second half of the twentieth century both a tremendous challenge and an almost unique opportunity. The challenge lies in the legacy of nineteenth century obsolescence; the opportunity is to make it one of the most productive, efficient and beautiful regions in Britain; a region in which future generations will be able to work in clean and healthy conditions, live in dignity and content and enjoy their leisure in invigorating surroundings. For Teesside already possesses in abundant measure those fundamental characteristics

> which provide the foundations for a full life. In few places does one find such modern industries, providing for man's [*sic*] economic prosperity, in such close proximity to a beautiful and spacious countryside, which can be the means of satisfying his recreational and spiritual needs.

Teesside's population was forecast to grow from 480,000 to 700,000 by 1991, with the creation of an additional 120,000 jobs. To local planners, at least, in this era of white-hot technological revolution, anything seemed possible. Cleveland County Council's chief executive in the 1980s, Bruce Stevenson, later commented on this as follows: '*Teesplan* was an extremely optimistic document but it really did reflect the views of the time. The availability of jobs was never in dispute. It was driven by a target population.' Expansion became an all-consuming ambition. As Mr Robson, president of the Teesside Industrial Development Board from 1958 to 1967 put it, graphically and fervently, in his 1966 presidential address: 'We must grow and continue growing. To cease growing is to start on the decline.'[6]

The task of promoting the virtues of growth and modernisation was often a delicate one, however, and the expansion of investment was often elided into growth in employment terms, temporarily concealing several conceptual and practical dilemmas. In so far as it *was* accepted that it encompassed growth in employment, modernisation was a project that could command support from key sections of labour as well as capital. In this way, support for modernisation was underpinned by drawing heavily on a local political tradition which presumed the existence of a local self-interest, grounded in a cross-class coalition. An appeal was made to localism which fell, by and large, on very receptive ears in many sections of labour and, especially, of capital. The image of Teesside was matched to the rhetoric of expansion. This self-promotional gloss was highlighted by Mr Robson, speaking in 1963:

> Teesside is traditionally an area which holds together, with industry supporting what might be called a Regional Chamber of Commerce and with local authorities who co-operate on several occasions and are more friendly disposed one to another than is common in certain other areas. This Development Board makes easier the collaboration between all the forces of development in the area and draws them together.[7]

By the late 1960s the modernisation consensus was cemented firmly in place. To challenge it verged on heresy. The promotion of Teesside as a suitable site for practically any capital investment project was well-established. A breathtaking range of bids for mobile investment took place. The Ironmasters District in the north of Middlesbrough was offered to the Ford Motor Company and a claim was made for the new Royal Mint. That so many of these propositions failed to bear fruit raised intriguing questions. The implications of this failure were to emerge only later, slowly and haltingly.

4. CONCLUDING COMMENTS

As the Labour Party gradually became more prominent within the formal political institutions of Teesside, it did so in a way that deeply marked its views on what was both possible and appropriate there. A history of compliant and deferential trades unionism prepared the ground for political strategies which were premised on the primacy of capitalist production in the chemicals and steel industries. When an embryonic critique of such policies, which pointed to social division and degraded environments within Teesside, tentatively emerged in the late 1940s, it was quickly submerged by a resurgent concern to prioritise the requirements of growth in the heavy industries. But the tensions were not eradicated, merely disguised.

In the 1960s, and for a time in the 1970s, however, Teesside did appear to 'hold together' – in terms, that is, of a cross-political party consensus and of an alliance between key capitalist and, to some extent, labour interests engaged in production there. But the widely proclaimed consensual view which was so inextricably bound up with economic growth was in marked contrast to the evident social fragmentation within Teesside. This was both an essential precondition for, and consequence of, the dominance of such a limited range of powerful interests and the particularly restricted nature of the political agenda. Modernisation (meaning investment and technological change in, and the continued prioritisation of, a few industries plus vague promises about diversification) was nevertheless (by and large) accepted because it was accompanied by more-or-less full employment over much (though by no means all) of Teesside. But it was also accepted because there was little else on offer. There were few effective and concrete alternative propositions from Labour and its representatives because most of them had been incorporated into a programme inspired by capital's requirements for profitable production. The character of the place continued to be decisively shaped by the requirements of chemicals and steel producers. In the course of the following decade, however, questions which had previously been glossed over became increasingly difficult to ignore. They posed a mounting challenge to the hegemonic ascendency of modernisation and to the ideological offensive of the 1960s and attempted to assert their own views of what the place should become.

NOTES

This chapter draws in part upon local government records held in the archives of Cleveland County Council. Where this is the case, a detailed reference is given below:

1. DC/ES12/36.
2. DC/ES12/150.
3. DC/ES12/154.
4. CB/M/C 35/16.
5. CB/M/C 35/16.
6. DC/LO 6 BOX 20.
7. DC/LO 6 BOX 20.

CHAPTER FIVE

Changing International Markets and The Old Economy from the 1970s

1. INTRODUCTION

In previous Chapters we have explored the origins and early expansion of the Teesside economy, concentrating on the political and economic role played by industries producing and using iron, steel and chemicals. This chapter investigates how the two main employers, BSC and ICI, subsequently reacted to changing international markets in ways which raised deep and fundamental questions both about the effectiveness of past modernisation policies and for the future of Teesside.

2. FROM GROWTH TO CONTRACTION AT BSC AND IN THE STEEL-USING INDUSTRIES

The early development of Teesside was intimately connected with the expansion of the iron and steel industry based on Durham coking coal and Cleveland iron ores. Like many of the seedbeds of industrial capitalism, the area's dynamism owed much to a location close to natural materials which became natural resources. By the 1960s, however, a new set of locational influences and competitive pressures had developed. These derived from the growing availability of, initially, low-cost high-grade iron ore and then, later, coking coal on a world market, coupled with innovations in maritime technology which made it possible to transport these raw materials cheaply over vast distances. In many developed countries this meant that a coastal location, not necessarily endowed with its own natural resources, was more cost-effective than an inland one. For an increasing number of developing countries, it also meant that the establishment of brand-new coastal steel works, as part of state planned and directed industrialisation programmes, became an attractive proposition. These trends were ultimately to lead – especially in the context of global recession – to a severe crisis of over-production, with dramatic consequences in many of the old steel heartlands.

Such tensions became clearly apparent following the energy

price increases of 1973 and 1974. As demand for manufactured goods subsequently slumped in many developed countries, less steel was required. Those goods which were still produced gradually incorporated less and less steel, as other products like aluminium and plastics (which were both lighter and used less energy to produce) came increasingly to be used as a substitute. Chronic over-capacity in the steel industry was revealed all too plainly in company balance sheets showing mounting losses, and became translated into dramatic cutbacks and workforce reductions. Within the European Community half of its 800,000 steel workforce lost their jobs in a single decade. Similar reductions took place in North America. Places which had been built up for more than a century around one industry saw their *raison d'être* wiped out almost overnight. Such was the scale of the crisis that even some of the newer, coastal steelworks of the first world came under threat. At the same time expansion programmes in newly industrialising countries continued apace, often modelled upon the phenomenal growth of steel production in Japan after the Second World War: Brazil produced 20 million tonnes by the mid-1980s (a threefold growth since the early 1970s); and South Korea produced 15 million tonnes, a fourfold expansion of output. A wholesale geographical shift in the balance of world steel production and trade was underway (see Hudson and Sadler, 1989).

There was considerable state involvement in the steel industries of the developed economies during this period of crisis. Trade restrictions were one indicator of this (especially evident in the USA) but in many countries governments were also drawn to give active support for reorganisation programmes (including financial assistance), or, in some cases, outright nationalisation. The European Community took an increasingly interventionist stance, culminating in a declaration of 'manifest crisis' in the industry in 1980. This gave its Commission sweeping authority to monitor prices and set production quotas for individual steel companies, order cutbacks and closures within member states in line with Community objectives, and enforce rules and regulations relating to the gradual abolition of state aid to steel companies. This set of supra-national regulatory powers remained in force until 1988, demonstrating both the unprecedented extent of over-capacity and the difficulties of successfully initiating a European Community policy response.

In the UK these changes were mediated by a distinctive sequence of changing national political priorities. In response to a crisis in profitability, and with long-standing trades union support, the government had nationalised the bulk steel-making side of the industry in 1967, creating the giant, monolithic British Steel Corporation (BSC) with a workforce of 250,000 and an annual output of 23 million tonnes. After a short period of reorganisation and consolidation, BSC embarked on a strategy very similar to that recommended (somewhat belatedly and only in the face of impending state-imposed reorganisation) by the private sector before nationalisation. This represented a further attempt at national state planning to give renewed viability to a key industrial sector. Under the *Ten Year Development Strategy* ((HMSO, 1973), a £3,000 million investment programme was to be concentrated on the five 'heritage sites' – at coastal or quasi-coastal locations – of Llanwern and Port Talbot in Wales, Scunthorpe and South Teesside in England, and Ravenscraig in Scotland, whilst smaller, inland sites would be closed. Annual capacity was expected to increase from 27 million tonnes to a figure in the range of 33–5 million tonnes by the late 1970s, and to 36–8 million tonnes by the early 1980s. This represented a clear attempt to mimic the Japanese model of cutting unit costs via producing steel in giant, modern coastal complexes at very high levels of capacity utilisation.

On Teesside, this strategy entailed dramatic expansion. Whilst iron and steel-making was to be gradually run down at Hartlepool, to the north of the Tees, with the loss of around 8,000 jobs, there was to be massive investment in a new steel-making complex on the south bank of the river. Together with enlargement of the existing Lackenby plant, this would result in a steel works with an annual capacity of 12 million tonnes by the 1980s. The proposed development of the new Redcar site was to be in five stages. The first was the completion of new iron ore unloading facilities at the sea terminal. The second was the erection of a huge new blast furnace at Redcar to replace older blast furnaces at Clay Lane, and an expansion of the capacity of the existing steel works at Lackenby. The third stage was to be a plate mill to replace older mills at Hartlepool and Consett. The fourth and fifth stages involved further iron-making capacity along with a new steel plant and rolling mills. The 1974 *Plan for Coal* linked the future of east Durham's coking coal collieries to the new blast furnaces – a link that subsequently was to be abruptly ruptured with severe consequences for both these areas (see Beynon *et al.*, 1991).

As demand for steel failed to grow as forecast in the 1973 White Paper, such proposals for capacity expansion became increasingly uncertain. Rather than expand, BSC's output slumped to 17 million tonnes in 1976 and small profits became mounting losses (see

TABLE 5.1: British Steel Corporation: key indicators, 1967–90.

Year	Profit (loss) (£m)	Liquid steel output (m tonnes)	Capital expenditure net of grants (£m)	No. of UK employees x 1,000, year-end (thousands)
1967–8	(22)	22.9	–	254
1968–9	(23)	24.2	–	254
1969–70[1]	12	12.3	–	255
1970–1	(10)	24.7	–	252
1971–2	(68)	20.4	–	230
1972–3	3	24.2	154	227
1973–4	34	23.0	155	220
1974–5	70	20.8	273	228
1975–6	(268)	17.2	462	210
1976–7	(117)	19.7	494	208
1977–8	(513)	17.4	401	197
1978–9	(357)	17.3	267	186
1979–80[2]	(1784)	14.1	261	166
1980–1	(1020)	11.9	148	121
1981–2	(504)	14.1	164	104
1982–3	(869)	11.7	122	81
1983–4	(256)	13.4	164	71
1984–5	(383)	13.0	210	65
1985–6	38	14.0	220	54
1986–7	178	11.7	269	52
1987–8	410	14.7	253	52
1988–9	461	15.4	307	52
1989–90	399	14.4	450	52

Notes:
1. Six-month trading period from October 1969 to March 1970.
2. Figures affected by strike action, January–March 1980.

Source: BSC *Annual Reports*.

Table 5.1). With the UK economy in deep crisis, a drive to cut public expenditure was initiated under pressure from the International Monetary Fund. The policy of expansion was switched to one of retrenchment (see HMSO, 1978). Stage two of the Redcar programme was completed with the commissioning of the Redcar No. 1 blast furnace in 1979, but plans for the new plate mill (stage three) and further iron- and steel-making capacity were abandoned.

The Basic Oxygen Steel (BOS) converters at Lackenby were, however, upgraded in line with stage two of the Redcar programme. This had implications elsewhere in the works. In 1978 the complex was entirely dependent upon the Clay Lane blast furnaces as all other blast furnaces on Teesside, associated with obsolete open hearth steel capacity, had been closed. The maximum annual output of the Clay Lane furnaces, however, was no longer sufficient to operate the expanded steel plant at full capacity. With the blowing-in of the new Redcar No. 1 furnace, the Clay Lane furnaces were shut down, resulting in the entire Teesside complex becoming irrevocably dependent upon one blast furnace for the supply of liquid iron. Since the BOS process required at least 70 per cent hot iron in the charge, the implications of this dependence upon one giant, technologically sophisticated but none the less delicate item of capital equipment were far-reaching.

The reliance upon a single blast furnace was both unusual and potentially disastrous and had only about come as a result of the truncated expansion programme. The original intention in 1973 had been to build three such blast furnaces (the steelwork for a second blast furnace was purchased but never assembled). Steelworks producing steel by the BOS route are usually supplied with hot iron by a series of blast furnaces, not just one. Since all blast furnaces require periodic renewal of the refractory brick lining which protects their steel shell from the temperatures within, this diversity of supply to the steel-making process is crucial. With more than one blast furnace, relining – a long and arduous process – can be accomplished in rotation, so that there is always iron available for conversion into steel. With only one blast furnace, routine relining or, still worse, unplanned closure, inevitably would mean that steel production has to cease.

All this led to considerable uncertainty on Teesside, particularly following the recent election of a new Conservative administration. At BSC, capacity was slashed from 21 million tonnes to 14 million tonnes in just three years, and employment fell by almost half, to 104, 000 by 1982. Major works such as Consett and Corby poured their last cast of steel. Yet those massive cutbacks were to give no guarantee of success and stability, with national losses reaching £8 million a week. In 1982 further closures appeared likely, especially at Ravenscraig. Concern also grew on Teesside, since a renewal of the Redcar blast furnace's lining was necessary, yet no plans had been announced and political opposition to closure at Ravenscraig was growing strongly. The conditions were set for competition between those places for survival. A specially convened local Steel Conference met in 1983 to discuss the issue (see Cleveland County Council, 1983b). The future of Ravenscraig was temporarily resolved, however, in a fashion which implicated all five major sites. They were given a three-year guarantee of continuing steel making, but no assurances were made with regard to rolling mills or to capacity utilisation levels. In such a situation, the future of the Teesside steel industry looked particularly suspect. Once the focal point of BSC's expansion programme, it had become a precariously imbalanced operation.

Faced with this position, Cleveland County Council commissioned a special report to investigate the options open to BSC on Teesside (see Hudson and Sadler, 1984). The company aimed to complete the reline in five months in the summer of 1986, keeping the rolling mills occupied with a stock of steel created before the reline commenced, and with supplies from Scunthorpe. Small quantities of steel would still be produced by converting two furnaces previously used to produce ferro-manganese to the production of iron. Export orders which were not of strategic significance would temporarily be discontinued.

The reline was successfully completed more or less in accordance with this strategy. However, it highlighted the deep-seated consequences of the premature truncation of the 1973 expansion programme. The emphasis on basic iron- and steel-making facilities on Teesside contrasted with under-investment in its rolling mill capacity. This was epitomised in the cancellation of the plate mill, originally intended as stage three of the Redcar programme, and by a further series of mill closures. One primary and six secondary rolling mills were closed in the late 1970s and early 1980s whilst no new rolling mills were constructed. This was in addition to the coke ovens, blast furnaces and electric arc steel-making furnaces made redundant around the time of the commissioning of the Redcar blast furnace. Employment fell from 23,000 in 1978 to just over 7,000 in 1984.

Closure of rolling mills with minimal replacement investment represented the greatest threat to the Teesside works in the long term. It meant that the complex was geared towards the production of relatively unsophisticated low value-added semi-finished steel (either continuously cast in large cross-section or only partly rolled from ingot). The market was already well saturated for such products. Following the closure of the Cargo Fleet rolling mills in 1984 and the transfer of their production to a newly modernised mill at Scunthorpe, only two main mills remained on the Teesside site. The beam mill, commissioned in 1958, operated in a major growth area for BSC, supplying the construction industry. The coil plate mill (opened in 1968) on the other hand, manufactured a product in considerable over-supply within the European Community. It was operating in the same product area – strip (essentially narrow-gauge plate) – as the three mills at Llanwern, Port Talbot and Ravenscraig, and these had been publicly threatened with closure in 1982.[1] The steel plant could make far more steel than the remaining rolling mills could handle. Together with the nearby Skinningrove works (which produced specialised sections) maximum rolling mill capacity amounted to just 46,000 tonnes per week, while the steel works was capable of producing 60,000–70,000 tonnes per week.

These changes involved Teesside playing a new role within a division of labour within BSC. It produced relatively unprofitable bulk steel for rolling elsewhere in the UK (at the pipe and tube mills in Corby, or the rail mill at Workington) or for direct export. This role was reinforced in 1985 when a long-term contract was signed under which BSC Teesside supplied Tuscaloosa Steel in the USA with 0.25 million tonnes of semi-finished steel annually. The logic behind such moves was clear. With a periodic necessity to reline the blast furnace and cease steel production, or at best to cut it to a trickle, new rolling mill investment was best concentrated elsewhere whilst Teesside was left to focus upon the bulk production of crude steel.

In 1986 BSC returned to profit after a decade of losses, and in 1988 the company was returned to the private sector via a stock market flotation, as one component of the Government's privatisation policy (see Sadler, 1990a). It had survived the worst years of recession via a combination of dramatic capacity reduction, intensified working practices and state support for new investment (amounting to £1,200 million in the five years before privatisation: Table 5.2). Much of this latter had gone to the Port Talbot works, which was emerging as British Steel's major new production focus. In contrast, the Ravenscraig works in Scotland had received practically no new investment of any sort, emphasising fears there over its continued future. These were heightened still further by the closure of the Ravenscraig plant's hot strip mill during 1991 and confirmed with the closure of the works in 1992.

British Steel was privatised at the top of the boom. By 1992 it was reporting plunging profits, down from a record £733 million in 1989/90, to £254 million in 1990/1 and £55 million in 1991/2. The UK recession combined with the worst recession in the global steel industry for over half a century. In these circumstances

TABLE 5.2: Major actual and planned capital investment projects at individual BSC works prior to and immediately after privatisation.

Period of major investment	Works and facilities	Cost expenditure (£m)
	Port Talbot	
1983–6	Hot strip mill modernisation	171
1986–7	Hot mill reheat furnace	16
1987–9	Blast furnace reline	31
Sanctioned late 1988	Second continuous casting plant	70
		288
	Teesside	
1982–4	Coke ovens rebuild	44
1984–5	Beam mill reheat furnace	17
1985–6	Blast furnace rebuild	50
1986–8	Ladle arc furnace	13
Sanctioned late 1988	Beam mill modernisation	69
		193
	Llanwern	
1986–8	Continuous casting plant	47
1988–9	Vacuum degassing facility	12
Sanctioned late 1988	Hot dip galvanizing line	59
		118
	Shotton	
1984–6	Hot dip galvanising line	30
1986–9	Electro-galvanising line modernisation	32
		62
	Scunthorpe	
1986–8	Sinter plant	45
1987–9	Ladle arc furnace	15
		60
	Trostre	
1986–8	Continuous annealing line	48
	Ravenscraig	
1986–8	Blast furnace coal injection plant	15

Source: Compiled from British Steel prospectus (1988).

questions were raised once again over the whole structure of the company's operations in the UK. Freed of territorial restrictions imposed by nationalisation and, on flotation, 25 per cent-owned by non-UK-based investors, the company looked to internationalise the scope of its activities (via joint ventures), and to develop an international product specialisation in areas, such as structural steels, in which it had established strengths. It hoped to break away from a dependence upon the UK market, which accounted for around two-thirds of its turnover. In this way British Steel was following many of its major customers in moving its centre of production out of the UK. The collapse of the UK market for steel during the late 1970s and early 1980s had been caused by precipitous decline in major steel-using industries such as motor vehicles, shipbuilding and engineering. In response to these pressures, those manufacturing companies which survived internationalised their operations still further, closing down production in the UK and increasingly emphasising bases in other countries.

As part of this process of change BSC began radically to redefine its links with suppliers to its Teesside complex. In 1992 it announced plans to cut their numbers from 3,000 to just over 1,000. 'Our theme is total quality partnership and strategic purchasing', is how Mr J. Campbell, Teesside's Works Director described the rationale for the changes, adding that the company was seeking 'just-in-time' services from its suppliers (*Northern Echo*, 15 January 1992). On Teesside, the combined effects of changing relations with customers and suppliers meant that the links between steel production and processing – once an integral and highly visible part of the area's economic strength – vanished, to be replaced by a wholly different environment in which separate operations took place in distinct, often widely-separated, locations. The production-led rationale of the old industrial complex had been savagely torn apart.

This was painfully apparent, for instance, in the demise of the shipbuilding industry on the Tees; the last yard, Smith's Dock, closed in the mid-1980s. It was evident in the disappearance of some famous old names, such as Cleveland Bridge and Engineering, and in the contraction of a firm which had once been the third great private-sector pillar of the Teesside economy after Dorman Long and ICI – Head Wrightson. This company, founded in Stockton in the nineteenth century as an iron foundry business, was taken over by the Davy Corporation in 1976. Davy then concentrated upon design and contract management, as it had been withdrawing from direct manufacturing from the 1960s onwards. Davy had acquired its one-time rival at a time when Head Wrightson's workforce had shrunk to 4,000, spread over many different sites. Davy continued to specialise in design and it found little use for many of the former Head Wrightson manufacturing facilities. A fresh round of closures followed, culminating with the shut-down of the remaining works, Head Wrightson Teesdale, in 1984. This was bought at the last minute by a locally owned offshore exploration company, ITM, saving 100 jobs until it went bankrupt in 1986 (for details see Peppin, 1990, pp. 292–310). Whilst some of this company's operations were salvaged, its collapse – and, more importantly, that of Head Wrightson – was a sorry end to a long history of engineering and fabrication. Its eventual closure in many ways symbolised an era of near-terminal decline in many sectors of Teesside's steel-using industries.

This picture of highly internationalised circuits of production with minimal local interconnection and scant concern for the local impacts of internationalisation was also evident with regard to one of the steel industry's major raw materials, coking coal. In 1979 BSC changed its ordering policies, switching to imported supplies of this commodity. This led to the loss of a major market for the National Coal Board, which had invested heavily in south-east Durham during the 1970s in the expectation of a guaranteed market supplying the planned new Redcar blast furnaces. Such a rupture between two state-owned corporations intensified the impact of decline and further weakened the links between the Teesside steel industry and the sub-regional economy (see Beynon *et al.*, 1986b, 1991). The new role for the Tees estuary is the mirror image of its position in the nineteenth century. Once the site of coal *exports*, in the late 1980s plans were announced for it to become a major steam coal *import* terminal, further displacing UK production. Furthermore, natural gas was brought to Teesside from the North Sea via a 250-mile pipeline, with a capacity of 1,600 million cubic feet of gas per day, and plans were announced in 1991 by Enron for a private gas-fired power station. This was to be located on part of the Wilton site, which had become surplus to ICI's requirements. Certainly, for ICI, this offered the promise of cheap electricity, steam and feedstocks for its remaining Teesside operations. But ICI will take only about 15 per cent of the power station's output of electricity: the rest will go into the grid, displacing more UK-produced coal from the power station market.

3. FROM IMPERIAL TO INTERNATIONAL CHEMICAL INDUSTRIES: ICI'S GLOBAL STRATEGY AND CHEMICALS PRODUCTION ON TEESSIDE

The 1950s and 1960s were an era of great expansion for chemicals producers in the industrialised countries. Output grew at rates double those for manufacturing as a whole – and these were high as part of the long post-war boom. This dynamism was strongly concentrated in the petrochemicals sector, for as process technologies developed, larger plants enabled greater economies of scale and encouraged the replacement of materials such as wood, metal and glass by plastic. Growth in such chemicals production was locationally concentrated in Western Europe, the USA and Japan. It was widely expected to continue.

It was in this context that local and national government policies paid so much attention to providing adequate land on Teesside for the needs of the chemicals industry, so as to smooth its continued expansion. If the chemicals industry – meaning not just ICI but other multinational corporations which might be persuaded to invest in the region – was to prosper, it had to have more land. So it seemed in the 1960s, which is why the reclamation of 2,000 acres of land at Seal Sands, on the north bank of the river, proceeded so rapidly (see Figure 3.5).[2]

Work on this was undertaken in partnership by various agencies of the UK state, the European Community and private capital. The Tees and Hartlepool Port Authority initiated much of the reclamation while the County Borough Council co-ordinated the timing and pace of progress via its development control and management functions. It also partly funded the land reclamation and provision of services but much of the finance for drainage, power supply and roads came from the European Regional Development Fund (ERDF). The Water Authorities, via their often controversial investment in the Cow Green (see Gregory, 1975) and Kielder reservoirs (the latter again substantially financed via the ERDF), ensured more than adequate water supplies. Finally, regional policy assistance from central government substantially underwrote the fixed capital investment cost of multinationals located there.

Seal Sands represented a prime location for chemicals companies seeking to expand capacity. The existing ICI complexes presented a potential source of feedstocks and raw materials, while products could be shipped out by the Tees. Several USA-based multinational companies located branch plants there in response to the opportunities it offered for profitable production. The first of these was Monsanto, which opened a plant in 1969. This produced polymers which were sent for conversion to nylon fibre at other locations. The plant represented Monsanto's largest single fixed capital investment outside the USA, amounting to some £200 million. Monsanto was followed by several other US chemicals multinationals, including Rohm and Haas and W. R. Grace. A further small plant to produce chemicals intermediates was set up by Seal Sands Chemicals in 1979. The cumulative total investment in chemicals plant and equipment on Seal Sands then stood at over £500 million, much of the cost of this being borne not by the individual companies but by the UK state through regional policy measures.

A further major boost to the development of Seal Sands arose through the discovery of oil in the North Sea. The most important single investment in response to this was by Phillips Petroleum in a terminal to store and provide initial processing of oil brought 200 miles by pipeline from the Ekofisk field. The flow of oil reached 400,000 barrels per day by the late 1970s. Initially, oil landed was re-exported without further processing to established oil ports in the south of the USA and Europe. With the completion of a separation plant in 1979 (over three years behind schedule), the oil was subjected to initial processing there. Propane and ethane were produced and shipped to the Rafnes petrochemicals complex in southern Norway. The cost of fixed capital investment in the terminal and separation plant and the associated tank farm at Greatham, which had an initial storage capacity of 7.5 million barrels of crude oil, totalled over £300 million.

Elsewhere on Teesside, ICI also seemed to be fulfilling growth prophecies with its continued investment. While the pace of technological change at Billingham was generally slower than in the early 1960s, further major developments took place at Wilton during the late 1960s, so that by then about one-half of the 2,000 acre site had been developed. These involved both expansion in capacity for existing products and the construction of plants for new products. Most fundamental was an expansion in cracking capacity. In 1965 this stood at 130,000 tonnes a year, from the original three olefine plants built in the 1950s. In 1966 a further cracker was added with an annual capacity of 200,000 tonnes, while in 1968 another cracker with an annual potential output of 450,000 tonnes was completed. This last, then the largest single stream ethylene unit in the world, meant that capacity to produce the basic building blocks of petrochemicals' manufacture – primarily ethylene but also propylene, butadiene and butylene – had increased sixfold in three years. The move towards larger plants reflected competitive pressures – the rate of return on one 450,000 tonne cracker was nearly twice that on three of 150,000 tonnes – and the need to cut unit production costs. At the same time, capacity to manufacture products such as nylon polymer and polyester at Wilton, using the output of the crackers, increased. Additionally, further plants were built for the manufacture of bulk plastics in the form of sheets, blocks and films.

The early 1970s was marked by a more muted pace of investment compared with the late 1960s; it represented a phase of consolidation between peaks in the investment cycle. Nevertheless, by the mid-1970s Wilton, together with the North Tees refineries, formed the centre of a complex of chemicals industries and companies linked by a complicated pattern of sales and purchases of inputs and outputs. Cumulative fixed capital investment totalled over £400 million and employment stood at over 13,000. In the (admittedly not unbiased) words of the chairman of ICI Petrochemicals Division, Dr Telfer, Wilton was 'the most modern petrochemicals complex in the UK [with] few equals anywhere in the world' (quoted in *Newcastle Journal*, 22 June 1976).

In order to try and maintain this position of pre-eminence, however, further major fixed capital investments were required. One element in this programme was the construction of a second tunnel under the Tees, to allow closer integration of Wilton with both Billingham and the newer operations at Seal Sands. A second component was the construction of further naphthalene and propylene plants at Wilton. The major development, though, was the construction of a sixth cracker at Wilton, initially jointly (50 : 50) owned by ICI and British Petroleum, which began in 1975 at a cost then estimated at £100 million. Construction of this 600,000-tonne capacity cracker did not proceed smoothly, only finishing in 1979 – over two years behind schedule and at a cost which had doubled to £200 million. In addition to this, in 1979 a new butadiene plant was brought into operation and the existing ethylene oxide and glycol plant was extended, making it the largest single unit in Western Europe for these commodities. Moreover, a further £140 million investment was authorised on new plant to make plastics, especially PVC.

In some ways, then, it appeared during the 1970s as though expansion and investment in chemicals production on Teesside were continuing much as before. In other ways, however, the global environment within which such strategic decisions were taken had changed, rapidly, especially with regard to petrochemicals. The oil price rises of the early 1970s gave a big incentive to many oil- and gas-producing countries, particularly in the Middle East, to develop downstream into processing operations. Other newly industrialising countries such as South Korea and Brazil also began to develop their own, protected, petrochemicals industries. Furthermore, the major oil companies expanded heavily into downstream processing, sensing the chance of a big return on investment (see Fayad and Motamen, 1986; OECD, 1985). The combined effect of the introduction of all these new producers was to create a situation of marked over-capacity by the end of the 1970s.

The major West European and North American chemicals companies were not unaware of such changes and began to reassess their global operations. ICI – then the UK's largest manufacturing company and the fifth largest chemicals manufacturer in the world after the US company Du Pont and the West German companies, BASF, Bayer and Hoechst – responded to this situation via a reassessment, often radical, of what it produced, how it produced and where it produced. It began further to adjust the geographical balance of its operations. Its traditional strengths lay in the UK and the protected markets of the former British Empire. Increasingly, it began to internationalise production, first in Western Europe, then in North America and South-east Asia (Clarke, 1983). This was based upon a clear recognition of the limited growth prospects of the UK market and much stronger demand projections elsewhere around the globe. This reassessment had marked impacts on Teesside.

The weakness of the UK chemicals market was starkly highlighted during the recession of the late 1970s and early 1980s. Demand for plastics in key sectors such as construction and motor vehicles fell dramatically, and the chemicals industry nationally shed 80, 000 jobs – one-fifth of its workforce. During one quarter of 1980 ICI even recorded its first-ever net loss, creating major shock waves in the City of London. Its response was swift and decisive, beginning with a round of plant closures and redundancies within the UK. As well as plant rationalisation ICI was involved in rationalisation of its product range, gradually withdrawing from the production of some chemicals, especially in the UK. In 1982 ICI and BP announced a joint programme under which they reduced their polyethylene and polyvinyl chloride (PVC) capacities. ICI closed one polyethylene plant at Wilton with the loss of 700 jobs, and handed over a second to BP. ICI's share of the 600,000 tonne capacity No. 6 ethylene cracker at Wilton went up to 80 per cent, enabling it to close the No. 5 cracker there. What had been intended as *additional* capacity in this product became instead *replacement* capacity. BP closed three plants at Baglan Bay in South Wales producing chemicals associated with the manufacture of PVC (with the loss of 500 jobs) and three PVC plants at Barry, also in South Wales (with the loss of 600 jobs), handing over to ICI the fourth PVC plant at Barry which had been opened only the previous year. In this way ICI (with its guaranteed supply of chlorine) increasingly specialised in the production of PVC and BP in that of polyethylene.

In 1985 a fresh round of rationalisation in these products took place. ICI completed a retreat not just from the UK but from European polyethylene production when it sold a plant at Fos-sur-Mer, near Marseille, to Shell. Other changes were announced for ICI's PVC business and completed in 1986. Heavy losses forced ICI to merge its PVC activities with the Italian state-owned chemicals group Enichem, creating Europe's largest company in the sector. The merged company, European Vinyls Corporation, supplied about 25 per cent of the European market. In an attempt to reduce over-capacity and increase profitability, ICI closed plants at Hillhouse in the UK and Waldshut in West Germany (with the loss of 300 jobs), whilst Enichem closed works at Porto Marghera, near Venice, and at Brindisi, shedding 1,000 jobs.

Increasingly, too, ICI became more selective in its policies towards different kinds of chemicals. It had always been one of the most diverse chemicals companies in the world, providing practically the full range of products. In the increasingly harsh competitive environment it placed more emphasis upon speciality chemicals. Geared more to small-batch production than the bulk output of so-called 'commodity' chemicals, this area was less affected by cyclical fluctuations. It was also technologically more sophisticated and less vulnerable to competition from newly industrialising countries. ICI gradually expanded its speciality chemical operations through a series of acquisitions, mainly in the USA: in 1984 it purchased Beatrice Chemicals, a major supplier of speciality chemicals; in 1986 it became the world's biggest paint maker with the purchase of Glidden; and in 1987 it purchased Stauffer Chemicals, for its large agrochemical operations. Through a highly sophisticated and selective process of acquisition, ICI expanded its interests in promising product segments and potentially lucrative geographical market areas.

Whether in speciality or commodity chemicals, investment was increasingly directed to new growth markets like South-east Asia, or to potential expansion areas within mature markets, such as the USA. During the 1970s, UK sales accounted for over three-quarters of ICI's profits; in the 1980s over half came from sales outside the UK (see Table 5.3). A similar shift took place in the global distribution of the company's workforce (see Table 5.4). While ICI's international labour force remained relatively stable, employment in

TABLE 5.3: ICI trading profit world-wide, 1978–89 (£m).[1]

	1978	1979	1980	1981	1982	1983	1984	1985	1986	1987	1988	1989
UK	370	470	137	216	176	390	578	394	487	617	613	612
Other Western Europe	(2)	31	–	(13)	(4)	49	66	76	134	184	270	225
Americas	30	37	44	63	53	114	214	270	224	271	315	382
Australia and Far East	65	77	85	94	72	64	105	104	119	156	182	236
Other countries	16	18	13	14	20	27	43	52	40	35	35	45
Inter-territory elimination	–	–	8	(4)	(11)	(21)	(23)	–	(31)	(28)	(9)	(33)
Royalties, government grants	25	22	15	55	60	70	80	82	76	62	64	–[2]
Total	504	655	302	425	366	693	1,063	978	1,049	1,297	1,470	1,467

Notes:

1. Export sales and related profits are included in the territories from which those sales were made.
2. From 1989, royalty income and government grants were included in the appropriate geographic area.

Source: ICI, *Annual Reports and Accounts*.

TABLE 5.4: Employment in ICI world-wide, 1975–89 (x 1,000).

	UK	Other Western Europe	Americas	Australia and Far East	Other countries	Total
1975	129	16	23	13	15	196
1976	132	12	20	13	16	192
1977	95	11	20	12	16	154
1978	93	11	20	16	13	151
1979	90	11	20	16	12	148
1980	84	11	20	16	13	143
1981	75	11	19	16	13	132
1982	67	10	18	15	13	124
1983	62	13	17	14	13	118
1984	59	13	17	14	13	116
1985	57	15	20	14	13	119
1986	57	15	23	15	13	121
1987	56	16	30	15	12	128
1988	55	16	32	15	12	130
1989	55	17	34	17	12	134

Note: Totals might not reflect regional figures due to rounding.
Source: ICI *Annual Reports*.

the North-east of England declined rapidly (see Figure 5.1). The change in priorities was mirrored at all levels throughout the company. In effect a cultural change was wrought, from a business conceived in the days of Empire to one with an international main board encompassing American and Japanese directors.[3]

On Teesside, such developments entailed a sweeping re-appraisal of ICI's operations there. ICI recorded losses in petrochemicals and plastics production from 1980 to 1983, raising question marks over the Wilton works, even after closure of one of the crackers in an attempt to cut unit costs. These were exacerbated by a problem of raw material supply. The basic feedstock of petrochemical production was typically either the crude oil derivative naphtha (as at Wilton) or ethane, a natural gas liquid. In the late 1970s and early 1980s, Shell and Esso constructed a major new petrochemicals plant at Mossmorran in Scotland to utilise ethane from the North Sea. They secured a lucrative taxation arrangement for the plant (set on the basis of internal transfer prices) with threats of cancellation of the project if such assistance was not forthcoming from government. In 1982 these taxation conditions

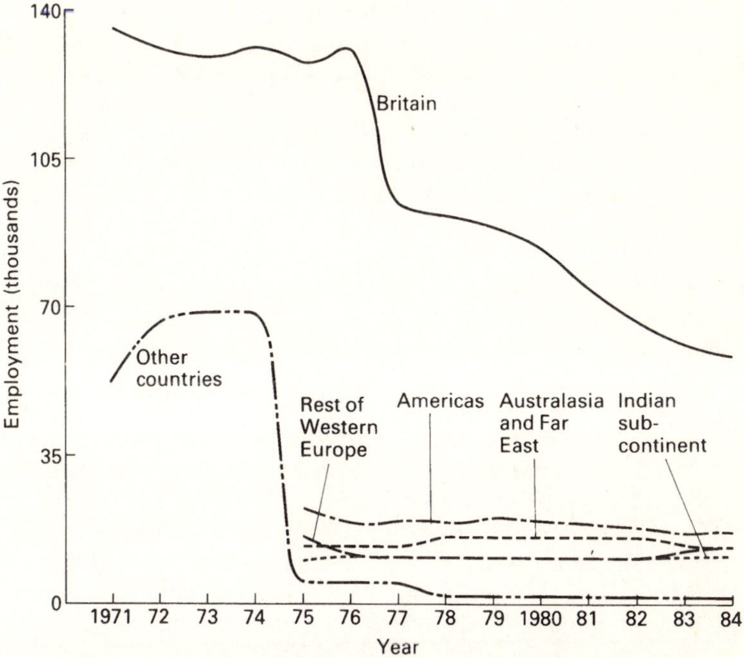

FIGURE 5.1: The international distribution of employment in ICI.

were also extended to cover BP's Grangemouth plant, which was converted at a cost of £25 million so that it could run on ethane rather than naphtha. ICI responded aggressively to these concessionary tax arrangements, arguing that they undermined the long-term viability and competitiveness of its existing, naphtha-based Wilton operation. In a letter to all Members of Parliament, the company warned that 'if ethylene production were so undermined by unfair competition that it had to end, manufacture of all co-products at the Wilton complex would also cease'. It took the matter to the courts, fighting a four-year round of legal battles, ultimately with success. The tax concessions granted to ICI's rivals were held to be unlawful.

Whilst this decision was significant, it did not guarantee the future of the Wilton site. Employment in petrochemicals fell from 10,000 to 6,000 as cost-cutting measures were implemented and selected plants closed completely. This process of contraction was as challenging as the lengthy court action and was closely linked to a reassessment of the Wilton site's international role. One consequence of ICI's internationalisation during the 1970s had been the construction of a new petrochemicals and plastics plant at Wilhelmshaven on the West German North Sea coast. In terms of its downstream use of ethylene, this was practically identical to the Wilton works. Moreover, it was better placed geographically to supply much of the crucial Western European market. ICI chairman, Sir John Harvey-Jones, remarked in 1986 that 'It was a big mistake to have invested equally at Wilton. We built the same plants; we had a dual strategy, but the one we can't load is at Wilton'.[4] Completion of an underground propane storage scheme in 1982, though, gave the Wilton site some opportunity to play the ethane/naphtha feedstock markets to its advantage (see Chapman, 1986, p. 94).

Whilst the Wilton complex had some problems, these were much more acute at Billingham, with its continued specialisation in the production of agricultural fertilisers from ammonia, itself produced from natural gas. The complex benefited considerably during the 1970s from a fifteen-year gas-supply contract signed in 1969. For, following the oil price rises of 1973–4, gas prices rose dramatically, and by 1974 it was estimated that ICI was saving some £90 million a year, paying well below current market rates. Despite a renegotiation in which ICI sought an extension to the length of the supply contract and British Gas a price increase, it was estimated that in 1982 ICI was paying only between six and eight pence per therm, compared to the going rate for continuous supplies to industry of 29.5 pence and for interruptible supplies of 25.5 pence.[5] ICI even supplied 150,000 tonnes of ammonia made from this cheap natural gas to one of its competitors, Fisons at Immingham.

In 1982, though, the UK fertiliser market became much more competitive when Norsk Hydro, the Norwegian chemicals company, bought Fisons' UK fertiliser business for £50 million. This new rival had the added advantage of access to abundant supplies of North Sea gas. Within the first year, Norsk Hydro's share of the UK nitrogenous fertiliser market increased to 17 per cent from the previous year's 13 per cent attained by Norsk Hydro and Fisons, with clear implications for ICI's position in this business area.

In response to this threat, ICI announced a £60 million project for two new ammonia plants at Severnside near Bristol in 1985. This was its biggest UK investment since 1978 (itself a profoundly revealing comment on the absence of major investment by ICI within the UK). The chairman of the Agricultural Division (quoted in *Financial Times*, 31 October 1985) explained that:

The market for nitrogen fertilisers will not grow as fast in the next decade as in the last, and there will be strong competition from foreign companies established in the UK and from imports. So we have embarked on a programme to reduce costs at every point in our business.

The two new plants had a capacity of 300,000 tonnes per annum. Those they were to replace were the oldest and least efficient of ICI's seven ammonia-producing works in the UK. At some twenty years old, the latter were about the same age as those at Billingham – raising questions over its continued viability.

Such doubts – at both Billingham and, to an extent, Wilton – were reinforced in 1986 when ICI announced its biggest organisational change for several decades (to take effect the following year). In response to the diverse profit potential of different product ranges (see Table 5.5), it formed a new group bringing together the four 'commodity' or bulk chemicals businesses of fertilisers, fibres, petrochemicals and plastics, and general chemicals. The new company, ICI Chemicals and Polymers, became a wholly owned subsidiary of ICI – an unusual departure from previous reorganisations. It employed 38,000 people concentrated within the UK in North-east and North-west England. Considerable speculation accompanied the move, with many financial analysts contemplating that it was a prelude to a sale which would give ICI a stock market rating appropriate to a speciality rather than commodity chemicals producer. ICI was at pains publicly to distance itself from such suggestions. It was clear, though, that the company faced key decisions about the areas of heavy chemicals in which it wished to remain in the 1990s. Nowhere were these concerns about ICI's future intentions (and the future of the UK chemicals industry) more keenly felt than on Teesside.

ICI's fertiliser operations were in especially deep trouble, reflecting declining demand across Europe and low-cost sales of Russian urea – an alternative form of fertiliser. In 1986 ICI was forced to drop its prices by 25 per cent in an attempt to maintain sales.[6] A programme of retrenchment was initiated across the UK. At Billingham this included plant closures and a fresh round of redundancies, estimated in 1987 to amount to 250 a year for the following five years. This would halve the 2,500-strong workforce engaged in fertiliser production. Decline became the keyword there in the late 1980s. The plant was in an unpromising geographical market (especially given changes in Western European agricultural policies) and a declining product range, exacerbated by environmental pressures to reduce the use of inorganic fertiliser. ICI's output of fertiliser in the UK fell from 0.7 million tonnes

TABLE 5.5: ICI profit (loss) by business activity and segment, 1978–9.

	1978	1979	1980[1]	1981	1982	1983[2]	1984	1985[3]	1986[4]	1987[5]	1988	1989[6]
Pharmaceuticals	68	66	66	90	138	199	249	271	287	306	306	399
Paints	24	30	27	27	22	26	39	42	47	92	98	100
Other effect products	- - -	- - -	- - -	- - -	- - -	10	14	60	175	176	143	69
[Organic and speciality chemicals	21	7	(34)	(30)	(18)	- - -	- - -	- - -	- - -	- - -	- - -	- - -]
CONSUMER AND SPECIALITY PRODUCTS SUBTOTAL							302	373	509	574	546	568
General chemicals	128	141	99	75	60	107	145	138	168	208	262	293
Petrochemicals and plastics	54	98	(79)	(54)	(139)	(7)	138	97	181	310	403	417
Fibres	(13)	(33)	(86)	(36)	(25)	(7)	22	16	58	41	49	27
Industrial explosives	22	18	19	35	33	26	41	34	26	38	47	48
[Plastics	39	56	- - -	- - -	- - -	- - -	- - -	- - -	- - -	- - -	- - -	- - -]
INDUSTRIAL PRODUCTS SUBTOTAL							346	282	430	595	760	789
Agrochemicals and plant breeding	- - -	- - -	- - -	- - -	- - -	- - -	82	82	28	52	117	152
Fertiliser and related products	- - -	- - -	- - -	- - -	- - -	- - -	136	99	(15)	(4)	(15)	(11)
AGRICULTURE SUBTOTAL	150	154	151	182	158	174	218	181	13	48	102	141
[Oil and gas	(16)	79	97	83	73	93	109	59	20	- - -	- - -	- - -]
Miscellaneous	2	12	8	–	–	5	9	–	5	20	5	(33)
Inter-sector elimination	–	–	19	(2)	4	(3)	(1)	1	(4)	(2)	(7)	(2)
Royalty income and government grants	25	22	45	55	60	60	80	82	76	62	64	–
TRADING PROFIT	504	655	332	425	366	693	1,063	978	1,049	1,297	1,470	1,467

Notes

1. In 1980 the plastics business was merged with petrochemicals. The organics business also encompassed speciality chemicals.
2. In 1983 'other effect products' encompassed decorative products from within the paints business and the 'organic and speciality chemicals' business. From 1983 to 1984 it was known as colours, polyurethanes and speciality chemicals, only acquiring its present label in 1985.
3. In 1985 ICI's activities were reported for the first time under four industry segments: consumer and speciality products, industrial products, agriculture, and oil and gas. From this date profits included sales made within the segment by different activities but these profits were excluded from the segment totals.
4. In 1986 the films business was transferred from the industrial products segment to consumer and speciality products. The effect this had on 1985 results was as follows (for comparative purposes only – with 1985 restated figures in brackets):

   Industrial products: formerly £282 million (£242 million) Consumer/speciality products: formerly £373 million (£413 million)

   The effective transfer of £40 m was made from the heading 'petrochemicals and plastics' to 'other effect products'.
5. In 1987, following the formation of ICI Chemicals and Polymers Group and the merger of ICI's oil interests with Enterprise Oil, a number of product reclassifications took place. Oil activities were included in Industrial Products; methanol transferred from Agriculture to Industrial Products; and a number of other transfers were made. The effect this had is shown by the restated 1986 results as follows:

	1986 reported result	1986 restated result
Pharmaceuticals	287	287
Paints	47	47
Other effect products	175	173
CONSUMER/SPECIALITY	509	507
General chemicals	168	166
Petrochemicals and plastics	181	216
Fibres	58	53
Industrial explosives	26	26
INDUSTRIAL	430	458
Agrochemicals	28	28
Fertilisers	(15)	(21)
AGRICULTURE	13	7

6. From 1989 royalty income and government grants were included in the appropriate business activity.

of nitrogen equivalent in 1985 to 0.4 million tonnes in 1989. In 1990 ICI agreed in principle to sell two of its three remaining fertiliser production sites (at Severnside and Leith) to the Finnish group Kemira, as part of a continued withdrawal from the sector. Another element involved further closures at Billingham. The proposed deal was blocked by the Monopolies and Mergers Commission on the grounds that Kemira's increased UK market share (rising to over 40 per cent) would unduly diminish competition (Monopolies and Mergers Commission, 1991), but the accelerated rundown of Billingham continued.

A slightly contrasting picture emerged at Wilton, although the prospects for growth there were still heavily constrained by ICI's global ambitions. It aimed to double the proportion of sales in South-east Asia to one-fifth within the 1990s, anticipating some 40 per cent of total world chemicals industry market growth to take place there. As part of this strategy, ICI announced its biggest single investment for a decade in 1989, a £150 million plant in Taiwan to make terephthalic acid, used in the manufacture of plastic bottles and film. Wilton remained, however, one of ICI's biggest global complexes, its sole supplier of ethylene in Western Europe (of which more than half the output was dispatched to other ICI sites) and a major centre of petrochemicals and plastics production. During the late 1980s, world prices for ethylene and these bulk plastics recovered strongly. There was even speculation about recommissioning the No. 5 cracker which had been mothballed at the start of the decade, although there were also worries of an impending downturn in the market for ethylene in the face of incipient over-capacity.

Instead, in 1990 ICI unveiled a £450 million international plan aimed at increasing its production of acrylic plastics, an up-market and fast-growing sector of petrochemicals. This involved an expenditure of £110 million at Wilton to expand methyl methacrylate (MMA) production, and ICI also planned to expand its only other MMA plant, in Taiwan – a revealing combination of global production locations. This material was then to be shipped across the globe for further processing. In the UK, this was ICI's biggest single investment for over a decade; significantly, though, it was expected to lead to the creation of just forty additional jobs. A substantial part of this investment in MMA production at Wilton was intended for a recycling plant to reduce waste emission. Environmental improvement had also become a growing concern for ICI. At Wilton this involved a planned expenditure of £80 million in the first half of the 1990s on anti-pollution measures, partly in response to growing local environmentalist pressures (pp. 113–19), a sizeable investment but with minimal job-creating effects. In any case, by the end of 1990 ICI had announced a 10 per cent cut in the planned 1991 global investment programme of £1 billion as the impacts of recession again bit deeply.

Whilst ICI's Teesside operations taken as a whole still represented the largest of all its production complexes, with fixed capital assets of £4.5 billion, almost half its global total, and, even in the 1980s, an investment of £850 million, employment had practically halved, from 23,000 in 1975 to less than 11,000 in 1992. At Billingham continuing contraction looked likely, especially as fertilisers production could be cut back without too much impact upon the rest of the Teesside operation. At Wilton (and the closely linked North Tees refinery complex), product diversification was in progress, backed by a new round of investment. Much of this, however, was likely to lead at best to stabilisation of existing employment rather than any major job growth and was to be accompanied by ICI withdrawing from particular product markets, either via portfolio swaps (such as that through which Du Pont took over ICI's Teesside fibre plants in 1992), disposals or capacity closures.

The contrast with the 1960s could not be sharper, and it was not just confined to ICI but was mirrored also on Seal Sands. There a parallel round of closures had taken place on an area of land which had been specifically created for the chemicals industry. Plants which had been established for just a few years withered in the harsh winds of global competition. In 1981 Rohm and Haas closed its Teesside works with the loss of 240 jobs, just six years after opening. Four years later Monsanto, the first major company to locate on Seal Sands, disposed of its plant to the West German group BASF as part of another round of 'portfolio swapping' and rationalisation. Across the river at Teesport, Shell closed its refinery (opened in 1968 and once its third largest in the UK) in 1984 with the loss of 600 jobs. Just as at the main ICI sites at Wilton and Billingham, the picture after 1980 was dominated by plant closure, job loss and retrenchment.

With a symbolism that extended beyond the company to Teesside as a whole, there could be no clearer illustration of the decline in ICI's fortunes than the interest of Lord Hanson's predatory asset-stripping conglomerate in the company in the early 1990s amidst continuing rumours of a radical restructuring of ICI's corporate anatomy. Whilst the unwelcome overtures of Lord Hanson were resisted in 1991, not least through vigorous political pressures from Members of Parliament with ICI plants in their constituencies and from trades unions, pressures for a break-up of ICI into separate profit centres remain as the logic of huge chemicals companies operating across a wide range of product markets is increasingly challenged. ICI more and more sees its future in greater specialisation and responsiveness to a smaller number of customers. As Mr. Tom Hutchinson, an ICI main board director, responsible for Europe, put it, commenting on the wave of mergers and joint ventures between ICI's customers (*Financial Times*, 7 September 1990): 'Overall the picture is one of few customers seeking fewer suppliers and expecting a total and highly responsive service package. ICI wants to meet these challenges and be a "preferred" or "front-choice" supplier'. Not even ICI, which once strode the globe as an industrial Hercules, was immune to the savage pressures of restructuring ripping through the global economy. While it is clear that ICI's diversification into speciality chemicals has been far from problem-free, it was also very evident that the portents for Teesside as ICI, like BSC, continues to disengage from the place are exceedingly gloomy.[7]

4. CONCLUDING COMMENTS

One consequence of steel nationalisation was substantially to confine BSC to bulk steel production and the national market. One result of an abandoned post-nationalisation expansion strategy was to leave the Teesside works specialising in the production of low value-added semi-finished steel, with a shortage of rolling capacity to generate profits for new investment. Additionally, much of the steel-using industry which underpinned the economy of Teesside for over a century was swept away by recession. The Billingham works of ICI, once a major source of the company's fertiliser production, faced concerted challenges from the declining use of fertilisers and alternative sources of supply. Whilst the ICI Wilton site continued to be an important centre of petrochemicals and plastics production, it was a shadow of its former self in terms of both capacity and employment. In effect, both steel and chemicals felt the effects of severe international competition in products where other, newer producer countries possessed many advantages.

The ways in which BSC and ICI responded to this situation were revealing. Whilst BSC was increasingly further forced into bulk production of ordinary steels by the 'Phoenix' mergers of the 1980s (Hudson and Sadler, 1987) and (at least until 1988) politically constrained to invest in steel production in the UK, ICI both sought out new products in speciality chemicals and, increasingly, new and more profitable investment locations. ICI scoured the globe in search of profits (and with some considerable success); BSC remained largely tied to the UK. Yet steel production there faced the same competitive challenge as chemicals so that the net result in terms of investment and employment in the UK was similar, if mediated politically in a different fashion: dramatic cutbacks and plant closures with the continuous threat of yet more to come. BSC's and ICI's responses to their corporate crises were decisive in creating a crisis for labour in Teesside, one that was made all the more acute by the fear that worse was to come. The uncertainty that such a situation generated was both debilitating and instrumental in the creation of a new, more precarious economy and employment base in the area.

These changes also raise questions about the nature and role of the state. The construction of a giant maritime industrial complex on Teesside was significantly and decisively underpinned by the UK state. Without such state involvement, it simply would not have materialised there. ICI and BSC selectively benefited from the provision of the basic general conditions of production by central and local government, whilst the chemicals companies on Seal Sands operated on land that was actually created via state activity. Regional policy underwrote investment but effectively cut jobs. BSC operated as a nationalised producer for twenty-one years, and its closest production ties within the region were initially to another nationalised company, the National Coal Board. Yet events in the 1980s, as the final intra-regional ties were torn apart, demonstrated graphically that none of these forms of state involvement could guarantee either continuing production or employment levels within the UK in the context of fiercely competitive markets. The limits to the state's capacity to manage a national economy – or at least its manufacturing base – were clearly exposed, a *fortiori* when, as in the 1980s, central government chose to define its industrial policy as an active embracing of the pressures of international competition as *the* mechanism through which to restructure the UK's productive base.

The effects of this were all the more acute on Teesside because of previous expectations and the former extent of alternative forms of state involvement. In the heady days of the early 1960s, a strategy for modernisation of the national manufacturing sector was devised which centred on petrochemicals – maybe *the* growth industry of the 1950s, ahead even of automobiles – and other 'modern' industries. Teesside was a focal location in this, identified as a place in which modernising investment was to be carried out. To a considerable degree it was – but not necessarily in a way or on a scale that, coupled with broader macroeconomic policies, guaranteed employment stability or internationally competitive industries. Instead, capacity and employment were cut, selectively at first, then more severely. Growing long-term unemployment on Teesside has to be seen in relation to the failure of 1960s modernisation policies to succeed, even in their own terms. The dominant political response to this at national level culminated in Thatcherite policies. These, combined with further international competitive pressures which government policies welcomed rather than resisted, meant faster and further decline in manufacturing in the UK. Such experiences raised quite profound and fundamental questions as to the future possibilities for national economic management in the context of increasing internationalisation of production in key industrial sectors.

NOTES

1. This was described as follows by Ian MacGregor, when Chairman of BSC (Industry and Trade Committee, 1983, para. 54):

   > Our biggest problem is the lack of strip business. We have three major strip mills and one light plate mill at Lackenby, so we have four essentially strip mills. We have business for one probably, running flat out.

2. Perhaps as a consequence of the speed of development, the implications of possible sea-level changes were ignored. Much of Seal Sands, and indeed other areas of industrial development on Teesside, are located at altitudes less than 1 metre above the highest water level recorded during the 1953 storm surge (Tooley and Jelgersma, 1992, pp. 229–31).
3. The leading figure behind ICI's recovery from recession in the early 1980s, John Harvey-Jones, highlighted these moves in his contribution to ICI's *Annual Report* for 1984:

   > ICI has an increasing presence in all the high growth areas of the world. We are more geographically diverse than any other major chemical company and have steadily strengthened our position in Europe and North America, the two major chemical markets of the world. In the Far East, where the potential is vast but business challenges are complex and difficult, ICI already has a substantial presence and we are making a major effort to increase our activity in this region. The increasingly international nature of the ICI Group requires us to ensure that we have an international outlook and perspective.

   In the 1988 *Annual Report*, new Chairman Denys Henderson could report that ICI

   > may look superficially like the ICI of ten years ago, but it is in fact very different. Since the start of the decade, we have radically restructured the entire business. We now operate in more countries than any other chemical company in the world. We're growing where the markets are growing –

fastest in Asia Pacific, but strongly, too, in North America and Europe.

4. Interviewed on 'Money Makers', BBC 2, 18 February 1986.
5. The Billingham works consumption of natural gas was estimated at 7 per cent of the total UK market (see Chapman, 1986, p. 91).
6. The reason was explained by ICI fertiliser's strategic planner, Ken Atkins, as follows: 'We cannot make money at that level and the only reason we've done it is to keep imported urea out' (quoted in *Financial Times*, 3 November 1986).
7. After we completed the text of this book, it was announced, in February 1993, that ICI was to be split into two companies. This is a decision which will have profound national and local consequences. No longer will ICI be the UK's largest manufacturing firm, whilst of the 9,000 jobs to be lost as an immediate consequence of demerger up to 2,000 will be on Teesside. This may well simply be a first stage in further job shedding; it has been estimated that up to 25,000 jobs would need to be cut from ICI's non-pharmaceutical operations to equalise the rate of return between them and pharmaceuticals (Adcroft *et al.*, 1991, p. 118).

CHAPTER SIX

The Failure of the Politics of Modernisation: Mass Unemployment and Environmental Concern

1. INTRODUCTION

In the 1960s Teesside was promoted as a major centre of new employment growth, capable of absorbing surplus labour from elsewhere in the North-east. *Teesplan* was insistent that this new growth was unlikely to come from the existing staple industries, however. Its forecasts envisaged the most substantial expansion being in other manufacturing activities and services. It anticipated that within twenty-five years factories producing consumer goods would be employing more people than Teesside's traditional heavy industries (implying a four-fold increase in employment in these new manufacturing industries) and that many elements of service sector employment would double (see Table 6.1).

The outcome was very different. As recession deepened, the pace of employment decline in Cleveland accelerated, employment falling from 246,000 in 1975 to 184,000 in 1984 (see Table 6.2). The first signs of renewed local political concern about continued dependence upon a few employers emerged during the 1970s. In 1979, as part of its Structure Plan reassessment programme, Cleveland County Council (1979, p. 15) explored the merits of wholesale land allocation to heavy industry (2000 acres had been so developed since 1966):

> it is questionable whether or not this is contributing at all to the achievement of the employment objectives; the vast land take and loss of visual and recreational amenity and the destruction of environmentally important areas has been accompanied by an overall job-loss in capital-intensive industry.

Such a reappraisal was particularly problematic for a local authority so heavily dependent upon these same companies, not just for goodwill but also more tangibly. They were both a considerable source of employment for many local people and of local authority income via their business rates. These difficulties were neatly encapsulated as follows by one appraisal of the Structure Plan process (Centre for Environmental Studies, 1976, p. 49):

TABLE 6.1: *Teesplan* estimates of employment of Teesside, 1966, and forecasts of employment for 1991.

Teesplan Industrial Group	1966 Estimated employment, 1,000s				1991 Forecast employment, 1,000s			
	Male	Female	Total	Percentage of regional total	Male	Female	Total	Percentage of regional total
Chemicals	29.8	3.3	33.1	16.8	30.6	6.1	36.6	11.6
Metals	29.1	1.5	30.6	15.5	20.2	1.7	22.0	7.0
Engineering and shipbuilding	14.5	1.2	15.7	7.9	12.6	2.4	15.0	4.7
Other manufacturing	8.8	8.4	17.3	8.8	57.1	17.3	74.3	23.5
Retailing	8.2	13.4	21.6	10.9	14.5	26.5	41.0	13.0
Other central services	11.0	9.9	20.9	10.6	20.8	19.6	40.4	12.8
Non-personal services	32.2	5.2	37.4	18.9	47.1	6.7	53.8	17.0
Health and Education	4.1	12.7	16.8	8.5	9.6	22.0	31.6	10.0
Agriculture and extractive	4.0	0.1	4.2	2.1	1.8	0.2	2.0	0.4
Total	141.8	55.7	197.5		214.2	102.3	316.5	

Source: *Teesside Survey and Plan* (1969), 21, 27. Figures amended from Ministry of Labour statistics by including estimates of civil servants and self-employed.

TABLE 6.2: Employment change in Cleveland County, 1975–88.

	Employment, 1,000s					Percentage of total	
	1975	1978	1981	1984	1988	1975	1988
Agriculture and extractive	4.8	5.0	5.5	4.5	4.6	2.0	2.5
Chemicals	27.9	28.6	22.6	21.3	19.6	11.4	10.5
Metal manufacturing	28.1	25.2	18.2	10.1	9.7	11.4	5.2
Mechanical engineering and shipbuilding	18.1	12.9	8.9	7.3	6.0	7.4	3.2
Other manufacturing	31.4	26.8	21.4	16.1	19.7	12.8	10.5
(Total manufacturing)	105.5	93.5	71.1	54.8	55.0	43.0	29.4
Construction	22.7	22.2	14.1	10.7	10.9	9.2	5.8
Services	112.5	114.5	109.6	114.0	116.4	45.8	62.0
Total	245.5	235.2	200.3	184.0	186.9	100.0	99.7

Sources: 1975–84 Census of Employment; 1988 Cleveland County Council estimates.

> There are necessarily constraints on any local authority that it will not wish to emphasise. There are industrial undertakings that are so important, as employers and/or ratepayers, as to make their interests a matter of special concern to the Council. There are inevitably lobbies suggesting the advantages of particular lines of policy. These constraints and influences are not necessarily suspect or reprehensible in themselves, but they lend themselves to political exploitation. Teesside, wishing to reduce its dependence upon a few basic industries, yet fearing to jeopardise its position with these firms, was in a particularly sensitive situation.

Nevertheless, by the 1980s it was impossible to ignore the declining significance of the heavy manufacturing base any longer as unemployment escalated.

For this deepening unemployment crisis was, in large part, directly attributable to the strategic decisions of major chemicals and steel companies. It was made all the more serious because the forecast employment growth in other activities failed to

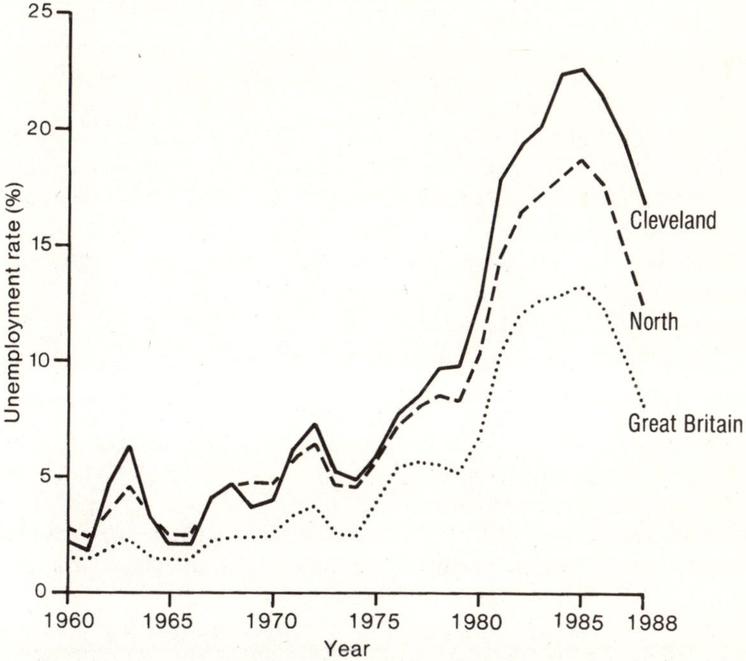

FIGURE 6.1: Unemployment rates in Teesside, 1960–88.

materialise. *Teesplan* had been formulated in the 1960s when unemployment rates of 5–6 per cent were regarded as unacceptably high; as impediments to further regional and national economic growth. In 1966 a mere 2 per cent of Teesside's labour force was officially out of work (see Figure 6.1). From the mid-1970s, though, unemployment rates began a steady increase – well above the rising national trend – reaching 10 per cent in 1978 and 20 per cent in 1982, peaking at 22–23 per cent in 1984 and 1985. These were the highest percentages for any county in mainland Britain and represented around 55,000 people registered as looking for work. As unemployment rose in the late 1970s and early 1980s, the proportion of long-term unemployed rose to over one-half of the total. The overall unemployment rates also concealed considerable variation within the area (see Cleveland County Council Research and Intelligence Unit, 1982). At times in the mid-1980s large parts of inner-urban Teesside had unemployment rates in excess of 40 per cent. Such conditions posed widespread problems, not least for local government. Despite out-migration, the growth of long-distance commuting within the UK and of Teesside residents becoming international migrant workers (see Hudson, 1989b) unemployment rates stayed stubbornly high – above 15 per cent – for the rest of the decade, declining only (partly) due to a limited economic recovery and (largely) due to changes in the basis of calculating unemployment statistics and to eligibility for unemployment benefits. The local authorities, along with many thousands of people in the region, had been burdened with some formidable problems, an all-too visible legacy of Teesside's economic collapse. The issue facing them all was how to respond to this situation.

2. THE FAILURE OF MODERNISATION AND DIVERSIFICATION POLICIES AND ITS IMPLICATIONS: NEW POLICY RESPONSES IN A CONTEXT OF RISING UNEMPLOYMENT ON TEESSIDE

The failure of state-inspired attempts at planning for growth within Teesside was deeply significant, not just in itself but also in revealing some of the contradictions in, and limits to, state policies in a capitalist society. Within the region a strong pro-growth coalition was prominent during the 1960s, built on the paternalist legacy and employer power of earlier years. This prioritised the interests of a few sectors and companies in exchange for promises about secure employment in them and alternative employment and diversification into new industries. Instead, the overwhelming dominance of these few large companies continued to make its presence felt, as ICI internationalised and BSC retrenched in response to deepening domestic recession and intensified global competition. Rather than expand, the economy of Teesside went into a spiralling decline. This raised fundamental questions about the earlier consensus.

The modernisation consensus of the 1960s had been grounded in a misunderstanding of the *international* context within which steel and chemicals production was and was to become situated. As ICI increasingly emphasised other growth areas of the global market, BSC was squeezed by the pressure on its operations from declining domestic demand and international competition. Whilst the forecasts of the 1960s had not anticipated any major growth in steel and chemicals employment, they had at least indicated that state-sponsored investment could preserve existing jobs. In the second half of the 1970s BSC and ICI received £180 million in Regional Development Grants, almost 13 per cent of *all* such grants within the UK (Cleveland County Council, 1988b). However, as the UK again slumped into recession, retrenchment, job loss and capacity closure became widespread – and were to remain so throughout the 1980s. The corporate policies of ICI and BSC directly led to a steep upward trend in unemployment. In the mid-1970s, BSC and ICI employed some 50,000 on Teesside; by 1992 this had fallen to just over 15,000 (11,000 at ICI; 4,400 at BSC). The failure of other components of the 1960s modernisation strategy (the promise of manufacturing sector diversification and service sector growth), however, meant that employment on Teesside was still heavily dependent upon BSC and ICI.

The goal of diversification in the manufacturing sector had largely been defined as the provision by the local authorities and others of industrial estates and factory units. This became interlinked with reclamation of derelict industrial sites, especially the trail of these left by the movement of the steel industry towards the mouth of the Tees. The newly formed Cleveland County Council had a programme to reclaim 2,000 acres in 1974 – 80 per cent of these disused steel-making sites. Restoration proceeded slowly, however, because of problems of land acquisition and financial constraints, the latter tightening from the mid-1970s as pressures on local government expenditure intensified.

During the 1950s the policies which prevented manufacturing industries competing in the labour market with the chemicals, steel and engineering companies meant that limited manufacturing diversification took place. New industries were confined mainly to those seeking female labour. As such clothing, food and electrical engineering companies located plants on 'new' industrial estates adjacent to working-class housing areas (for example, see Boulding, 1988; Centre for Environmental Studies, 1985; North, 1975). During the 1960s and 1970s employment growth on such estates continued to be very modest. Robinson and Storey (1981) reported that only 11,400 new jobs were created in this way between 1965 and 1976, whilst Cleveland County Council Planning Department (1982) extended the period to 1978 and identified 14,225 jobs. There was an evident shortage of new companies responding to the ready availability of land, labour and financial incentives. New manufacturing jobs were swamped by the effects of closures (-14, 374) and job losses at plants remaining open (-32, 301) resulting in a net loss of over 27,500 over the period (Cleveland County Council Planning Department, 1982). By the latter half of the 1970s the supply of new large branch plants had all but dried up on Teesside (see Cleveland County Council, 1985b). Those already there were prone to closure not expansion. Manufacturing employment fell in total by almost 40,000 between 1978 and 1984 (Table 6.2).

From 1979 onwards, local government on Teesside – as elsewhere – became increasingly involved in policies which provided direct financial assistance to small companies (see Centre for Environmental Studies, 1985, pp. 65–8). These were constrained by financial restrictions and from the outset it was recognised that their contribution to employment creation was likely to be marginal. Cleveland County Council (1979, p. 28) argued that 'we cannot look to [new small manufacturing] firms to make substantial inroads into our unemployment total at least in the short or medium term'. Yet the local authorities continued to pursue 'small firm' policies as vigorously as they were able, successfully lobbying for the designation of parts of Hartlepool and Middlesbrough as Enterprise Zones (in 1981 and 1983, respectively). Local politicians felt the need to be seen to be doing something about mounting unemployment, and could see little alternative to 'small firm' policies. Something – however limited – had to be found to replace 'big firm' developments.

Such local pressures intersected with central government ambitions to promote the virtues of a small firm enterprise culture. As MacDonald (1991, p. 3) correctly notes, if an enterprise culture of flourishing new small firms could be fostered in Cleveland, 'enterprise policies would most probably work anywhere'. Consequently, during the 1980s Teesside witnessed an 'amazing proliferation of government sponsored schemes' intended to foster the emergence of such an enterprise culture. Such new firms were, however, overwhelmingly in a narrow range of 'one person' service sector activities. In this, they reflected a broader reality. In the final analysis the effect of such employment policies (both for jobs and self-employment) was very limited. By the end of 1988, the net increase in employment of all kinds on the Hartlepool and Middlesbrough Enterprise Zones was, respectively, 836 and 844 (Department of Environment, 1990). Many of these had resulted from short-distance relocations. This serves to place into sharper focus the emphasis upon service sector expansion, and, in particular, the 1960s idea of redeveloping Middlesbrough as a major sub-regional commercial and financial centre.

Hailsham's strategy (see HMSO, 1963) had placed great emphasis on this town centre redevelopment. This reflected pressures from commercial and financial capital for new investment opportunities to be created outside London (Marriott, 1967). The road lobby (Hamer, 1974) also had a role in this, as did other construction interests and professional planning organisations. The White Paper argued that town centre redevelopment would help diversify employment opportunities, by service sector growth and by presenting a more favourable image to potential in-migrant manufacturing companies. While emphasising the redevelopment of central Newcastle in its role as regional capital, it also advocated similar changes in central Middlesbrough so that it would become a commercial and social focus for the Teesside conurbation.

In *Teesplan*, estimates were made of demand for central area land for civic, commercial and retail uses, based on trend forecasts of population, income and service sector employment. Middlesbrough and Stockton constituted Teesside's two, historically-established shopping centres and there was considerable rivalry between them, especially in local government circles. However, neither offered a particularly good range or quality of services. Concentrating future growth in Middlesbrough seemed to those responsible for *Teesplan* to be the most effective way of deploying public expenditure. Likewise, new office developments were to be concentrated there for it was recognised that Teesside had not experienced the post-war office boom characteristic of regional centres such as Newcastle. As a result, a considerable part of the forecast increase of up to 70,000 jobs in service sector activities would be concentrated in central Middlesbrough (HMSO, 1969, vol. 2, p. 69). Redevelopment of the town centre was, therefore, intended significantly to diversify the occupational and employment base of the area as well as help improve the range and quality of available services and the conurbation's overall image.

Implementing the policies to achieve these goals was, however, extremely problematic. It became evident that local authorities lacked the powers and resources needed to implement them as planned. The redevelopment of central Middlesbrough began in 1968 but severe difficulties subsequently arose. It failed to gain universal support among local residents who organised a series of petitions expressing concern over the effects of planning blight, produced by uncertainty over the future of the area (Gladstone, 1976). Others, dissatisfied with the representation of their interests by local councillors, formed residents' associations to contest redevelopment proposals and even publicly to challenge the local authority and propose 'alternative' plans (Lynch, 1976).

There was more serious opposition to the proposed policies from political and economic interests which would be adversely affected by concentrating development on central Middlesbrough. Not least, this was true of Stockton, for even at the beginning of work on *Teesplan*, there were proposals to redevelop its town centre via a joint local authority-private sector partnership (Gladstone, 1976, p. 52). It was only with some difficulty that agreement was reached to focus commercial redevelopment on Middlesbrough to the detriment of Stockton.

A further problem was posed by the reluctance of the major retailing chains to move into central Middlesbrough. This was only (partially) overcome once the local authority indicated in 1972 that it would not permit the development of 'out of town' superstores. By the late 1970s, however, it could no longer sustain this position. The Asda group proposed building a major superstore at Eston but Cleveland County Council refused planning permission. A powerful lobby of local residents and politicians emerged, arguing that Eston had poor retail provision and high unemployment, both of which would be alleviated by the Asda development. After a Public Inquiry lasting five weeks the Inspector overruled the County Council's objections.

The promotion of Middlesbrough as a sub-regional centre was also undermined by changes in central government policy. This was most evident in the abandonment of a proposal to relocate the Property Services Agency there. The possibility of a major central government office being relocated in Middlesbrough had been floated in *Teesplan* but it was not until 1976, after considerable lobbying, that central government decided to move the Property Services Agency there, with its 3,000 jobs, as part of a more general decentralisation of government offices from London. A 13-acre site was acquired and cleared. After the 1979 General Election, the new Conservative Government precipitately reversed the relocation decision, providing a severe setback to the development of Middlesbrough as a sub-regional centre. In a strikingly similar sequence of events a decade later, hopes were raised about the transfer of 1,600 jobs in the Ministry of Defence's Quality Assurance Unit, only to be dashed after three years' uncertainty when the project was abandoned by central government in 1992.

The redevelopment proposals for central Middlesbrough were completed in 1982, with the opening of the Hill Street Centre, a decade after the completion of the first major phase, the Cleveland Centre. There had clearly been problems along the way. Whilst Middlesbrough had become the focal point of location for the branch offices of many financial services, supply of office space considerably exceeded demand. Moreover, the town's prospective role as a cultural and entertainment centre had simply not materialised. Employment opportunities had failed to occur as planned. Service sector employment growth (much of it in part-time jobs) was only two-thirds of that assumed in *Teesplan*. Services employment in Teesside remained heavily dependent upon the public sector, and activities such as local government, education, health and social services (for example, see North, 1975). This remained the case *despite* the failure of proposed public sector projects, such as the transfer to Middlesbrough of the Property Services Agency.

The failure of these diversification policies meant that job losses at BSC and ICI posed intractable problems for the local economy. As the consequences of their corporate restructuring became all too painfully apparent in steep rises in unemployment, these companies were increasingly drawn to provide their own responses to Teesside's economic difficulties. Whilst these policies had only limited impact in reducing the numbers of unemployed, they were significant in deflecting criticism of the companies and their continued operations on Teesside.

From the mid-1970s onwards BSC nationally operated its own job-creation subsidiary, BSC (Industry), aimed at supporting the creation of a new generation of small businesses in steel-closure areas. Within Teesside this was active first at Hartlepool, then subsequently on the south bank of the river. ICI directed similar attention to smoothing the path of its employment decline on Teesside during the 1980s. Local managers adopted a subtle and sophisticated approach to lowering employment levels at Wilton. They began with a strategy designed to establish the levels of surplus labour at the site. In May 1981 Mechanical Maintenance Groups were introduced around the site. While the plants were run with a skeleton staff, these maintenance workers sat down in the works canteen all day, every day doing absolutely nothing. One manager later revealed that this was: 'a process of management finding out what manning levels should be, of proving whether there was a manpower surplus' and how 'we could have found work for them, but we would have been generating non-urgent work. We were prioritising work much more, generating a more effective use of resources. We were fighting for the survival of the works'. At this time the ICI Board was opposed to compulsory redundancy because of the effect this would have upon the company's image. In their fight for survival, managers had, through the immobile maintenance groups, succeeded in convincing many people that the works was over-manned. Thereupon they initiated an extensive programme of 'resettlement', encouraging workers to leave the Wilton works on a voluntary basis. 'Resettlement' meant a whole range of activities, from support for new small businesses to early retirement and retraining, or placement in a new job. The main scheme ran from March 1981 to October 1983. A second phase aimed only at instrument tradesmen and artificers ran from June 1984 to September 1985. Management was given a free hand to encourage workers to leave provided it kept to the company's policy: 'honest, fair, morally right and in keeping with the image'. Although the area had among the highest unemployment rates in the UK, considerable effort was devoted to convincing workers that they had a future outside ICI. The company's very own Job Shop was established in the works, holding the same cards as the Job Centre in town. In these and other ways, craftsmen in particular were offered the lucrative possibility of employment offshore or abroad. Three managers visited the Middle East, seeking contacts and vacancies, which were to involve over fifty people. A similar number went into business on their own. In all this the company was seen to be concerned, to be spending money, to be leaving no stone unturned – 'keeping up the image'. This helped sustain and augment the aura of the resettlement programme. For most, though, the outcome was 'early retirement'. Throughout, the trades unions were very much in the background. Their influence was confined to attempting to reduce the pressure put on individuals by the company.

When the resettlement scheme at Wilton finished, ICI continued to show concern for its image. A senior manager was seconded to Whitby to form a local enterprise group, the Whitby and District Business Development Agency. He too later left ICI and joined the Agency payroll. In the late 1980s, as the Billingham complex entered its phase of gradual run-down, the company created a new science park development on some of its unwanted land on the fringes of the Billingham works. This estate – named Belasis Hall Technology Park, and run in conjunction with English Estates – was advertised as a suitable seedbed location for prospective small chemical or high-technology companies, offering access to ICI feedstock and/or research and development capabilities. It created new jobs but it was more to do with public relations than a serious attempt to redevelop the local economy. It was another gambit in a concerted and highly astute campaign to minimise the adverse local political consequences of decline on Teesside.

In this way over twenty years the emphasis switched from public policies aimed at diversification and service sector growth to reindustrialisation policies led by the very corporations at the forefront of job losses. The mismatch (between projected employment and reality) was on a par with the outcome of the industrial plans made in the 1960s. In the 1980s, however, the policies adopted by BSC and ICI helped to encourage the creation of a particular kind of 'new' economy on Teesside, one characterised by insecurity and uncertainty.

3. FURTHER CHALLENGES TO MODERNISATION POLICIES: FROM UNEMPLOYMENT TO ENVIRONMENTAL CONCERN

The modernisation consensus centred on a series of political trade-offs, mostly relating to jobs. During the 1950s and 1960s, concern had grown over the impacts of pollution arising particularly from chemicals and steel production on Teesside. This was effectively suppressed by local politicians, many of whom had close connections with the major companies involved (see Gladstone, 1976). 'Jobs' were the trade-off for a poor physical environment. By the mid-1970s, the opposition from environmental groups to the further reclamation of Seal Sands (intended to create still more land for the chemicals industry) was considerable and this was not so easily contained. Initially, it was triggered by the Tees and Hartlepool Port Authority (THPA) announcing plans for land reclamation in an area which had been designated one of Special Scientific Interest, because of its unusual bird population. The THPA lacked the necessary statutory powers to develop the land for 'port related industry' and it sponsored a Parliamentary Bill for this purpose. This Bill was overtaken by events as the required powers were provided by the Teesside Structure Plan. However, strong opposition continued, and this protest came to a head at the structure plan examination in public. The report of the panel of this examination substantially accepted the conservationists' protests, recommending that the vast majority of the land should not be allocated for future port development.

This decision produced a furious reaction. The main trades unions and employers' organisations united to lobby in favour of the original Structure Plan proposals. Their platform was based on the slogan: 'jobs not birds'. This lobby was influential, persuading the Secretary of State to overturn the panel's decision and heavily re-emphasise the central role of such developments on Teesside in relation to attaining national economic priorities:

> the Secretary of State considers that the continued development of the port and port-related industry on Teesside is vital both at a national and at a regional level. He accepts that the need for port development in this area may arise

unexpectedly and that, in this situation, it is very important that there shall be freedom for development to proceed. He has concluded that, despite the importance of the nature conservation considerations, it is of great importance for employment in the region and the overall national economic interest that plans should make provision for the potential need for deep water facilities by making this land available for 'port-related industry'.

The conflict continued to simmer, however. For example, in 1979 the Secretary of State for the Environment proposed making some 440 acres of land at North Gare/Seaton Channel, adjacent to the Seal Sands area, available for 'port-related industries'. The justification for this was an asserted need for further deep water facilities to meet 'national port-related industrial requirements'. This land had once more been designated an Area of Special Scientific Interest, on ornithological grounds. As before, the main trades unions and employers' organisations closed ranks: 'jobs not birds'. Teesside Chamber of Commerce argued that 'Hartlepool must strike a balance between pollution and jobs', while the Middlesbrough District Secretary of the Transport and General Workers Union added that Hartlepool must not 'put birds in front of human beings'. In contrast, both Hartlepool Borough Council and Cleveland County Council objected to these proposals. They were concerned with environmental change, and by the fact that no case had been made for increasing the acreage of land already zoned in the Teesside Structure Plan for port-related industry. The worm had turned. No longer were environmental groups alone in opposition to big capital, organised labour and the state. The failures of the growth coalition on jobs had brought out divisions within the state between central and local government.

The pressures from the THPA to reclaim more land at Seal Sands continued, however. The powers that it possessed to reclaim land were due to expire in 1984. Accordingly, it sought to extend them beyond this date, and Cleveland County Council, Stockton Borough Council and various conservation groups, objected. After much correspondence and consultation, the councils agreed to withdraw their objections. The THPA had agreed to include in the Bill assurances that it would consult with the councils and the Nature Conservancy Council before applying for consent to reclaim land at Seal Sands. Furthermore, it agreed that the Secretary of State would consult the local authorities before giving his consent under the Bill. However, there was no guarantee that the THPA or central government would then take their views into account in deciding on a course of action. This was far removed from the corporatist 'fix' of the post-war years.

Officers and councillors within local authorities were becoming increasingly concerned about environmental pollution and safety hazards. They were becoming suspicious of land use policies which prioritised the needs of major chemical, oil and steel developments. As these industries became increasingly associated with large-scale job losses, the 'jobs at all costs' philosophy became increasingly difficult to sustain. Local authorities began to re-evaluate their land use planning and economic development policies. In this they began to assess not only the environmental costs of further large-scale oil and chemical projects but also their 'employment effects'. As early as 1972 Teesside County Borough Council (1972, p. 103) had raised questions about the compatibility of growth in these sectors with other local government policy objectives:

> the image of Teesside as a growth area with an improving environment and widening job opportunities could be adversely affected by the persistence of a labour market dominated by chemicals and steel and an environment under continuous threat from pollution resulting from the development of large capital intensive plants.

The tone was conjectural, however, and at that time these reservations were set aside. More serious doubts were raised from the mid-1970s onwards, as it became clear that the Structure Plan documents had over-estimated both the direct and indirect employment creating effects of oil and petro-chemical related investment (Cleveland County Council, 1975, p. 61). One consequence of this was a proposal to allocate more land for 'labour intensive' manufacturing activities and for 'small firms'. The council suggested, that in view of the dangers and problems inherent in promoting chemicals, oil and steel expansion 'it might be argued that diversification of employment should be the *main* objective of Structure Plan industrial policy' (Cleveland County Council, 1975, p. 64, emphasis added).

These proposals to emphasise other forms of industrial development were strongly resisted by the powerful lobby of the THPA, the major private sector companies and the trades unions. As unemployment continued to rise, it became increasingly difficult for this old coalition to survive. In its reassessment of existing Structure Plans, Cleveland County Council (1979) recognised that many objectives were far from being fulfilled. The rise of unemployment since the late 1960s had been very similar to that of the rest of the North-east, *despite* so-called growth zone status

(Figure 6.1). In terms contrasting sharply with previous optimism, it suggested that 'the future outlook for employment' was bleak (p. 21) and argued 'it seems likely that high unemployment is here to stay, at least for some considerable time to come' (p. 23). It went on to consider the implications of a policy that prioritised heavy industry. In addition to the requirement for vast areas of land and the adverse visual impact, it concluded that such development might well deter other investors, and create a vulnerable local economy. It argued that 'there is some doubt that the presence of capital-intensive industry is beneficial in the long-term to the Cleveland economy' (p. 6).

By the mid-1980s (in the context of now soaring unemployment rates) Cleveland County Council prepared a new Structure Plan (see Cleveland County Council, 1985c). The prospect of low economic growth and high unemployment had a pervasive influence on all aspects of the process of policy reassessment. In addition to the slump in manufacturing, the service sector had seen only hesitant growth. The equivalent of twelve major office blocks stood empty. Priorities changed.

In 1986 the Council set up an Unemployment Working Party. To the extent that this acknowledged that producing local 'full employment' via modernisation policies was no longer a credible option, it represented an important ideological break. It was no longer viable simply to claim to address the needs of the unemployed indirectly via policies to encourage private capital within Teesside; there was a need for policies which addressed the needs of the unemployed, as citizens, directly. They did this in only a very limited and partial way, but in recognising the need to do something they had registered an important political transition. A member of this committee, County Councillor David Walsh, explained what brought it about:

> The early 1980s saw a change within Cleveland County Council. There was a growing recognition of the shifts in power within the country to the south-east, and of a Government ideology which felt that Teesside had played its historic role. There was a recognition that we could no longer rely on government intervention, that we had to take things into our own hands.

In 1987 the Working Party produced an 'unemployment strategy' (Cleveland County Council, 1987). Its priorities were to address the needs of the individual more effectively, improve communication with the unemployed, and establish 'Community Action Areas'. It was, however, barely scratching the surface of the problems of mass unemployment, constrained partly by the legacy of past Labour politics and partly by the real financial constraints on local authorities in the 1980s.

In this new political climate major companies on Teesside, such as ICI, began to cultivate a much more environmentally friendly image and to increase expenditure on pollution control measures. Whilst atmospheric pollution was reduced, however, discharge of pollutants into the river Tees and the North Sea remained a major issue. A report compiled by Greenpeace in 1992 listed ICI Wilton and BSC Redcar among the twenty industrial plants contributing most to marine pollution within the UK. ICI Billingham, BASF, Tioxide and the Tees Storage Company joined them in the top fifty. Mr David McClean, Minister for the Environment and Countryside, responded to this by saying (quoted in the *Northern Echo*, 16 September, 1992): 'It is unrealistic to suggest that we can simply tell industry to stop discharging waste to the rivers and seas overnight; the only way to do that would be to shut it all down'. Shortly afterwards, in November 1992, the Department of the Environment approved a proposal by Cory Environmental to build an industrial waste incinerator at Seal Sands. There was considerable local opposition to this project and environmental concerns were voiced increasingly loudly. They became enmeshed with the impact of unemployment to raise serious questions over the path which Teesside had taken in the 1960s, and of the political consensus upon which it was based. The environmental consequences of previous developments were pointed out and they became increasingly difficult to defend. This process was described as follows by Mrs Maureen Taylor, County Councillor and environmental campaigner:

> It was always my argument that the sort of development which is on Seal Sands now wouldn't create a load of jobs, and that is why the trades unions got at me because they said, here lay the future of Teesside in terms of jobs. What tipped the balance in favour of the kinds of industry we have now was the argument that 'jobs had to come'. It was a false argument but nevertheless it was one which won the day. So the pollutant industries came to Seal Sands in the 1970s, spilling their muck. By the late '70s even some of the livelier proponents against what I was arguing were heard to say 'enough is enough'. And I think that was linked not only to the pollution but also to the point that in they come, they take the regional policy grants, and at the first sign of something that doesn't suit them, off they go.

It was a further sign of changing times on Teesside in the 1980s that a local campaign was successful in preventing the dumping of nuclear waste in old ICI anhydride mines, but the fact that the company embarked on such a plan is revealing in itself. Public opposition resulted in 83,000 people in the Billingham area alone signing a letter of protest to the Prime Minister, opposing the dumping proposals. No longer were such 'pollutant industries ... spilling their muck' wanted there. It was no coincidence that the most vociferous campaigners against the polluting effects of industrial development were women. Claims such as those about the priority of 'people over birds' or that 'jobs had to come first' were, in essence, claims about the priority attached to *male* employment, to the need for 'jobs for the boys' in industries such as chemicals and steel. However, the impact of these industries extended beyond jobs and beyond the factory gates. They had ordered the division of labour between men and women for decades. They had also polluted the atmosphere and the environment of those who lived around their works. They had helped to damage health, and mounting evidence confirming this was becoming available in the 1980s. In the 1980s the residents of the area along the south bank of the Tees experienced some of the poorest health in the North. In a population of 86,000, there were 370 deaths per year of people aged under 65, of which 145 would not have occurred had this area experienced the mortality rate of England and Wales as a whole (Townsend *et al.*, 1988, p. 50). Only one other area in the Northern Region had such an extremely high level of premature mortality. Townsend *et al.* (ibid., p. 50) observed that 'there cannot be more than a very few such areas in the country'. Whilst the concentration of high death rates and illness was partly due to severe poverty and deprivation, it also reflected 'the possible consequences for health of air pollution emanating – especially in the not so distant past – from the massive chemical and steel complexes' (ibid., p. 127).

The collapse of the consensus which prioritised 'jobs at all costs' therefore posed a considerable challenge to established forms of politics, both nationally and, especially, on Teesside. The dilemma was neatly and inadvertently encapsulated in 1979 by Mr James Tinn, MP for Redcar. When further steel works closures were being considered, he 'reminded the House' during a parliamentary debate (Hansard, vol. 973, 7 November 1979, col. 490) that

> over the last decade no less than 10,000 jobs [in steel] were lost on Teesside. In only one closure was there a massive and

> well-organised protest, and that was not in my constituency but across the river. The Teesside workers recognised that modernisation was inevitable and that a price had to be paid for it. They paid the price before they got the new works.

Accepting the inevitability of job losses associated with modernisation investment at Redcar during the 1970s, his concern was the possibility of *further* job losses. Such a trade-off had, of course, become central to the politics of labourism both nationally and locally. Yet subsequent events, and further massive reduction in BSC's workforce during the early 1980s, proved it to be flawed. Coming to terms with the failure of previous policies was to be especially difficult.

Throughout the 1980s the challenge to the old consensus emerged in a variety of ways. At one level, it led to some sharp changes in patterns of party political support; the local electoral map underwent some significant changes, for example. Within local government it resulted in a thorough-going reappraisal of previous conventionally accepted wisdoms. With the benefit of hindsight, many confident assumptions of earlier years were subjected to critical scrutiny. Head of Cleveland County Council's Research and Intelligence Unit, Reg Fox:

> The problem we've got is that we've been the forerunner of changes in manufacturing, and I don't think society generally and the national political scene has caught up with the fact that this is going to be happening in the rest of manufacturing. Until the country comes to terms with that, we'll not have the resources to tackle our problems.

Chief Planning Officer, John Gillis:

> The sad thing is, for at least the last ten years we've been telling people this. We must cope with these people who are unemployed. What are we going to do with them?

Answering this question was one of the most pressing issues informing politics on Teesside in the 1980s and into the 1990s.

4. CONCLUDING COMMENTS

As Teesside entered the 1980s, then, much of its old economy had been decimated. The political consensus and modernisation policies constructed around assumptions about future prosperity based upon restructuring the chemicals and steel industries and upon diversifying Teesside's economy became subject to growing pressures as unemployment rose and the environmental consequences of such forms of activity became better and more widely understood. As unemployment rose to, and remained at, high levels, previous constraints which had suppressed discussion of the undesirable environmental consequences of chemicals and steel production weakened significantly. Not least, environmental dereliction was itself increasingly seen as a barrier to economic and employment diversification. Moreover, the growing salience of environmental issues provided space into which gender relations within Teesside could be reappraised, as 'jobs for the boys' became seen as 'pollution for the girls'. But as an old order, political and economic, was thrown into deep crisis, questions arose as to what would – or could – be put in its place.

CHAPTER SEVEN

Flexibility and New Forms of Work in the Teesside Economy in the 1980s

1. INTRODUCTION

In the late 1980s the presence of substantial numbers of unemployed people was used by employers forcefully to push through new forms of employment relations. These changes were not introduced at the edges of the employment system by 'cowboy employers'. They were at the very heart of employment on Teesside. The chemicals and steel industries were clearly implicated in this process, as formerly held notions of 'jobs for life' were rudely ruptured. Offshore construction (one growth industry which evolved from the ruins of engineering and shipbuilding) joined them at the forefront of such development. Trades unionists, socialised into a culture of compliant co-operation, found great difficulty in coming to terms with the new adversarial climate and in finding effective ways of resisting managements' demands. In other industries, with weaker traditions of unionisation (or none at all), there was even less opposition to change. Small firms and new branch plants successfully sought similar concessions from their workers and the search for flexibility spread to the service sector, to both old and new, public and private sector activities alike. In so far as an enterprise culture emerged on Teesside, the new generation of would-be entrepreneurs tended to be self-employed and self-exploiting, confined to a restricted range of service sector activities (see MacDonald, 1991, for example). As with 'modernisation' in the 1960s, the search for flexibility emerged as a shared goal for employers in the 1980s. While their workforces might be unhappy with these developments, they had little choice but to comply.

2. THE IMPACT OF UNEMPLOYMENT ON TEESSIDE'S LABOUR MARKET

Much of the context for the changes which took place in the Teesside labour market during the 1980s related to the existence of very considerable numbers of unemployed people looking for paid employment. In some areas the continued impact of successive rounds of redundancies became particularly acute. The outer estates of East Middlesbrough, for instance, had levels of unemployment three times the national average, with resultant pockets of severe social stress (see CES, 1985). Scattered throughout Cleveland County there were another half a dozen similar areas characterised by permanent high unemployment and deprivation (Cleveland County Council Research and Intelligence Unit, 1982; also *Independent on Sunday*, 23 August 1992). Some very real and striking parallels were drawn with the experiences of the last great depression of the 1930s (see Nicholas, 1986). The existence and experiences of large numbers of unemployed people filtered through more generally to changed labour market conditions (see Foord *et al.*, 1985, 1987) and to the conditions of work of those with jobs.

One view of unemployment in the UK in the 1980s held that, in areas such as Teesside, there was no longer any stigma attached to being unemployed because so many were out of work. This portrayal, however, ignored many very real problems and was not one shared by those out of work. The social worlds of the unemployed and employed may have been separate ones, but this was not necessarily through choice, as one young unemployed man explained:

> I don't know if this is just a coincidence – but I have some friends and five of them go out together and they're all working, and there's a load of us that go out and we're all unemployed – and if I was with them five lads, say for a night out, I think I'd be embarrassed to say I'm unemployed. With the other lads I'm not bothered.

Another, aged 51 and unemployed since 1978, commented:

> I feel like bloody scum, like I've been put on a shelf and forgotten about. Scroungers off the country, that's what we're called. We're not scroungers, we're human beings like everyone else.
>
> I go out and can't buy a round. I feel guilty when I see my daughters because I can't give much to the grand-kids. As far as I'm concerned, I don't have a life.'

Lack of money, then, limits activities and undermines independence in a variety of ways. Paula, an unemployed factory worker, commented:

> I don't like the indignity of being out of work. I don't like it, say, if the giro doesn't come in the middle of the week, and

> you have to borrow from your mam. It makes you wonder what you did with your money when you were at work. I have the odd day at the seaside, but you know you can't spend when you get there. You have a meal at the cheapest cafe and just enjoy the fresh air.

For those who had experienced a working life, the sense of social exclusion could be acute; for those just entering the labour market on leaving school, this can be powerfully compounded by frustrated ambition (see also Coffield *et al.*, 1986). Marco, an unemployed 17-year-old, summed up his situation in this way:

> There's nowt to do around here. We just walk around all day, do circuits like, hang about the shops. The bobbies come up and take our names, just to hassle, we're not bothering no-one. The bobbies are shithouse. They just want to get you down the station and bang you up.
>
> I was on YTS but I gave it up. The bosses got on my nerves. I go down the dole shop but they all want over 21 or experience. I'd do anything, me'.

It speaks volumes that, at the age of 17, Marco had already been reduced by cumulative frustrations to the point where he was ready to 'do anything'.

Many of the tensions associated with unemployment – especially on a long-term basis – were refracted through the household, although with varying connotations for different individuals. One young school-leaver talked about when his father was unemployed as follows:

> He was unemployed for more than a year. He got very depressed, he took up golf, but couldn't stick it. He just started getting depressed and niggly. You couldn't blame him really. You could understand. He was used not so much to a lot of excitement, but pressure. I think my parents nearly did split up at that time.

In many households where men were unemployed, women's wages took on a new significance. Yet the assumption of 'appropriate' roles for men and women remained very strong, despite such changes. The patriarchal traditions of a male-dominated society, emphasised by the central importance of male employment in Teesside's heavy industries, were deep-rooted. One woman, working as a supervisor in a large chain store, commented:

> I think the man is the breadwinner – or we'd like to say that. With the unemployment situation now he might not

> actually be the breadwinner – but I like to feel I have the option to pack in work any time. A man doesn't have that option'.

Such views made the loss of a job keenly felt by many men. They also generated a new set of tensions for many women, who felt their own role under threat. Kathleen worked full time in a department store and her husband had been unemployed for over three years:

> He has taken on my job – sometimes, I'll be honest with you, I get depressed, I walk home and he says to me I've done so and so that means I've nothing to do. Sometimes it gets me. I want to do it myself. The first two years weren't so bad, but in the last year I've noticed I can go home, walk up the stairs and he's behind me – he's wanting to talk. Everywhere I go he's behind me wanting to talk.

In such circumstances the pressure on the unemployed to search for paid employment extends beyond a need for money. It is intensified by the fierce competition for such jobs as are available. In addition to formal Job Centre placings or government training schemes, unofficial information networks become increasingly significant in the search for work – even if on a temporary basis. Contacts and reputation become almost as important as qualifications and experience, at least in some segments of the labour market. For some, an alternative route was to leave Teesside either for overseas construction projects, or for other parts of the UK. But such solutions could be problematic. In the international labour market, competition from other migrant workers was intense, especially in the Middle East and those contracts were often not as lucrative as they appeared. The housing market made it difficult to move from Teesside to the South of England, and working there temporarily frequently led to personal, family and social difficulties. Nor was self-employment an easy option. Despite powerful government encouragement, the creation of a new small business in a depressed local economy was no easy task. Even for those who do succeed 'enterprise means ... a twilight world of hard work, low pay, casualised labour and insecurity ...' (MacDonald, 1991, p. 2). Moreover, such new firms are overwhelmingly 'one-person' operations confined to a narrow range of service activities and reinforce existing gender divisions of labour. In short, the implications of industrial decline permeated all aspects of Teesside's labour market.

In this situation, people sought work and income at almost any price, and often their opportunities were limited to the informal sector or casual work in the so-called 'black' or 'fiddle' economy. A popular media image in the 1980s was of Hartlepool's 'new' coal economy, as unemployed people illegally collected coal washed up on its beaches. Such 'black' jobs were characterised by a total lack of security and proper safeguards for working conditions, and also by the fear of getting caught by government authorities. One skilled unemployed construction worker explained how:

> I could have plenty of jobs on the fiddle, but it is a bit risky. I could fiddle for thirty quid a day. In the present day and age I don't blame a bloke who does fiddle, but I feel I'm just too well known.

Another unemployed man put it this way:

> There's a lot of people on the fiddle – but then again a lot are jealous of the money they earn. There's a lot of anonymous phone calls to the DHSS. I wouldn't tell on anybody myself, but I would not take part either for fear of being caught.

The pressures to become involved in the informal sector or even to cross the boundaries of legality, despite the risks, were and are substantial, coming from many directions. Doubtless, there were some who simply wished to avoid paying taxes. This was, after all, nothing new, and it applied to a degree in almost all occupations and industries. For many others it was an understandable reaction to low wages or benefits. But a more recent – and in many respects more disturbing – phenomenon on Teesside was the active collusion of employers in the arrangements: manipulating the black economy, playing upon people's experiences and fears of unemployment and thereby adding further pressures which stimulated insecurity. Local news reports talked of perhaps one in ten of Teesside's registered unemployed being involved in such activities by the early 1990s. One woman working in a canteen believed that:

> You can get a job in any trade on the fiddle – on market stalls, in shops, in garages, anywhere. Of course the employers aren't bothered are they – they don't have to pay the stamp [National Insurance contributions].

An unemployed man pointed to his own experiences:

> I worked for a security company full-time over the Christmas holidays. They said sign on as part-time and get your benefit as well. It meant they could pay me less in wages. I wouldn't have got the job if I hadn't agreed.

This avoidance of regulation and job protection in a labour market characterised by high unemployment mirrored the casualisation of employment occurring on the periphery of the formal sector through contract work and sub-contracting. High unemployment meant increased insecurity and more intense exploitation in all kinds of work (including self-employment). Companies built on their newly-found strengths to assert the 'right to manage'. They did so secure in the knowledge that people in the pool of unemployed were desperate for work at practically any price, and engaged in an increasingly competitive and divisive struggle to try and get it. In these ways unemployment – both the reality and the threat – became a vital and active constituent in much of what happened to people on Teesside during the 1980s.

One middle-aged man, himself in work, put it like this: 'The authorities are pushing people into a situation of anarchy. People just don't see justice being done.' He continued:

> 'I know a lot of bent people, a lot a rogues. You can get anything you want knocked-off. It's the poor robbing the poor. The gear turns up at car boot sales, it's all stuff that can't be traced ...
>
> I've had three cars stolen. I went after one with a baseball bat and put him in hospital. Now they tell me I could be done for GBH. The lad next door had his lawnmower pinched three weeks ago. The police virtually accused him of doing an insurance job ...

Such views represent a particularly savage indictment of what life had become for many on Teesside in the 1980s; a life blighted by the spectre of mass unemployment, with growing divisions between those in formal employment and those seeking alternative survival strategies threatening the fabric of civil society.

3. EMPLOYMENT IN THE 'OLD' MANUFACTURING ECONOMY

Steel

At BSC, changes began soon after the defeat of trades unions in the national steel strike of 1980. The arguments surrounding this dispute have been rehearsed at length elsewhere, but many workers on Teesside were clear that the Iron and Steel Trades Confederation (ISTC) had been selected as an easy target for the newly-elected Conservative Government's anti-trades union strategies. The political priorities of the incoming government had a clear and almost immediate impact on Teesside, as 'softening-up' the unions became a central component of national employment policy. Tony Cook, a member of the ISTC's national executive committee in 1980, argued later that 'the steel unions were targeted –

absolutely no doubt about it'. He went on to describe the aftermath: 'We lost men, we had closures, and the eyes across the negotiating table had steel shutters. They were enjoying it'. In the minds of many, these changes were associated with the management style of the new BSC chairman, Ian MacGregor. Tony Poynter, ISTC branch official:

> MacGregor was a completely different kind of guy. He met the stewards and management early on Teesside, and said there'd be no more pay rises without productivity increases. He was very abrasive. 'People have got to go', he said. Every year, they were coming back for more redundancies, more changes in working practices – things that had never been put to the unions in this area before.

These demands for changes 'that had never been put to the unions in this area before' marked a significant break from recent experiences of employment in the steel industry, both on Teesside and more generally in the UK. If nationalisation had hardly secured existing employment in the 1970s, it had at least seemingly offered a route through which new and 'better' forms of representation of employee interests could be explored, culminating in the 'worker-director' scheme (for conflicting views on this, see Bank and Jones, 1977; Brannen *et al.*, 1976). Whilst the practical impact of such developments was limited, the contrast with events in the 1980s could not have been sharper.

From 1982 onwards steel workers faced the perpetual threat of redundancy and the possible closure of the whole complex. Such a prospect was a major impediment to active opposition to employers' demands, and management utilised this to assert what it saw as its 'right to manage'. In many parts of the works this created an atmosphere of fear and uncertainty. Alan Deans, an ISTC official, gave one example:

> Management are going absolutely berserk on time-keeping. If you have two shifts off or you're late twice, you'll get a written warning. If it happens a third time inside thirteen weeks, you're out. That's what I call whipping the workforce into line. You're classed as a bad case now if you've had six shifts off in a year. That's what I mean by a frightened workforce.

Whilst such concerns were by no means insignificant in themselves (especially in such a physically strenuous industry), they were also symbolic of broader and more momentous changes. In this process (playing on a well-established tradition of territorial chauvinism within the steel unions), management was keen to foster competition between individual production sites. Information was used to engender a collective fear of greater success at other BSC plants as a means of 'whipping the workforce into line'. Trades unions were unable to prevent burgeoning inter-plant competition, even when they recognised the threat that it carried for labour solidarity and collective organisation. Ron Agar, AEU convenor:

> The four BSC divisions now are running businesses separate from each other. We're competing with each other. If Ravenscraig were to close, that would be to our benefit, because on certain items customers would come to us. The same goes for Llanwern. As a trade unionist I never wish to see these works close. But from a purely selfish point of view it would help us – and you'd get the same reaction from my counter-part at Ravenscraig. That's how MacGregor got it organised. Every business must be self-financing.

A central element of this new approach lay in devolving responsibility for labour costs (but not, significantly, for capital investment) to plant level. After sixteen negotiating sessions, local agreement was reached in March 1981 for 3,800 redundancies as part of a scheme in which the remaining Teesside workforce would receive 3 per cent lump sum bonuses in March, June and September, provided that the job losses were carried through on time. This was subsequently extended on Teesside and at other BSC works to include other efficiency improvements. Local deals came to form the major, and for a time the only, source of wage increases. From 1981 to 1984 there was no national pay rise at BSC. A deal agreed in January 1985 provided for only a 4.25 per cent increase on basic rates for fifteen months. In May of that year Teesside pioneered a further extension of BSC's decentralised bargaining. Local negotiators concluded agreement on a bonus scheme linked not only to productivity but also – for the first time – to works' profit. Following this, employees would receive lump sums each quarter rising to a maximum 9 per cent of basic pay if quarterly works' profits reached £5.75 million.

The introduction and subsequent strengthening of locally-negotiated wage increases was important in emphasising local labour productivity as *the* means of securing local works' viability (even though many elements in the bonus calculation, including works' profit, depended partly or wholly upon central decisions concerned with production, marketing and capital investment). The unremitting emphasis upon labour costs was indicative of management's newly-found strength. A further manifestation of this was a growing demand for labour force flexibility – both in numerical and functional terms. The clearest expression of this was at the BSC Hartlepool works, on the north bank of the Tees.

After a long run-down in the 1970s, only a plate mill and two other mills capable of rolling pipes up to 20 and 44 inches in diameter, respectively, remained in operation there. In January 1983 BSC announced its intention to close the 44-inch pipemill and, in May, to close the plate mill. Subsequently, however, an alternative plan emerged (as explained in a letter from Mr Broxham, BSC Teesside's Personnel Director, to Bill Sirs, General Secretary of the ISTC, on 22 June):

> shortly after making that announcement (in May) it became clear that a decision on the placement of a major order for pipe would be made in early August which if it could be secured for the Hartlepool 44″ mill would provide nearly six months' work on 10 shifts for the 44″ pipe mill. The plate requirement for this order would similarly provide nearly six months' work for the Hartlepool plate mill on 5 shifts operation. On the basis that there was a possibility of getting this order the Corporation put forward the proposal that instead of a full stand-down the Hartlepool plate mill should be demanned from approximately 1000 covering 15 shifts to a crew of approximately 250 who could man a single shift pipe production operation. This crew would be retained until August in the hope of getting the pending order.

This order was subsequently successfully secured on 23 August. It involved an £18 million deal with Shell to supply 70 per cent of a 180-mile pipeline to carry gas from the Fulmar field in the North Sea. To fulfil the order BSC indicated its intention to recruit 220 workers for the 44-inch mill (which had been idle since February) and give them contracts until February 1984. The order also guaranteed the jobs of the remaining 260 plate mill workers until then.

The nature of the short-term contracts offered to those working on this order proved to be particularly innovative, and made chilling reading for workers asked to accept them. The letter of appointment, dated 23 August 1983, stressed that:

> collective agreements between the Corporation and any of the recognised trade unions are not applicable to your short term employment, with the whole exception of the 'Memorandum of Enabling Agreement' made on 27 May 1983 between the British Steel Corporation and the TUC Steel Committee with regard to Short Term Employees working in Hartlepool 44″ Pipe Mill.

The 'Memorandum of Enabling Agreement' made only too

apparent the conditions under which waged employment was being offered. To quote:

2.1 Employees will be required to work any system, days or shifts according to the needs of the business.

3.1 *Maximum* flexibility and mobility shall apply.

4.7 Employees will not be entitled to a redundancy payment, employment and income security benefit or any other severance pay.

5.2 There will be no minimum holiday entitlement.

5.4 It is accepted that priority will be given to operational requirements and that holidays will normally be paid as cash on the completion of the employment contract.

In order to make the message absolutely clear, the memorandum also included a seven-side, sixty-six point schedule of working practices which included the following:

12 Craftsmen will maintain the cleanliness of their work areas and own amenity facilities (e.g. meal cabin).

13 Craftsmen will be expected to operate production equipment and machinery as the need arises.

24 Semi/non-skilled grades will perform any work as directed.

59 All grades will undertake cleaning duties as instructed.

63 Production grades will undertake tasks for the maintenance department within their own skills.

66 It is in the interests of all employees to complete any pipe contract at least cost, on time and to the customer's specifications. This criterion necessitates the employment of the minimum number of people working together as a team and operating sensible flexible working practices which contribute to maximising the production operation.

The original agreement was to cover any contracts starting before the end of August 1984. When further production contracts were signed after that date (despite the cancellation of the Shell Fulmar order in March 1984 because of poor quality), local union officials met BSC seeking changes in employment terms and conditions. The company, however, had no interest in varying the agreement. In particular, it refused to recognise continuity of employment across two or more contracts, claiming that each new order represented a break in service. Thus, BSC had secured via its earlier threatened and actual closures, transition from a workforce employed under standard agreements and procedures to one employed on a rolling series of temporary contracts under radically different working conditions. No clearer illustration of the effects of high unemployment in the local labour market could have been given; and this was not lost upon the rest of the BSC Teesside workforce.

In other parts of the giant complex, BSC followed a variation of the theme practised at Hartlepool. The use of sub-contracted labour grew enormously in the UK steel industry during the 1980s. Teesside works director, Mr Ward, explained the rationale behind this as follows: 'The spine of our operation is iron and steel production. We had to look at other activities, work out their fixed and variable costs, and sub-contract accordingly'. A whole range of such activities was contracted out to other companies, including catering, cleaning, transport, wrecking and bricking of furnaces and computer support. One of the most contentious issues was the use of sub-contracted labour in maintenance work. For in a process industry such as steel, it was often difficult to distinguish between production and maintenance tasks. The wrecking and bricking of steel converters, for example, was a 'maintenance' operation performed regularly and essential to continued steel production. Indeed, in many other countries the use of sub-contracted labour in operations such as this, and even in direct production, was not unusual. Yet this ran against the history of labour organisation and work allocation within Teesside's steel industry. Concern over the extent to which BSC had cut back on its own labour force for essential maintenance was expressed by Bill Purvis, AEU district organiser: 'BSC say they can't carry a full maintenance crew on a permanent basis. But maintenance really has been cut beneath the bone. If anything serious crops up they just can't handle it'. Another view came from Mr Davey, the ISTC's senior organiser on Teesside: 'Let's face it, we can't say to BSC, "you can't have that contractor". We're really just the policemen of agreements. What we are concerned about is contractors taking regular jobs of BSC employees on the production side. We have resisted that most strongly.'

Whilst these different emphases reflected varying membership bases, there was no doubt that, for discharging their role as 'policemen', the steel unions had relatively limited powers. The encroachment of sub-contracted labour upon production tasks was gradual and insidious. It even included instances of BSC employees being laid off, forming their own company and successfully tendering for their former jobs. Furthermore, the unions' weakness was apparent not just in the scope of sub-contracted operations but also in the conditions under which sub-contractors employed labour.

These conditions were important. The expansion of sub-contracting was an integral part of the Corporation's drive to reduce its core workforce, shed some of the burden of employment costs as pensions, retirement and sickness benefits, and at the same time tacitly accept, if not encourage, a redefinition of working practices. It is very difficult to be precise about this impact of sub-contracting – partly because BSC wished it to be so. Mr Ward, Teesside works director, told us that he 'would be very unhappy if there were to be any discussion over the terms of our agreements with sub-contractors'. But it is nevertheless clear that there were considerable grounds for concern.

On Teesside, the conditions under which the growth of sub-contracting took place were supposed to be regulated by a 'Contractors Agreement' signed between BSC and the steel unions in 1981. This was meant to ensure that contractors paid nothing less than the agreed minimum rate for a job. Much evidence suggests, however, that this was observed only in passing. Moreover, there was growing concern about the illegal use of labour from the ranks of the unemployed by sub-contractors. The ISTC's senior organiser, Mr Davey, recognised that: 'There's no doubt that contractors do employ people off the dole. Some of them recruit a dozen or so people in a pub, and offer money in the back pocket' whilst Ron Agar, AEU convenor, was even stronger in his views, and fully conscious of their implications:

> A lot of the men that come in to work for contractors are claiming DHSS benefits. I have proof of this, and I'm in close contact with management on it. BSC claim not to know. Certainly they wouldn't condone it. But they've used the economy of this country to help the profitability of the steel industry. They've used the black economy, indirectly – although they wouldn't admit it. There's no way that a contractor coming in for one day would sign off – he'd lose all his benefit. And in a week he could earn more than a skilled craftsman. That's a sore point.

It was not just a sore point locally, but also a point not lost upon others. When BBC TV's 'Panorama' programme visited Middlesbrough in June 1986, it focused upon the issue, claiming that 'many of those employed by the contractors are on the dole and not signing off'. BSC spokesman Mr Adamson responded that 'at present no one who is on the dole is on this site' (*Middlesbrough Evening Gazette*, 17 June 1986). A letter was despatched to all contractors warning them not to employ such labour. But others were showing interest, including a special team of Department of

Employment investigators. After a four-week enquiry the front-page headline words of the local newspaper announced a 'dole swoop on 100 at BSC' (*Middlesborough Evening Gazette*, 28 August 1986). The article continued:

> More than 100 people face prosecution for false benefit claims after an anti-fraud swoop on men working at British Steel. Some of the men netted by Department of Employment investigators were allegedly being paid up to £180 a week working for sub-contractors. But they were also receiving as much as £60 a week in unemployment or supplementary benefit.

Such a high-profile inquiry (it was formally announced by a Government Minister) was significant in a number of ways. Not least for those anxious to cut public expenditure, it raised the issue of the *real* extent of unemployment in Teesside while at the same time it sent out a message to the rest of Teesside's unemployed about the burgeoning surveillance activities of the state. It also apparently vindicated many of the steel unions' claims. But the deeper reasons behind the growing black and dark grey economy remained in the shadows, hidden from public view. For a large part of the potential for abuse lay in the fact that sub-contracted labour was casual work – and the transition from stable to casual employment in the steel industry had been actively and positively encouraged by BSC. Part of the reason for this lay in the use of outside labour to encourage changes in working practices within the remaining core workforce. Ron Agar, AEU convenor:

> On the one hand you do away with the direct labour, on the other you bring in the indirect labour. It's not seen on the balance sheet, but it's a matter of balancing the books. We could muster three or four hundred craftsmen within twenty four hours on Teesside. The contractor hires and fires these men at a minute's notice. They pose a threat to us every day of our working lives. We don't know whether we've a secure future. It's an uphill battle all the way. It seems we can never get security of employment, because of the contractors.

The elision here between contractor and contracted is significant. For in the minds of many core employees the sub-contracted labour force became the challenge, the threat to their own jobs. The focus was always upon them rather than the managerial practices through which sub-contracting had grown and the economic imperatives that pushed management down this track. This perception of the situation was by no means unwelcome to BSC and it had also been actively promoted by the contracting companies. For core workers seeing the process in this way had the advantage of promoting fragmentation within the labour force, facilitating its continuing recomposition and changes to working conditions.

An early sub-contracting agreement involved the transfer of catering services from BSC to Gardner-Merchant. As it involved changes in service occupations within manufacturing industry, the results of this change are of a broader significance in terms of the generalisation of sub-contracting across the Teesside economy in the 1980s. One of the few women branch officials in the ISTC, June Milburn, described the consequences:

> Our girls today don't like to fight. They don't want to argue. You get the area manager telling our girls what to do and they'll do it, because they're frightened to lose their jobs. When we were with British Steel, the men backed us. They don't today, they say we're contractors. I believe they would come out if it came to a real fight, but only some of the men back us now. We're on our own, more or less, and the girls are frightened of that. The managers play on the fact that the girls are frightened. They're splitting us up into little families.

At the same time the content of the job had become more demanding:

> You can't do the job properly, you can't finish a job you set off to do. The standards of service have gone right down. The managers know the standards are well below par, they're putting us under pressure to up the standards, but we can't do it. We've not got the time. There's not enough staff to cope.

And the rewards were more uncertain:

> We haven't got half the fringe benefits we used to have. We were supposed to stay on the same terms as British Steel, but that got waylaid for the first two years. And the pension scheme we've got now is no way up to British Steel's standards.

At the same time, active trades unionists like June found themselves increasingly discriminated against:

> We were all interviewed for our jobs by Gardner-Merchant. Some of us had been there ten or twenty years. It was a case of 'if your face fits'. Mine nearly didn't. They offered me a shift job and said if I didn't take it, I was out. It took me two years to get off shift-work. The night-shift was no good for my union work, and they knew it.

Such active discouragement of trades union activity was a further clear manifestation of the increasingly bold reassertion of managerial power. Making this point was the rationale for the changes in employment conditions in steel introduced on Teesside.

Competition between and within works to stay in employment was underwritten by two things: fear of unemployment in an area experiencing a profound employment crisis; and knowledge that some workers were on short-term contracts or were ignoring customary skill boundaries and job demarcations, probably for an outside contractor. The reward to those who remained as individual core employees for increased labour productivity was only too tangible, in the form of lump-sum bonuses. The pressure on workers to reduce costs and increase productivity via intensification of the labour process perhaps took its clearest institutional form in the Total Quality Performance programme, introduced in 1989. By 1992 this was reportedly reducing costs by £32 million a year. Moreover, the works director introduced Phase Two of the Programme with the slogan 'If you don't have time to do it right first time, when will you find the time to correct it?' This stressed that cost savings over the next three years would have to match those of the previous three (*Northern Echo*, 15 January 1992). The message was clear – continuously increased labour productivity was a necessary condition if the works was to have a chance of survival. The price of heightened exploitation, in terms of individual job control, quality of work environment and solidarity, was one that many workers in and around the steel industry were prepared to pay because they saw, and were offered, no alternative.

Chemicals

The character of employment in chemicals on Teesside went through a series of changes which were similar to those at BSC. In some ways, however, ICI went even further in the redefinition of labour relations and conditions. In one sense, in doing so, it was merely carrying on in its long-established tradition of conscious and careful attention to the detail of work organisation and industrial relations, one which had already made a deep impression on Teesside. In the 1960s ICI pioneered the introduction of sophisticated packages of work measurement schemes aimed at tightening management control over the labour process, in return for incentive payments on a series of widely differentiated scales. These packages – the Manpower Utilisation and Payment Structure (MUPS) and the Weekly Staff Agreement (WSA) – met with considerable opposition, especially at Wilton. This works, at that time, presented a marked contrast to the more stable 'company-town' environment at Billingham. The conflict at Wilton turned after a reorganisation which strengthened the site management committee, and after a leading shop steward was dismissed. This was one further indication of the character and influence of ICI's labour relations policies, despite opposition from within formal trades union structures or a more informal 'combine committee' made up of representatives from various ICI sites (see Chapter 3, Section 4). More often, though, ICI secured agreement through gentler – if no less persistent – forms of coercion. One local AEU official, Bill Purvis, reflected on this as follows:

> ICI kill you with kindness. They consult so far ahead, it doesn't register. You don't think what's going to happen in twelve months' time – you might be dead by then. Then before we know where we are, twelve months later, ICI say there's been no response so they assume it's alright to carry on. It's like wading through cotton wool. At times I've sat down at night and thought, 'I've been conned'.

Like BSC, then, ICI followed a conscious strategy of reducing its workforce and sub-contracting maintenance tasks during the 1980s. The implementation of the resettlement scheme at Wilton in the early 1980s slid easily into this strategy. A hard core of ICI maintenance workers remained, but for large jobs ICI either called in the contractors or, more radically, employed temporary workers on short-term contracts of six weeks' to six months' duration. Recruitment to permanent jobs at Wilton ceased. Management and unions agreed that if 'permanent' employment fell below a certain number, new staff should be recruited from the contract workers. There clearly remained, though, a marginalised workforce of casual employees only partially attached to the company and a visible reminder to ICI's permanent workforce of the realities of the wider labour market in the 1980s.

Equally, like BSC, ICI consistently emphasised the need to increase functional 'flexibility' and interchangeable skills within its workforce. One manifestation of this was a drive to dismantle demarcation lines. In 1984 ICI management proposed that process workers should do some maintenance work traditionally undertaken by skilled fitters, in return for which they would be upgraded under the terms of WSA. At Wilton the site manager emphasised the need for change (quoted in *Newcastle Evening Chronicle*, 27 November 1985):

> There are certain things we are not good at. We have very outdated working practices and we know it. A number of

competitors and outside firms are getting into agreements with unions and employees about changes. And we have to do that here.

The kind of flexibility which ICI sought from its employees produced a strong and hostile reaction from the trades unions but they could also see that precedents were being set in other companies. The goals of ICI managers were increasingly apparent from the employment practices of its competitors. Shell/Esso's Moss-morran complex was opened and operated with multi-skilled or, more accurately, multi-tasked, workers outside the TGWU's traditional process grades. During the mid-1980s plant after plant offered job cuts and labour flexibility as an alternative to total closure. Union plans to save BP's Llandarcy refinery in Wales offered to cut restrictions on demarcation and called for a joint investigation into the further use of outside sub-contractors. Management and unions at Shell's Carrington plant agreed a package to prevent closure of part of the works, by cutting employment from 1,200 operating and maintenance crew to 500 technicians, a uniform grade, flexible in terms of jobs performed.

In some instances this drive to flexibility went further than at BSC and became intertwined with the negotiation or imposition of single or non-union deals. In 1985 the company's major rival in fertilisers, Norsk Hydro, imposed a single-union deal upon the TGWU at its Immingham complex. This was part of a package which included reduced demarcation, uniform status for all workers and an advisory council of management and workers' representatives at works level (see Linn, 1986). In 1987 Tioxide (then a joint venture company between ICI and Cookson) stripped trades unions of all negotiating rights and secured voluntary acceptance of staff status by the workforce at its Grimsby plant. This move to non-union status was achieved with the co-operation of local union officials after a ballot. It was described by the group's personnel manager as follows (quoted in *Financial Times*, 19 March 1987): 'The unions have not contributed much to the well being of our company or to the well being of the employees. The unions have disappeared, in effect.' Later that year a wholly-owned subsidiary of ICI, Scottish Agricultural Fertilisers, also withdrew collective bargaining rights from trades unions at its Leith fertiliser plant. On this occasion the move was resisted, but with only limited success. After lengthy negotiations the trades unions involved – GMBU, TGWU and AEU – secured some recognition. The package of related changes, including new working arrangements and multi-skilling, remained intact, however.

Such changes fostered a growing climate of uncertainty within the ICI workforce. One indication of this came in 1986, in the first ever national ballot on strike action over pay at ICI. This resulted in a majority of two to one in favour of accepting the offer, but the fact that the ballot was held at all and the sizeable minority in favour of industrial action were indicative of deep change in a company previously renowned for its relatively harmonious industrial relations. A more significant portent, though, especially to many workers on Teesside, was the creation of a new Chemicals and Polymers Group, and the potential scope for redefinition of industrial relations agreements within this new company. These fears were expressed by one TGWU shop steward at the Billingham works, Arthur Nevens:

> Why form one limited company, why not form one division within ICI? That's the real worry. I wouldn't be surprised if they don't even recognise unions in this new set-up.

He was equally conscious of the limitations on what the trades unions could actually do:

> ICI have been planning this for at least five years. Our biggest enemy is silence from ICI, and we're very worried about getting a response from the workforce. Management are openly saying, if you don't want a job, there's four million out there that would readily take it.

In such a climate of fear and uncertainty, it seemed as if almost anything was possible. Such suspicions appeared to be confirmed in 1989 when talks opened on what was described as the most radical set of changes to working practices at ICI since the WSA was introduced in 1969. In a reversal of the previous codification of different jobs and working practices – one which neatly reflected the new broader economic environment and labour market conditions – ICI sought greater worker flexibility and team-working through the elimination of job distinctions. And in seeking the redefinition of working practices, especially on Teesside, ICI could all too easily point to the changing character of work elsewhere: not just in steel, but also in the one major growth area of manufacturing employment on Teesside – the offshore construction industry.

Offshore Construction

The discovery and subsequent exploitation of oil in the North Sea led to the emergence of a small number of locations in which the oil and gas rigs and associated equipment for the offshore industry were produced and serviced. Teesside was one of those locations. Offshore construction, inherently highly susceptible to fluctuation in the price of oil, has seen two major periods of dynamism separated by a deep trough of cutback and decline on Teesside. In the early 1970s Laing Offshore ran a major yard at Graythorp on the north bank of the Tees for the construction of jackets (the 'legs' on which oil and gas platforms stand). At the same time, local engineering companies like Whessoe and BSC's heavy engineering subsidiary, Redpath Dorman Long, diversified into the construction of topside modules, the superstructure of platforms. At its peak Graythorp alone employed 2,500, but this yard closed in 1976 and the industry experienced a drastic rundown in the late 1970s and early 1980s. It was not until the mid-1980s that orders really picked up again; although when the upturn came, it was dramatic. Contracts for Shell's Tern and Eider fields announced in 1985, for example, provided continuing employment for 2,700 at four Teesside yards, and these were far from the only orders on their books.

This jobs growth in the mid-1980s was significant in a number of ways. It represented the only major expansion in employment in 'traditional' manufacturing industry on Teesside for over a decade. It took place on terms which shaped and reflected the evolving labour recruitment and management strategies of the times. They were acutely different from the industrial relations practices that had characterised the offshore industry, and the construction sector more generally, just a decade previously. For in the 1970s the whole Teesside area – but especially the Graythorp yard and the BSC Redcar site – was affected by a series of industrial disputes. Teesside acquired a bad name among major industrial construction companies. One local offshore manager recalled how this period saw 'virtual warfare' between management and workforce. Revealingly, much of this was blamed by Teesside workers on the fact that the big companies brought in their own labour from outside the area. In the 1980s, with unemployment on Teesside creating a readily-accessible reservoir of skilled and unskilled labour, most of the offshore contractors recruited locally. The most common characteristic of labour relations became not conflict, but its virtual absence.

The much greater control exerted by site management stemmed in the first instance from the role played by the giant oil companies. Such an impact was recognised by one manager as follows:

> It's a closed shop between the oil companies, they invite people to tender. They've definitely made us more efficient.

> There's no way we can afford to be complacent. We can compete with anybody in the world, including the Japanese, on productivity.

For every tender each yard was required to send a full profile of orders in hand and completed, employment, labour relations and site agreements, covering every conceivable aspect of running the yard. Oil companies could, and did, even interview the fabricator's employees as part of the appraisal process. Once an order was awarded, the oil companies' control was also very detailed. Pre-specified on-site offices were provided for the client by the contractor and documentation was required on literally every weld.

It was also apparent that the oil companies deftly prevented any alteration in this balance of power between producer and purchaser, through the controlled way in which they allocated and released orders to different yards. One sub-contractor spoke from years of experience in analysing this process:

> What the oil companies tend to do is look at one another, look at the projects coming on-stream, and nobody then fights for the yard locations. If the module yards know two people are fighting to put the work in there, they can obviously accelerate their prices. So what the oil companies try to do is make sure the projects are coming out enough to feed the yards, without putting themselves in a lion's cage where the yards can dictate what's going on.

In these ways, both directly and indirectly, the oil companies instigated radical changes in the social organisation of Teesside's 'traditional' metal-fabricating skills. This was clearly apparent in strategies to hire and fire employees, and in the social relations of production.

As with any building site, employment in offshore construction is by nature transient. Every worker at each yard had a contract of specific duration for the purpose of completing an order. Should a new order materialise, and if the work had come up to standard, the employee would probably be taken on again, as two managers described:

> Men accept that they're going to be made redundant, but they know that when we get the next contract they'll be reporting back. Very few of the people we take on are strictly redundant, they've moved on from other jobs.
>
> If a man says he's worked at such-and-such a yard, we write to them and ask 'would you re-employ this man yourself ?'

> If they say no, we say no. We have a very close relationship with the other module yards. The men have to keep proving themselves. The pressure is on to keep work. These here are the elite – this industry is like the first division of fabrication construction.

A further source of 'pressure' was the extensive use of subcontractors, just as in the steel and chemicals industries. Many tasks, including electrical installation, pipework, scaffolding, painting and shot-blasting, were put out to external contract. During the completion of a module most yards employed at least as many contractors as their 'own' workforce, and sometimes more. Under these conditions, industrial disputes were kept to a minimum in the 1980s. The employers knew that a serious delay would severely prejudice the chance of future oil company contracts. The employees knew that it would seriously jeopardise their own chances of finding future employment at any yard. The result, expressed quite simply, is that managers found it difficult to recall the last time they had to deal with a strike.

That this was true despite the extent to which working practices had been altered revealed much about the character of recent changes in Teesside. For the offshore construction industry went even further than the steel and chemicals industries in the redefinition of working conditions and the reduction of demarcation on the basis of differing skills. This process took on a significance that varied with a worker's former skills and created new potential cleavage planes within the workforce. One man, Geoff, worked for Whessoe as a plater and illustrated the point well:

> Over the last three or four years the plater has become basically the top trade. The welders carry the power, but the plater reads the drawings, sets it out and builds it – we're responsible for the job. The welders hold the power, because it doesn't matter how much I do, Whessoe don't get paid a penny until it's welded. But having said that, it's the platers that's responsible for the job. Chippers, burners, they're all serving trades to me. When flexibility came in on our site, there was a lot of talk, but basically it was aimed at the platers. The welders did a bit of grinding, they were asked to clean up after themselves – but if there was a lot of welding, there's no way they'd do that. That's flexibility for welders. The chippers were promised all sorts, a welding job, a bit of plating. The burners too, but everybody knew it was down to us. We even had to go in the welding school for tests – it qualified us to 3G, down on plate, vertical plate and

> overhead plate. We use the grinder a bit, we push the burning gear up if nobody's available.

Within the content of *his* job, flexibility meant it was easier to get things done around and for you:

> The servicing trades are much more keen to do the job for you now than they were before. It was the plater's farewell, you used to spend more time trying to find somebody to do the job for you than if you did it yourself. He'd say, I'm not doing that – ask him – and he'd say the same. Now, with flexibility, there's not so many burners, and when you ask for something it's done. It's a case of if you don't do it, I'll do it myself. It's made my job a lot easier, but it's also harder because there's more work. The way I balance it is that we're doing more work now than we were four years ago with less men. That might sound anti-union but it's not, if you're doing it cheaper you'll get more work.

For the plater, then, flexibility brought a new, more central role. This also meant that more platers were retained during those periods when employment at the yard was being run down as orders were completed:

> Years ago, they kept one, two or three platers. When flexibility came in they kept eleven, and paid more chippers and burners off. Now, they'll keep eighteen. All the time the balance has changed in favour of platers. I suppose that's why I agree with flexibility. It's certainly made me.

Not all workers, therefore, saw increased flexibility as a bad thing, indicative of the way that this both reflected and reproduced divisions within the workforce. In a number of other areas (such as bonus payments and supervision over specific jobs), 'flexibility' benefited the company quite substantially. Because most offshore orders were one-offs, there was no such thing as standardised production and little scope for the introduction of computerised work-booking and control. Instead each task was allocated a number of man-hours which was amended by a system of allowances, where, for example, conditions meant that continuous working was out of the question. Under certain circumstances this could be highly exploitative: Geoff again:

> On the last job the heat was terrific. The stewards went in and said the time's not good enough. You get allowances against the time if it's hot work, to cool off. They upped the allowances on the last job, on this one they're knocking 34 per cent off the allowances. The union have registered a failure to agree. There's times when welders are practically passing out. There's

> one lad they took to the first aid and they had to bang fluid into him – he'd dehydrated. It's at least 150°, at the actual weld it's 250°. They've got to have full leathers on, screen and gloves, and it's like working in a blast furnace.

Conditions such as these were perhaps extreme. But poor working conditions were sadly only too common in the other recent area of manufacturing employment growth on Teesside, the new small businesses and assembly plants of the new manufacturing economy.

4. EMPLOYMENT IN THE 'NEW' MANUFACTURING ECONOMY

As we have shown, there has been considerable emphasis within state policies on diversifying sources of manufacturing employment in Teesside, both via the attraction of branch plants and the promotion of local small firms. In the late 1940s and again in the 1960s there was some limited attraction of manufacturing firms outside the 'old' chemicals, steel-making and using industries, often quite explicitly in search of female labour. In the 1980s such branch plants sought to enhance productivity via strategies designed to promote greater workforce flexibility. Likewise new companies attracted to Teesside in the 1980s against a background of high unemployment there and Nissan's well-publicised recruitment and new working practices at its new factory a few miles north of Teesside (Hudson, 1992) sought to impose flexibility on their new workforces from the outset. Once again, however, new branch plants were often explicitly attracted by unemployed women on Teesside rather than men. In these instances, there were marked similarities between the 'old' and 'new' manufacturing industries in the strategies that they adopted in pursuit of greater flexibility in their use of labour.

This search for flexibility began with the initial recruitment of workers. Given the prevailing high levels of unemployment, companies were able to exercise great selectivity in whom they chose to employ. Established branch plants were able to restructure their workforces in this way. KP Foods (which opened its potato crisp factory at Billingham in the late 1960s) required production line operatives with no formal qualifications; its main recruitment criteria for such unskilled workers related to a person's physique, manual dexterity, health and personal hygiene. Because of high levels of unemployment and its demands for readily available unskilled labour, KP offered only six-month initial contracts to all new recruits, allowing management to 'screen' additions to the 'permanent' labour force.

Those companies first locating on Teesside in the 1980s were also able to exercise great selectivity in assembling their workforces. An example in Hartlepool was PMA Textiles. No less than 3,500 people applied for the first twenty-four jobs there (Boulding, 1988, p. 232). Successful applicants were interviewed up to six times at various hours of the day, night and week to ensure that they had the 'appropriate' attitudes, rather than aptitudes.

Tabuchi, the first Japanese company to locate on Teesside, followed a similar recruitment strategy. All new recruits to its electronics components plant began on temporary (three or six month) contracts, which included a three-month probationary period. Unsatisfactory performance while 'on probation' could lead to instant dismissal. In December 1986, before beginning production in 1987, Tabuchi none the less received over 2,000 applications for the 240 jobs it then had on offer (largely assembly line jobs offered to women). Given the numbers applying, the personnel manager was able to be very selective. Potential recruits took three tests, two for dexterity and one for memory. On average, three of every four applicants so tested were rejected. One expression of this was the average age of production operatives – 21 years of age on the day shift, for example – as the company sought young, fit and 'green' labour. Even so, with subsequent expansion of capacity and output, at times the company was forced to relax these strict requirements slightly to ensure that new lines started on time. And also to alter them; for example, the average age of female production operatives on the evening shift was 26 years, reflecting a preference for older, married women, less likely to move from this particular shift. Moreover, the main channel of recruitment was via word-of-mouth and this resulted in existing workers themselves screening potential applicants for jobs. One female production operative put it like this:

> I've got people into jobs here – but they've got to be prepared to work. The one downfall is that if they're no good, it comes back on you. That happened to me with a couple of the younger ones. I'll not be getting any more application forms.

Thus, via a variety of formal and informal recruiting channels, there was a careful selection process to ensure that, from the company's point of view, the 'right' people got the 'right' jobs. Careful selection and composition of workforces was informed by a desire to increase productivity via the introduction of more flexible methods of working. Companies pursued this objective in a variety of ways, seeking both numerical and functional flexibility in the numbers of people employed at any one time and the range of activities that they would undertake in the factory. New companies sought functional flexibility from the outset: in Hartlepool, for example, PMA Textiles required its 'associates' to work very flexibly, carrying out any of a wide range of tasks at any time of the day or night, on literally any day of the year (Boulding, 1988, p. 232). For some well-established small companies, such as Glamal Engineering, functional flexibility was nothing new. Work there was allocated in relation to the skills of the seven 'turners' employed (Peppin, 1990, p. 236): 'the best man for the job is chosen ... for each job that needs some drilling, one person does all the drilling down to his experience, not because of demarcation or anything'. Indeed, this sort of flexibility was, and long had been, a pre-condition for the survival of such companies. Others aspired to it. Larger established companies such as KP sought to secure a degree of functional flexibility in the late 1970s, via an agreement with the trades unions which provided for workers agreeing to carry out any function that they were capable of performing.

Another company seeking to achieve such flexibility was Sarek Joinery. Originally established as F. Hills in Stockton in 1847, it was taken over by the Bowater Group in 1969, which in turn was taken over by Ralli International in 1972 and then by Sarek Wood, a consortium of Swedish sawmills in February 1986. In this way, via a process of centralisation of capital, a locally owned company became a global outpost of a Swedish multinational. This in turn had implications for the Teesside factory. Sarek sought to introduce functional flexibility 'at the margin', by using external training centres for its apprentices to avoid trades union opposition to the training of 'multi-skilled' workers. In this way it sought to 'create a supply-side pressure for reduced job-demarcations (as multi-skilled workers are unlikely to agree to restrictions being imposed on the machines they are allowed to use)' (Peppin, 1990, p. 157). More generally, Sarek sought to blur the boundary between unskilled labourers and skilled joiners and machinists, to bring its Teesside plant into line with one in Hedingham in East Anglia, where a 'semi-skilled' grade had been introduced. It threatened to move production there if the Teesside plant resisted such changes.

The greatest pressure for job losses, however, arose as a result of a widespread pursuit of numerical flexibility, managers' capacity to hire and fire workers. First, some companies introduced and then subsequently dropped shifts in response to fluctuating demand. At Tabuchi, for example, increases in demand were met by recruiting whole new lines to work on evening and night shifts. Recruitment rather than substantial overtime (though the two were not necessarily independent) reflected both the scale of the desired increase in output and the low levels of skill and training demanded by the job. As Peppin (1990, p. 288) noted, in such a situation the quantity of available labour was more important than the quality, 'but the latter can be more or less assured because of the ability to be selective in recruitment'. This emphasised the connections between the capacity to be selective and that to dictate terms and conditions of employment.

Secondly, there was an increase in part-time, temporary and casual working. Perhaps the most extreme example of casualisation in the new factories concerned CDL 44 Foods frozen cake factory. In its first year in operation in Hartlepool, its owner, Mr Chris Liveras (who, despite two fraud convictions was given considerable grant aid to set up his factory), sacked his entire workforce over the long Christmas and New Year period. He then re-employed them on 2 January. In this way he avoided paying his workforce over the holidays. In a non-union factory, in a town with mass unemployment, the workers saw no choice but to accept such treatment. Other companies adopted less draconian but no less successful tactics.

KP, for example, following a decision taken at national level in 1980, moved from one full-time day shift to two part-time ones during the rest of the decade. The change was achieved gradually by replacing full-time leavers with new part-time workers. The rationale underlying this was a particularly interesting one. For by part-time KP meant 25 hours per week, well above the level at which it would avoid paying statutory entitlements to part-time workers. Moreover, KP specifically protected the rights of workers and kept hourly wage rates unchanged in the transition from full-time to part-time. Despite this the change related to the company's target of a 5 per cent annual reduction in labour time per unit output. It sought this via a combination of investment in new machinery and changed working practices. The switch to part-time work offered great advantages because it reduced 'down-time' (for example, because of meal breaks) and increased capacity utilisation, helping to overcome problems caused by reductions of the working week leading to reduced capacity utilisation (for example, because the plant previously closed on Friday afternoons). The new policy increased productivity through faster working in shorter shifts, reduced absenteeism and injury. It widened the pool of potential female workers at a time when demand from other new firms for full-time female labour was growing. The availability of the government's job splitting scheme subsidised the switch to part-time (provided one of the new part-timers was previously registered as unemployed). Moreover, by replacing overtime payments to full-timers with 'extra time' to part-timers, paid at the standard rate, the company cut its direct wage costs still further. Furthermore, it made the full-time night shift financially more attractive than the part-time day shift and so helped reduce staff turnover on it.

In this way, KP responded to pressures to reduce costs and cope with short-term (daily) fluctuations in product demand at leading retail outlets. In addition to the switch to part-time work, it also increased use of temporary labour – a characteristic it shared with many other companies in Teesside. By concentrating fluctuations in the level of employment among temporary workers, changes were made to seem acceptable, while maintaining a 'cushion' of labour at the margin if sales dropped. At the same time, though, recruiting *all* new workers on temporary six-month contracts allowed management to 'screen' workers over that period and carefully select those who made the transition to the permanent, core workforce. As Peppin (1990, p. 95) remarked, 'local labour market conditions and the issue of gender are ... significant factors enabling the change over' – and not only at KP.

Both Sarek and Tabuchi also made increased use of temporary workers. Throughout the 1980s Sarek used them to compensate for 'over large' losses through redundancies. Since at that time the factory was owned by Bowater, which offered redundancy terms that exceeded the legal minimum requirement, there was no difficulty in getting volunteers to accept redundancy, despite high levels of unemployment on Teesside. As some of their 'temporary' replacements were kept on for four or five years, there was more than a suspicion that 'over large' losses were a deliberate managerial tactic to cut labour costs. Tabuchi sought to deploy temporary workers at its non-union plant from the outset. At this plant, 'training' of new workers consisted of sitting alongside an experienced operator for three, two-hour sessions. Recruiting new workers on temporary three-month contracts allowed Tabuchi to alter labour demand in direct relation to the changing pattern of product demand. In 1986 Tabuchi recruited temporary workers specifically to its evening shift. By classifying the evening shift as 'temporary', employment levels were varied with little opposition from the workforce. This 'temporary' evening shift worked to the company's advantage in other ways, too, and the parallels with KP are striking. In utilising temporary labour in this way Tabuchi could 'screen' workers for full-time employment. It could also cut direct labour costs as temporary workers were excluded from fringe benefits such as the company's pension scheme. It was also able to use the evening shift as a place where new recruits picked up their work speed without interfering with output on the day shift. Individuals who performed satisfactorily on the evening shift were *offered* day shift work on the basis of length of service, attitude and attendance records. No one could *apply* to move to the day shift. Finally, by using the 'temporary' evening shift, Tabuchi increased the intensity of use of machinery and reduced the turnover time of fixed capital.

A further way in which many companies in Teesside sought numerical flexibility was by an increased and more systematic use of sub-contracting. This process, indicative of a changing social division of labour, undoubtedly accounts for at least some of the limited expansion of service sector employment that occurred on Teesside in the 1980s. Even small companies sub-contracted. Glamal Engineering, for example, employing less than thirty employees, contracted out some manufacturing work, plus all its office cleaning, washroom supplies and laundry services (to Initial Services). The economic rationale for increased sub-contracting was succinctly spelled out by the manager of another Teesside engineering company, Harkers:

> Every single thing we do for them, they can do for themselves. As activity has reduced, so they have cut capacity – so people are now sub-contracting at what used to be 80 per cent of their activity level, but they'd reduced capacity to 70 per cent. The thing they're not going to do again is go through all the hassle of recruiting and laying off men. *There are now more conscious decisions to subcontract*. Traditionally our business has been dragging people out of holes. *Now this is not casual subcontracting but planned subcontracting.* (Emphasis added.)

Tabuchi, for example, sub-contracted some wire bending to a firm in Hartlepool. Sarek, too, increasingly made use of sub-contracting: office cleaning, transport, catering and security were all sub-contracted out between 1980 and 1984. Moreover, both the latter contracts changed within four years, indicative of Sarek's continuing quest for cost reductions and the consequent uncertainty for the sub-contracting companies within the services sector (many of them new and small) and those employed, often precariously, in them.

Not least, sub-contracting companies themselves engaged in fierce price competition to win contracts, with particular consequences for the wages and working conditions of their employees, especially where companies were able to recruit 'off the cards' labour. Such situations were described within the Hartlepool area by two people caught up in them:

> The big companies and the little ones are cutting each other's throats for the work and, of course, it all comes back on the men – half of them are on the fiddle anyway. Keeps the costs down you see, and if you're a bloke on the dole, what choice have you got? If someone offers, you jump at the chance. (Quoted in Morris, 1986, p. 149.)

The second one put it like this:

> In the end the numbers dropped off and the companies didn't want to pay the prices the big firms were asking, so they went to the smaller companies who were prepared to undercut. They could do this because they'd use mostly part-time workers or self-employed (that is, off the cards) and just call them in when they wanted them ... if you want the work you've got to be prepared to take what's on offer, and if you don't accept it you don't get the work.

Such examples graphically illustrate the price that workers paid in terms of precarious employment and low wages as a consequence of the growth of sub-contracting.

Indeed, sub-contracting is but one element in a wider picture which depicts the 'new' manufacturing economy as *predominantly* a low-wage one, in which pressures to decrease wages further (or at least to contain wage increases) were strongly evident. In the clothing industry, which employed 3,800 people in Cleveland in 1988 (of whom 90 per cent were women) wages typically ranged from £80 to £120 per week (see Cleveland County Council, 1989a). Boulding (1988, p. 230) remarked of Hartlepool that the prevalence of small firms among those established there since 1975 was linked 'to a tendency towards low wages and poor conditions of work'. This was also true elsewhere in Teesside. At Glamal Engineering, for example, labourers were paid between £1.50 and £2.15 per hour. Low wages, especially for women, were also common within the larger of the newer firms. Boulding (1988, p. 229) stated that 'the personnel association reports that in some newer firms a 40 hour week is rewarded with £60 or £70', whilst his own surveys revealed wage rates of £1.60 per hour for established workers in companies such as CDL 44 Foods and Isocom (both of which employed about 180, mainly female workers). Wages were higher at PMA Textiles, at around £2.50 per hour, though this involved working twelve hour shifts (PMA was subsequently taken over by the Coats Viyella group and employment halved to ninety). Low wages were also much in evidence in the firms that Peppin (1990) studied. Operatives at KP Foods in 1986 and 1987 were paid a starting rate of £2.37 per hour, rising to £2.56 per hour after six weeks and their promotion to grade one. Night shift workers received a 25 per cent premium. At Tabuchi at this time production operators, quality control operators and warehouse employees aged 18 or more began on £2.25 per hour, rising to £2.43 per hour after three months and £2.60 per hour after six months. There was no differentiation between the rates paid to day and evening shift workers. Overtime rates varied from one and a third time for the first two hours to double time on Sundays. In addition, however, Tabuchi paid a range of bonuses and supplements. Team leaders (first-line supervisors responsible for keeping discipline within their team of six and overcoming problems on the line) received a £35.00 per week supplement. Bonuses were also paid to reward unbroken attendance by all workers: £30 after four months; £50 plus a certificate after sixteen months; £50 per month for the seventeenth and subsequent months (all net of tax). Even so, such wages in manufacturing were often higher than those in, say, retailing, whilst many women workers lacked the qualifications for other, better paid jobs. This, plus the need to combine domestic with waged work, pushed many women into low-wage part-time factory employment.

Not all the 'new' manufacturing companies paid such low wages, however. In Hartlepool, Tolaram paid its seventy-nine full-time male workers between £160 per week for process workers and £180 for craftsmen. Whilst higher in absolute terms than the wages paid to many women in new companies, though, these were still lower than the rates paid elsewhere in the chemicals industry on Teesside. Occasionally, in response to effective trades union campaigns, companies paid above national rates. Whilst the national minimum wage agreed by the Timber Trades Federation in 1987 was £118 per week, Sarek paid well above this: £133 for labourers, £160 to £170 for craftsmen, for example. When the company tried to contain wage pressures by incorporating bonus payments into the standard basic wage, having first cut the bonuses, the trades unions resisted, adding a work-to-rule to a long-standing ban on overtime in response to a continual stream of redundancies throughout the 1980s. Peppin (1990, p. 171) argued that 'Sarek was confronted by well-organised unions, anxious to defend their members' wages and jobs'. Whilst successful in terms of wages, the price of this was failure in terms of protecting employment: Sarek cut 600 jobs in an attempt to reduce costs and increase competitiveness.

If Sarek, an old-established company, was characterised by well-organised unions, anxious to defend wages and jobs, it was relatively unusual on Teesside in the 1980s. Even so, the trades union position over redundancies at Sarek revealed ambivalence:

> If the jobs are no longer there, we must accept the fact, but if it's an avoidable redundancy we'll fight it. In the past they've cut back too far and this has caused problems. The unions will fight any further compulsory redundancies on the shop floor from now on (quoted in Peppin 1990, p. 163)

But by this time the workforce had declined to less than 400 over an eight-year period.

In the unionised plants the workers were often on the defensive, often in retreat. Many of the smaller plants and companies (both new and old) were characteristically non-union; Glamal, for instance, was a non-union company. Furthermore, many of the larger new manufacturing plants were established from the outset as non-union plants. Five of the larger firms locating in the Hartlepool Enterprise Zone – Lab Systems Furnishings, PMA Textiles, CDL 44 Foods, Isocom and Tolaram – were explicitly hostile to any suggestion of trades union organisation. Working conditions in these non-union factories were often especially harsh. At Tabuchi, eating and talking were forbidden on the production lines. Two clauses from a 1986 contract at CDL 44 illustrated the situation vividly:

> 8. There will be one 15 minutes break and one 30 minute break (15 minutes of which is unpaid) during an 8 hour shift.
>
> 17. TIMEKEEPING
> Anyone late more than 5 minutes in any one day will automatically be sent home before starting work and will lose any attendance or productivity bonus, or both, for that week.

Such conditions conjured up images of confrontational relations between owners, managers and workers, with the balance of power tilted very firmly against the last group.

Tabuchi, too, was a non-union factory, but in this case non-unionisation, together with its Japanese ownership and plans for quality circles and consultative committees, was suggestive of a 'Japanisation' strategy for the workplace and industrial relations.

Work might be no less exploitative than at, say, Isocom but the implications of non-unionisation were *perceived* differently; as Peppin (1990, p. 267) put it: 'a sense prevails ... that employment at Tabuchi *is* somehow a "little bit different" by virtue of Japanese ownership'. Nevertheless, it was in the non-union plants that recruitment procedures tended to be most rigorous, discipline within the workplace most severe, the intensity of work greatest and wages the lowest. Non-unionisation was clearly an important influence on these aspects of work and its imposition was made possible because of the prevailing high levels of unemployment on Teesside.

5. THE SERVICE SECTOR

In private service sector activities such as retailing, employment on Teesside was subject to the same sorts of pressures as were seen elsewhere, with a substitution of part-time for full-time jobs in a low wage sector. Peppin (1990, p. 235), for example, reported wage rates in retailing of £1.50 to £2.00 per hour in Billingham and Stockton in the mid-1980s. More unusual, and so particularly interesting, was an expansion of employment in financial services and, in particular, in Barclaycard. For this was symptomatic of Teesside's relationship to the rapidly growing financial services sector (Leyshon and Thrift, 1989), a back office for paper processing that was closely analogous to the routine component assembly of many of the new manufacturing branch plants. In both cases, Teesside's role in these emergent divisions of labour was to carry out unskilled tasks, while the skilled jobs and centres of power and control were located elsewhere (see Allen, 1988).

The Middlesbrough office of Barclaycard opened in 1973 as part of a strategy to decentralise operations from its headquarters in Northampton to regional centres (others included Birmingham, Leeds, Liverpool and Manchester). Subsequent further expansion saw offices opened at Stockton in the following year. A major reason for this decentralisation lay in a problem of labour recruitment at Northampton (see NEDC, 1975). The search for suitable alternative locations therefore concentrated on areas with a potential pool of 'under-utilised labour, particularly young females regarded by the company as suitable for clerical work – as indicated by high unemployment and low activity rates' (ibid., p. 2).

Teesside, with its history of low female activity rates in formal waged employment, was a very suitable area, judged against these criteria of desirability. The work which was transferred was the least skilled task of remittance processing: 'work that is inevitably routine and repetitive, in fact it has to be handled almost on a production-line basis' (ibid., p. 3). Then, in 1976, Barclaycard's activities nationally were re-organised and customer services concentrated into work groups known as 'musters'. Each of these was responsible for some 200,000 accounts, comprised some 30-35 staff of varying seniority, and was located within a regional centre. In this reshuffle Middlesbrough acquired two musters and Stockton six. A further change in 1980 involved the transfer of the handling of sales vouchers from Northampton to Middlesbrough and Birmingham; the Middlesbrough/Stockton regional centre then undertook three major functions.

The scale of employment growth at Barclaycard was considerable. In 1985 the offices at Middlesbrough and Stockton employed nearly 700 people. One-half of these were 'permanent' staff and half were part-time 'auxiliaries', with more full-time staff in Stockton (reflecting the greater number of musters there). All of the 330 'auxiliaries' and 240 of the 340 permanent staff were women. It was important also to distinguish carefully between the 'shopfloor' type tasks of data entry and the musters. The latter generally employed permanent staff working a seven-hour day, and involved the more skilled and varied work such as credit enquiries and delinquent accounts. Data entry took place only at Middlesbrough and involved predominantly women working part-time on four-hour shifts with one fifteen-minute break, processing vouchers and remittances via visual display units (VDUs) on to a central computer system. By far the worst working conditions were there. Workers were expected to reach a speed of 14,000 key depressions/hour, or 2,400 vouchers on each four-hour shift, within three months of completing the initial 20-hour training course. Should they fail to do so, they faced the sack. For those who reached this standard, though, there were considerable attractions in working at Barclaycard. Wages were relatively good, there were few other office jobs available in the area, and the shift pattern could be welcome to school-leavers or, especially, older women with families. The possibility of overtime was by no means unwelcome, either. One woman, Anne, described how and why she once worked on sales vouchers:

> When the overtime was on I practically lived there, simply because I wanted a video. I worked all day Saturday, all day Sunday, and every night. I bought the video, and a portable colour telly for upstairs. If there was overtime now, I'd live there again, just for the money.

On the other hand, this money was not easily earned, and many employees only stayed because they needed the wages and had nowhere else to go to. For Doreen: 'It's the worst job I've had. I hate it.' The main source of pressure was in the monitoring of vouchers inputted – the number of keys depressed per hour. This is both a very tedious and stressful task. One operator described it as follows:

> I think when you're at the VDUs you're like a robot. In a lot of ways it made me ill because I was so uptight. All those numbers running through your head. You're not thinking what you're doing. You do it automatically.

It is also a task made constantly more difficult by the raising of performance standards, increasing the number of vouchers to be processed per shift. This is a process of work intensification similar to an increased assembly line speed in a factory. The 'figures' were very important as another operator, Catherine, explained:

> The standard thing is that they're always going to up the figures. It started at 1,800 vouchers/shift, then 2,100, then 2,400. You wouldn't believe the things they've gone through to make you get the figures. They had a competition – whichever individual got the most inputted could have a night off. Then they'd give each of us a tray of work which they said held 2,400 but that was rubbish – I'd finish a tray and know it held 3,000 or 3,200. So they started pulling up those who didn't get 2,400 for three days running, and really push them about it. We have a union we can go to – BIFU (Banking, Insurance and Finance Union) – and we suggested that rather than individual figures, we worked on group figures. The supervisor argued about it, we had a meeting, and in the end we had to accept individual figures. 'You're not arguing with me', she said 'you're arguing with Barclays.'

Dissatisfaction with the conditions of work, however, was not confined to data entry workers. There were also frequent complaints from those on higher-grade permanent contracts. For one woman working in a supervisory capacity on one of the musters, the job was interesting, but repetitive, and she always lacked sufficient staff in her sub-section:

> If you want to have a personal touch you can't use a computerised, standard letter, you have to telephone the cardholder or dictate a letter. Then there's the pressure to reach your targets, and even when we beat them they raise the targets again and we still beat them, but they never give you extra staff.

For other staff, a major problem was the limited potential for promotion, the lack of a clear career structure within Teesside. As Margaret, a clerical worker one grade below supervisor in musters put it:

> People know there's not much promotion without going to Northampton. There's only eight grade fours at Middlesbrough, but there's plenty of grade threes and grade fours aren't that old – so we're stuck. I can't see a way through now. I'd be very surprised if I get promotion.

But ultimately those working on musters developed a fundamentally different view of Barclaycard as an employer from that of those on data entry, as this woman continued:

> You couldn't fault Barclaycard as an employer, it's a good job. It doesn't tax the brain too much and there's so many perks – profit sharing, bonuses, and the chance of a bank mortgage on good terms. There's not much I can think of that can compete.

This contrast between the two views of Barclaycard – from the factory floor of data entry and the office environment of musters – encapsulates the divisive impact of private service sector employment growth on Teesside. Much of it consisted of low-skilled routine work taken by women eager for a wage, despite the conditions. A minority of the new jobs fell into a recognisable career structure with better conditions, but this was a structure which ultimately led out of the area for many of those who wanted, and were chosen for, promotion. The whole operation meanwhile was subordinate to the national strategy of Barclaycard (which in turn was constrained by the pressures of an increasingly international market in financial services for consumers) and could at any time be undermined by decisions to prioritise other regional centres. The route to such limited private service sector employment growth as there had been was thus precarious and partial.

The public sector, however, had been the main source of growth in services employment in the Teesside economy in the post-war period, despite the limited extent of central Government office employment – epitomised in cancellation of a proposed relocation of the Property Services Agency in 1979. A major element in this expansion was the 1,000-bed North Tees General Hospital, first contemplated by the Regional Health Board in its 1962 Hospital Plan. Townsend (1987, p. 25) emphasised how it was linked to broader modernisation policies in Teesside:

> it is indicative of the priority attached to the Teesside [industrial] development that the Teesside HMCs [Hospital Management Committee] were the only HMC in the region for which new hospitals were to be provided (on new or previously undeveloped sites).

The hospital was located to the north-west of Stockton town centre, allowing it to draw labour from the surrounding housing estates. By 1975 construction was complete and the hospital fully operational.

In the 1980s powerful pressures built up for changed employment conditions and levels. Some of these related to demographic change and the poor health of Teesside's population (Townsend *et al.*, 1988). Others related to managerial changes following the Griffiths Report and the growing use of performance indicators in evaluating hospitals whilst at the same time (after 1985) attempting to switch from hospital to community care. In this context, moves towards compulsory competitive tendering and the imposition of cash limits, with their implications for bed and ward closures, became particularly significant.

The Department of Health and Social Security (DHSS) introduced rules to cover the provision of catering, cleaning and laundry services by compulsory competitive tender in September 1983. At North Tees the initial (1986) contracts were won in-house, with an estimated 20–30 per cent cost reduction. As Peppin (1990, p. 183) argued:

> the threat of competition *has* produced 'savings' by forcing in-house providers to lower their costs ... but this has been achieved at the expense of an already low paid workforce, through reductions in bonuses, sickness allowances and paid holidays, and in the number of hours of work available per week.

The new 'in house' cleaning contract saw employees retaining their jobs, but changes in work organisation were introduced and all domestic cleaners were switched to three year contracts – the length of the service contract. The changes in work organisation required an intensification of effort by domestic workers: 'we never used to do [put away] linen or [clean] the landing. They expect us to do all this – and the towel holders – it's just built up and up after the tender'. Even so, the tender proved to be too low, resulting in later cuts in night-time domestic staff. In turn, this put pressure on nurses to accept greater functional flexibility. Management argued that costs had been under-estimated because high levels of sickness among staff had prevented intended wage bill restrictions – but absenteeism was at least partly caused by the increased pressure of work and low morale.

In catering, too, the new in-house contract was for three years. Whilst there were more redundancies, labour cost savings were achieved by use of a relief 'pool', drawn upon as and when required. In contrast, the in-house laundry contract did necessitate job cuts (since an outside contractor had been allowed to tender on a marginal cost basis, using the hospital's own equipment, with no allowances for depreciation). Ward closures then subsequently cut throughput, raised unit costs and increased pressures for more job cuts.

The government also introduced cash limits after the 1983 General Election. In October 1984 the Regional Health Authority sent letters to each District Health Authority (DHA) specifying a target of 15 per cent cost improvement by 1995. In turn, the North Tees DHA identified a saving of 6.5 per cent (or £1.5 million, 1985/1986 to 1994/1995) in the cost of providing existing services. This had a 'substantial impact on recruitment and labour utilisation at North Tees hospital' (Peppin, 1990, p. 190). The North Tees DHA had only 89 per cent of the money needed to pay all the nurses it required. As it is a single hospital DHA, the only way it could cut expenditure was to close wards. The first ward closed in September 1987; by December 20 per cent of the hospital's beds were closed, with direct effects on nursing employment and indirect ones on employment in services such as laundries.

Such changes had widespread impacts on levels and conditions of employment in the hospital. Although the stock of workers remained at around the 3,000 level in the 1980s there were considerable flows in and out – around 10-15 per cent a year of 'leavers' and 'starters'. These flows were concentrated in three groups of workers which accounted for 70 per cent to 90 per cent of change: ancillaries; administrative and clerical; nurses and midwives.

Ancillary workers were most affected by the introduction of competitive tendering but even before this there were powerful pressures to reduce their numbers, which fell by 27 per cent between 1978 and 1986 because of non-replacement of leavers. A further twenty-five jobs were cut in the year to March 1987, reducing the number employed to under 700, of which almost 70 per cent were part-time female workers. It was in this group of part-timers that turnover was greatest, partly because of the replacement of full-time with part-time staff. But instability of employment for them was also linked to the creation of a pool of up to twenty part-timers, who worked on an 'as and when required' basis as relief workers. This process of casualisation was seen as a cheap solution to the problem of providing cover in the event of sickness, holidays, maternity leave and so on. It was made possible by the high levels of female unemployment in the surrounding housing estates. Nevertheless, there were limits to the extent of casualisation. Whilst there was a reluctant trades union acceptance of a small pool of casualised workers, there would have been opposition to any attempt significantly to increase its size. In addition, management admitted that use of the pool

> is a difficult subject contractually ... we try to make sure people aren't called in too often – or else you'd have problems of people claiming regular employment [for the purposes of unfair dismissal]. Also that means the work's shared out better. (Quoted in Peppin, 1990, p. 204.)

Equally important were supply-side constraints. Women with unemployed husbands refused to work for more than a certain number of hours per week, as this would then affect their partner's benefit entitlement.

Among the administrative and clerical group, recruitment was generally to replace leavers but here, too, there were pressures to cut labour costs. As people left, some posts were abolished, others down-graded or reduced to part-time status. In cases where the allocation of posts or hours for a job was reduced, the inevitable consequence was work intensification for those remaining in employment.

Whilst the full-time equivalent of nurses and midwives rose from 1,251 to 1,289 over the period March 1986-8, this was wholly due to the knock-on effects of the reduction of nursing hours from 40 to 37.5 per week. The vast majority of nurses were female, with full-timers outnumbering part-timers in the ratio of 2:1. Numerical flexibility among nurses was achieved via use of a 'nurse bank' – again a strategy of casualisation to reduce labour costs. However, by the end of 1987 this strategy had reached its limits as the 'nurse bank' was virtually unused. This led to public protests by the fifty or so nurses in it. At the same time, partly as a consequence of this but more importantly because of faster 'throughput' as a result of seeking to meet performance targets, there were growing pressures for greater functional flexibility. This emerged in two forms: firstly, between different grades of nurses; secondly, between nurses and other occupations, at both ends of the skill continuum. Thus, there were pressures on nurses both to take over cleaning work from ancillaries and to take over routine functions previously or usually carried out by doctors. Increasingly, nurses were resistant to such pressures.

Clearly, then, changes in the direction of enhanced numerical, functional and financial flexibility were not confined to the private service sector. Despite what appeared to be rigid national job evaluations, grading procedures and collective bargaining, there was a considerable blurring of job boundaries and pay differentials, alongside a marked shift to part-time work and even casualisation at the margins, at local level. Peppin (1990, p. 220) concluded that 'there is little to distinguish labour market adjustment mechanisms in the NHS from mechanisms used by private sector employers'. But whereas in the private sector the driving forces for such changes came directly from increasingly competitive product markets, the driving forces for such change in North Tees hospital – as elsewhere in the public service sector – were institutional and legislative, a consequence of very direct state involvement and choices over political strategy.

6. CONCLUDING COMMENTS

It would be misleading to suggest that, before the 1980s, the only form of employment relation in Teesside was full-time or part-time work on a formal, legal contractual basis. There was, in Teesside as elsewhere, a variety of other forms of informal and illegal work. However, in the decisive sectors of manufacturing (chemicals and steel) trades unions had negotiated forms of employment relation that were relatively progressive from the point of view of labour, both in terms of wages and conditions of work. In general, these were national agreements applicable within these industries on Teesside rather than locally negotiated ones. Although the wages were lower, this was also the case in the major public service sector activities of education and health. In major sectors, therefore, well-established regulatory frameworks existed which set the terms of the bargain between employer and employee.

The insistent and growing pressures by companies for enhanced flexibility, as they sought to contain costs and/or restore profits, had a severe impact. The search for flexibility took many forms: functional (in terms of 'multi-tasking' or reduced job distinctiveness), numerical (with a marked increase in sub-contracting and casualisation) and financial (as wage determination shifted to a plant and individual basis). But the rationale remained the same – cutting costs and/or boosting profits. There was no question here of greater flexibility heralding some new golden age of greater worker autonomy and job satisfaction in new high-tech and flexibly specialised workplaces. The drive for flexibility was a very visible expression of management's newly found assertiveness in its dealings with workers, as the balance of forces between capital and labour tilted decisively towards the former against a background of high and rising unemployment. In a sense, rather than the dawning of desirable new times, it was a return to undesirable past practices. Seemingly abolished forever, they not only returned but returned with a vengeance and became increasingly prevalent, penetrating widely into both manufacturing and services, private and public sectors alike. From the point of view of the workers experiencing it, the meaning of the rediscovery of flexibility was very clear. It entailed intensification of work, deteriorating working conditions and, often, cuts in wages.

Trades unions, socialised into a culture of compliance and co-operation with management, found it very difficult to oppose this managerial offensive in search of flexibility. Even when they could see the danger all too clearly, though there were the occasional exceptions, they were usually unable effectively to resist the trend. But even in such exceptional cases, wages for those in employment were often protected only at the price of job shedding; unemployment for some was traded off against wage increases for others. This partial and limited form of opposition, however, only emphasised the more general lack of effective resistance. Moreover, many of the new plants were established as non-union operations from the outset so that the question of trades union opposition to working practices and methods of wage determination simply never arose.

There is no doubt, then, that burgeoning managerial desires for greater flexibility from their workforces in the new labour market conditions of the 1980s graphically revealed the limits to the sorts of trades union tactics and forms of organisation that had characterised Teesside before that decade. In this sense, the growing demands for 'flexibility' posed important questions about future forms of trades union activity and organisation. But in so far as the politics of the workplace flowed outwards into wider political discourse through the politics of labourism, then these too were called into question in the 1980s.

CHAPTER EIGHT

Reconstructing a New Consensus Politics?

1. INTRODUCTION

While there were significant changes occurring in Teesside's economy and labour market in the 1980s, so too were changes emerging in the spheres of party politics and state policies towards the area. The maturing crisis of modernisation policies called into question the bases of support for consensus politics, especially amongst Labour supporters and sympathisers. It seemed as if the costs of industrial decline were to be heaped upon those arising from past industrial growth. Nevertheless, so deep was the influence of consensus approaches within Teesside's political culture that a new, though in crucial respects very different, political project began to emerge which again projected a shared vision of the area's future.

2. THE CRISES OF MODERNISATION POLICIES AND OF LABOURISM: PARTY POLITICAL CHANGE ON TEESSIDE IN THE 1970S AND 1980S

During the 1970s, increasing doubts about the effects, unintended as well as intended, of implementing modernisation policies on Teesside found some expression in both national and local elections there. At national level, the four core Teesside constituencies (Cleveland, Hartlepool, Middlesbrough, Stockton) returned Labour Members of Parliament in the elections of 1974 and 1979. Even in the latter election, Labour won each of these constituencies with over 50 per cent of the vote. At local government level, the pattern was more variable and volatile. The swings between the main parties continued as before, with control alternating between elections. There was, however, no simple correlation at local level between growing doubts over modernisation policies and electoral swings between Conservative and Labour. A substantial measure of cross-party consensus still existed on the modernisation project. Switches in control of first Teesside County Borough Council and then Cleveland County Council

TABLE 8.1: Political composition of Cleveland County Council, 1973–89.

Seats held by	Election year				
	1973	1977	1981	1985	1989
Conservative	35	49	27	19	19
Labour	52	36	61	51	48
Liberal/SLD	0	0	0	7	10
Others	2	4	1	0	0
Total	89	89	89	77	77

Note: Electoral boundaries reorganised from 1985.

Source: Cleveland County Council Research and Intelligence Unit.

(Table 8.1) had no appreciable impact on the content of local modernisation policies. The challenge to these was coming from within the Labour Party and from environmental groups rather than being an issue between the two main parties. Local election results were shaped more by swings in the national popularity of the main political parties. Through this, changes in control at local level would be characterised by continuity rather than dramatic change in local authority policies. As such, there were marked swings away from Labour (as in the 1977 County Council election) and Conservative (as in 1981). Indeed, in 1981 as the deep recession in the national economy provoked by Thatcherite policies bit deeply into the remains of Teesside's manufacturing economy, Conservative representation on Cleveland County Council was dramatically reduced.

In national elections, however,Teesside's party politics also became more complicated in the 1980s. In part, this reflected boundary reform and the creation of the new Langbaurgh constituency. More importantly, however, it reflected divisive tensions within the Labour Party nationally, with some Teesside Members of Parliament playing a key role in creating them. When the Social Democratic Party (SDP) was formed in 1981, two of the founding 'Gang of Four' (Rodgers and Wrigglesworth) were prominent Labour politicians on Teesside. In 1983 the SDP gained Stockton South and just failed to win Stockton North (Table 8.2). This was a very strong reminder of the essentially moderate social democratic character of labour politics on Teesside. Here the new party sought to distance itself from what it perceived as 'hard left' tendencies of growing significance within the Labour Party. The emergence of the SDP as a new centrist party was in turn to have

TABLE 8.2: General Election results in Teesside, 1979–92: percentage of constituency votes obtained by political parties.

1979	Hartlepool		Middlesbrough		Stockton		Cleveland	
	Lab.	55.1	Lab.	51.4	Lab.	53.1	Lab.	53.7
	Con.	38.4	Con.	31.0	Con.	36.2	Con.	36.7
	Lib.	6.5	Lib.	9.3	Lib.	9.2	Lib.	8.9
			Other	2.3	Other	1.5	Other	0.7

1983	Hartlepool		Middlesbrough		Stockton North		Stockton South		Langbaurgh		Redcar	
	Lab.	45.5	Lab.	50.7	Lab.	37.1	SDP	36.7	Con.	41.6	Lab.	40.6
	Con.	39.2	Con.	27.6	Con.	33.3	Con.	36.6	Lab.	31.4	Con.	33.7
	SDP	15.3	Lib.	21.2	SDP	29.6	Lab.	26.3	Lib.	26.9	SDP	25.7
			Other	0.5			Other	0.4				
1987	Lab.	48.5	Lab.	59.7	Lab.	49.2	Con.	35.0	Con.	41.7	Lab.	47.3
	Con.	33.9	Con.	25.0	Con.	32.5	SDP	33.7	Lab.	38.4	Con.	31.3
	Lib.	14.0	Lib.	15.3	SDP	18.3	Lab.	31.3	Lib	19.9	SDP	21.4
	Other	3.6										
1992	Lab.	51.9	Lab.	64.1	Lab.	52.3	Con.	45.2	Con.	45.4	Lab.	56.0
	Con.	34.9	Con.	25.7	Con.	32.7	Lab.	39.8	Lab.	43.1	Con.	32.1
	LD	13.3	LD	10.2	LD	13.7	LD	15.0	LD	11.5	LD	11.9

Source: Wood (1983, 1987, 1992).

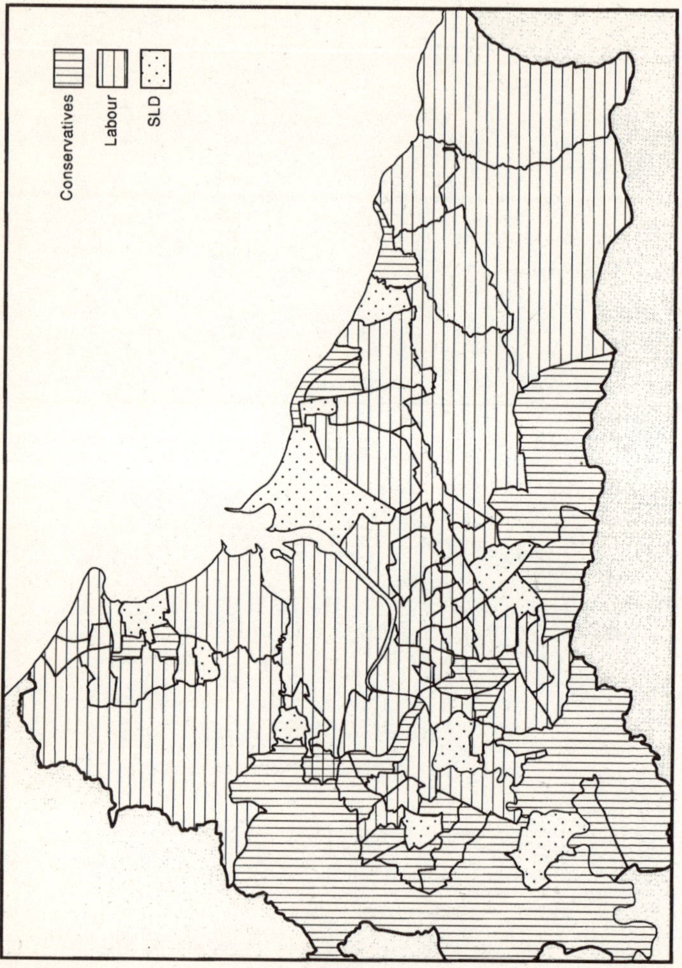

FIGURE 8.1: Cleveland County Council elections, 1989: ward results.

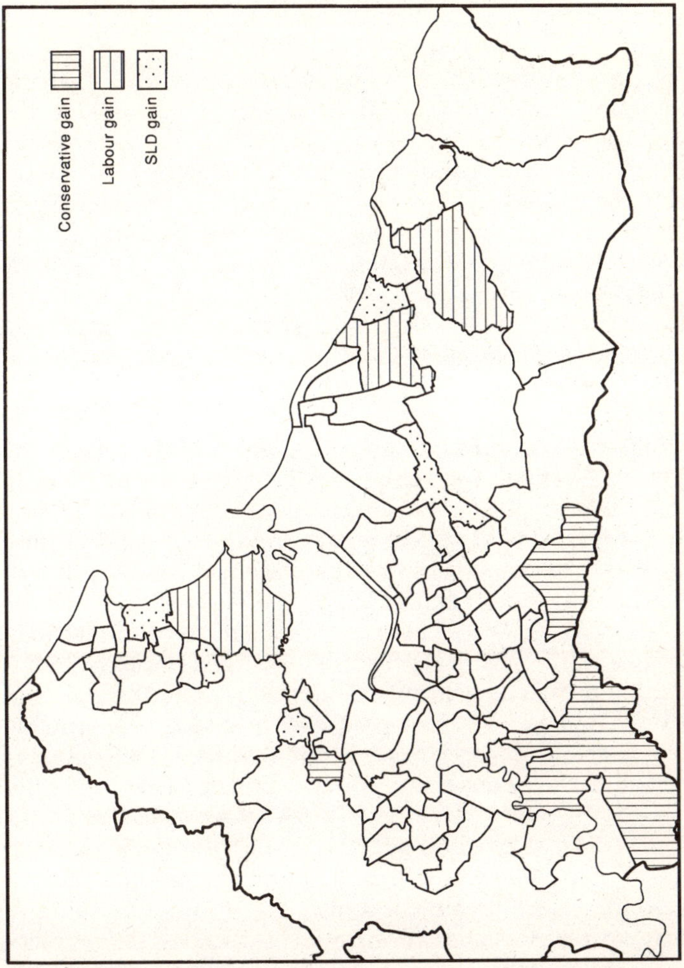

FIGURE 8.2: Cleveland County Council: changes in party control at ward level between 1985 and 1989.

important impacts on conflicts and debates within the Labour Party on Teesside and upon Teesside's electoral geography, throughout the 1980s. The SDP, and in due course the Social and Liberal Democratic Party (SLD), was very prominent in the Stockton constituencies; it was also winning 15–30 per cent of the vote elsewhere in constituencies on Teesside. Such support tended to be concentrated in particular places and this had great significance at local electoral level. In the 1989 Cleveland County Council election the SLD won ten seats (Figures 8.1 and 8.2). At the same time, the emergence of SLD support was linked to and reinforced established patterns of social and spatial division between the urban industrial strongholds of Labour and rural districts and small towns where Conservatives had great support (Figures 8.3, 8.4 and 8.5).

Labour MPs generally increased their share of the vote in the 1987 general election, as the political polarisation between 'North' and 'South' intensified (Hudson and Williams, 1989). Locally, Labour retained its overwhelming control of Cleveland County Council, and the dominance of Labour seemed complete. However, changes were emerging in the content of its policies and the style of its politics. These changes were incremental rather than dramatic or transformative; often they emerged through painful public disagreements over quite minor issues. But the cracks in the old 'machine' of politics were there to be seen. The growing local challenge of the SDP/SLD and the disaffection of previous Labour activists was one thing. Another was that Labour politics had been built around a number of certainties – rules and norms which gave a clear guide to political action: 'loyalty' and obedience to the party line was a basic assumption, and the SDP split shattered this. The attraction of council house sales to sections of the party's supporters raised even more profound questions relating to policy matters. The Labour Party was the party of state provision. It was the party which provided for *its* people and did deals with big business in this general interest. The libertarian strand in Thatcherism undermined Labour councillors at their very core. All this combined with the obvious failures of modernisation policies to generate powerful forces for change within Labour politics on Teesside. The Unemployment Strategy in 1987 was one aspect of this. In part this can be seen as an important ideological break; it can also be interpreted as an attempt to preserve and rework some of the social democratic concerns in a society now dominated by the priorities of Thatcherism. But such attempts to bridge the gap between old and new worlds were often

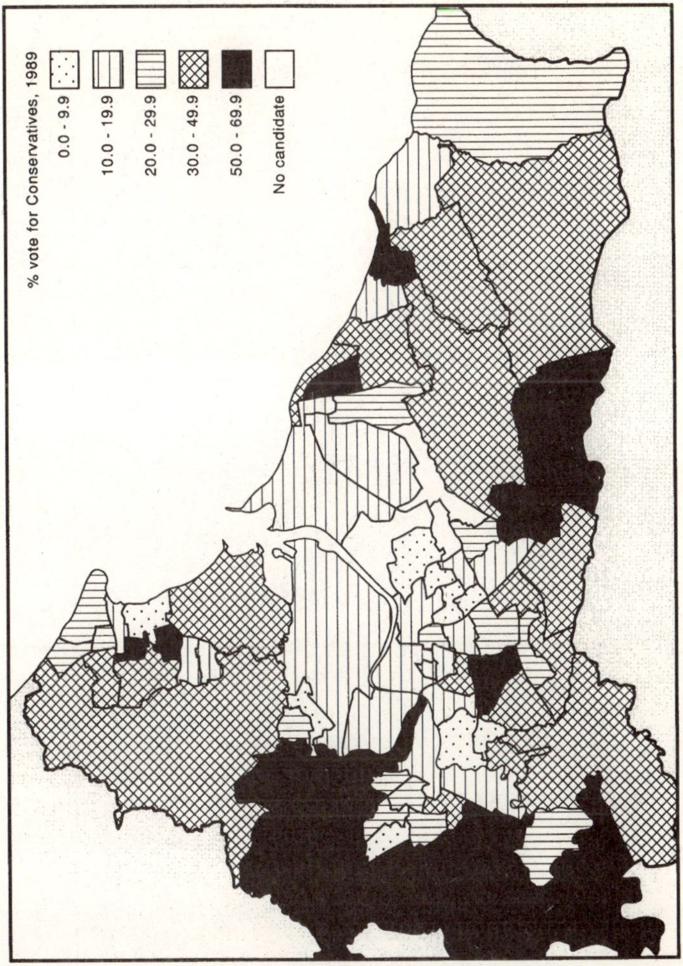

FIGURE 8.3: Voting support for Conservative Party, Cleveland County Council elections, 1989.

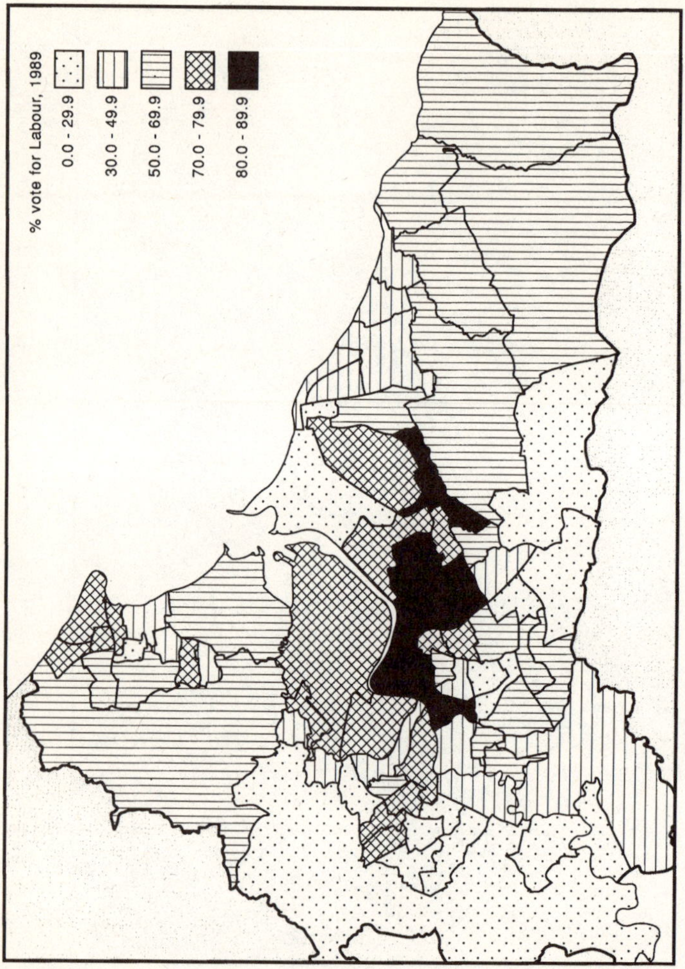

FIGURE 8.4: Voting support for Labour Party, Cleveland County Council elections, 1989.

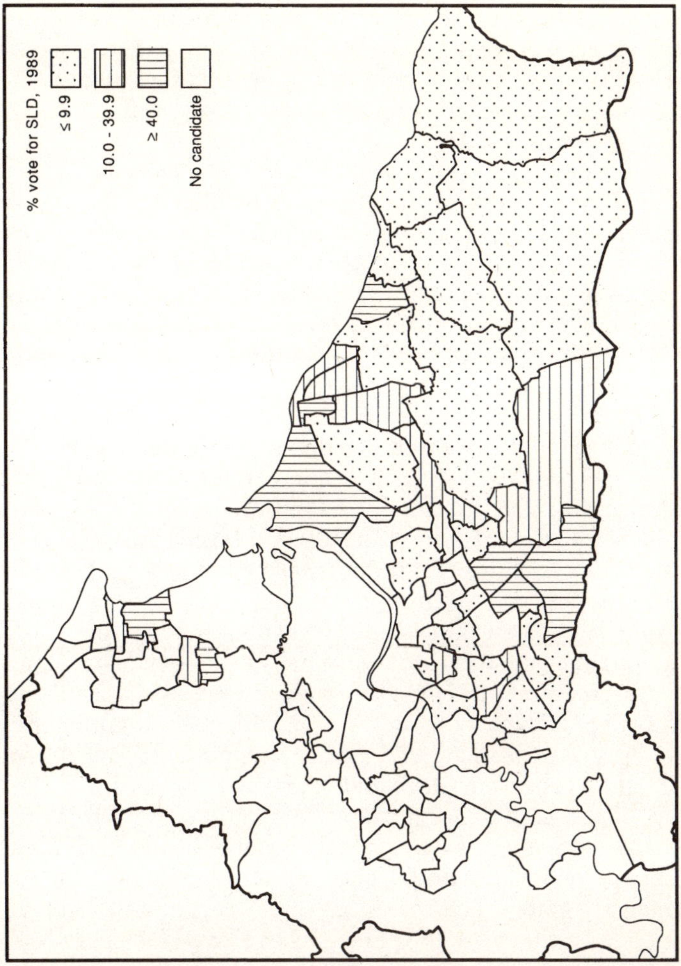

FIGURE 8.5: Voting support for the Social and Liberal Democratic Party, Cleveland County Council elections, 1989.

problematic. To recognise the realities of permanent long-term unemployment was clearly preferable to pretending that it did not exist. Equally an attempt to work *with* rather than *for* the unemployed was certainly a progressive move, and very different from the old-style deferential machine politics, which centred on councillors informing their constituents of what was happening. But that very difference itself created problems. Many of the young unemployed people in the area remembered well their previous experiences of alienation and rejection by the old Labour politics. This had been grounded in a world of work, of trades unionism, industrial relations, committee meetings: a world in which the unemployed did not really fit. As County Councillor Maureen Taylor put it:

> I think you can guess that there is a degree of contempt for us as Labour politicians from the unemployed, particularly the young. There's a feeling that 'none of you care'. And it's a slow uphill battle to change that attitude. Out of the unemployment working party came a whole host of ideas, some of them very exciting, and it does mean a fundamental shift in the traditional way of looking at it. Some of the Labour group haven't the faintest idea what it's all about. They think it's just a question of throwing money at it. But it takes a long time. You can't just barge into a community which has been neglected, which is suffering from all kinds of deprivation, and say 'we are going to do something for you'. There are a few little pockets in Cleveland where there is a slow building up of self-confidence within the community itself. What worries me are the ways in which some of the traditional Labour politicians might take this. I don't think some of them are going to be able to make the leap, and in that case we need a change in the personnel of elected members.

Such local participative forms, let alone strong grass-roots action, were scarcely encouraged by many of the old-style bosses of the Labour political machine.

Some of these tensions and problems can be illustrated by reference to events in Langbaurgh and Redcar. Labour lost and then regained ground in both of these places in both national and local elections. Here the painful process of compromise and change was very publicly displayed amidst charges of left-wing extremism, Militant penetration and the influence of the 'loony left'. It combined with a resistance to changes in policy on council house sales, at a time when, nationally, these issues had a very high profile. Local Conservatives involved themselves, often mischievously, in these affairs, occasionally combining with old established Labour opponents in unholy cross-party alliances. Prominent Labour leaders, swinging to an even more right-wing politics, seemed not in the least embarrassed by support from their previous political opponents. The 'old consensus' was being openly defended. In these battles, the enemy was very much 'the enemy within' the party.

Langbaurgh, on the south bank of the Tees, encompassed the extremes of wealth and poverty in North-east England; prosperous commuter villages amidst rolling hills sitting uneasily with an expanse of industrial dereliction and urban decay along the river. This variation ran deeper than job prospects. It was also reflected in social divisions and patterns of political support. The parliamentary constituency, created at the 1983 election, was held by a Conservative, Richard Holt, with a majority of 6,000 in 1983 and 2,000 in 1987. Although Ashok Kumar won it for Labour in a by-election in 1991, following Holt's sudden death, Michael Bates regained it for the Conservatives in the 1992 General Election. Langbaurgh returned County Councillors from all three main political parties in the 1985 and 1989 County Council elections (see Figures 8.1 and 8.2). The Borough Council, created in 1974, was also controlled by both Labour and Conservative parties at various times. From 1983 it was controlled by Labour, a party dominated locally by its right-of-centre leader, Arthur Seed. At this time the Langbaurgh Conservatives had some difficulty mounting serious opposition to a Labour leader who so willingly embraced much of their own national government's policies. After local government elections in 1987, however, Langbaurgh became a hung authority with no clear majority party. In the run-up to these elections, Seed began to lose his hold upon power in the Labour Party and an acrimonious struggle developed. The Conservatives saw in this their chance to obtain overall control of the council once again.

Under Arthur Seed Langbaurgh Council was an enthusiastic privatiser, not least of council houses. During the 1980s, over 3,400 council houses were sold, some 19 per cent of the 1980 council housing stock. Langbaurgh was not particularly unusual in this. Hartlepool (24 per cent) and Stockton (21 per cent) – boroughs in which the SLD and Conservatives, respectively, made gains in 1989 (Figure 8.2) – privatised a bigger share of their 1980 stock. Only Middlesbrough (18 per cent) of the Teesside boroughs sold off a smaller proportion. There is no doubt that for many tenants, in particular types of council dwellings, becoming an owner occupier under the Conservatives' 'right to buy' legislation was an attractive prospect. Dealing with such aspirations was to prove politically problematic for Labour. In Langbaurgh this problem was exacerbated by a decision to extend privatisation of council houses beyond those who wanted to buy, to include those who did not. The entire Spencerbeck estate, in need of some renovation, was sold to a private developer, with an agreement to evict any households unwilling to see their tenure altered in this way. In March 1986 this produced a furious political storm within the party. This was soon eclipsed by the news that the authority was poised to sign a *second* partnership deal with private builders to renovate and sell 242 council houses in south Grangetown. This deal would provide Wimpey with a return of 8.5 per cent on a £4.5 million investment. The remainder of the revenue would be spent improving council houses elsewhere in the borough. The precise sums here would depend upon house sale prices. Some Spencerbeck residents affected by the earlier deal had refused to move and this was jeopardising the new proposal. Seed reacted angrily to the possibility of a delay. 'People have got to make up their minds if they want decent quality housing', he said: 'we cannot finance all the schemes which are urgent from the money we have and must look to the private sector' (*Middlesbrough Evening Gazette*, 22 April 1986). In June the District Auditor issued a damning judgement on the Spencerbeck deal, criticising members of the council for failing to investigate its financial implications, in particular the loss of 229 houses at an annual cost of £175,000.

In 1987 it emerged that a 'secret' enquiry had been held by Seed, Conservative group leader Ron Hall and the only Alliance member, Brian Williams, into the housing committee chair, Terry Collins. It was alleged that he had acted beyond his powers in that Labour Party members had been dealt with more favourably than others with rent arrears. The panel concluded that there had been some irregularities. Councillor Collins immediately denied this. As far as he was concerned: 'this is about someone who is being persecuted because he does not see eye to eye with this council's ruling Labour group' (*Middlesbrough Evening Gazette*, 13 February 1987).

The issue came to a head at a full council meeting, in a row which 'culminated in the rare spectacle of the controlling Labour group tearing itself apart in public' (*Middlesbrough Evening Gazette*, 20 February 1987). Labour members challenged the panel's validity but failed to have its findings declared inadmissible. Several protested bitterly that the panel was little more than a witch hunt, but a proposal to reject the panel's findings was defeated. On 1 March an extraordinary meeting of the Labour group, attended by thirteen of its thirty-one members, expelled Councillors Seed and Docherty for voting with the Conservatives to remove Collins from the post of housing chair. Seed replied that the meeting 'was not convened properly' (*Middlesbrough Evening Gazette*, 2 March 1987), and that he intended to remain as leader until the impending elections. He added that he was considering whether to renounce an earlier decision to retire and threatened to expose Militant infiltration in his South Bank ward. In April Seed blocked a move to have Collins re-elected housing chair in the committee room, with support from Conservatives and some Labour members. In immediate retaliation seven more councillors were expelled at another extraordinary Labour group meeting.

As campaigning for the May 1987 local elections began in earnest, Labour faced a challenge in three seats from Seed and his supporters. Several official Labour candidates also declared their support for Seed after nominations closed. In the event the polls produced an indeterminate outcome. Seed failed by 25 votes in his bid to be re-elected. Labour was the largest single party with 29 of the 60 seats, but four of these councillors were not in the group. The Conservatives had 24 seats and the Alliance seven. Within a week of the election, however, two of the unofficial Labour councillors joined the Conservative group. With some justification, Seed's replacement as Labour group leader, Arthur Taylor, branded the decision a 'cynical betrayal of the voters'. In reply one of the defectors, Councillor Keith Cook, argued that 'it was the dirty tricks of the left-wingers which forced us reluctantly to join the Tory group', whilst Councillor James Readman explained 'we will not resign because the people know we are fighting the loony left' (*Middlesbrough Evening Gazette*, 15 May 1987).

Whilst these political machinations reflected personalities as well as policies, there were some important broader issues involved. In particular, they clearly revealed the limited differences between the dominant brand of Labour Party politics and the Conservative Party's agenda. In this Langbaurgh was far from exceptional. Labourism on Teesside was grounded in a very centrist political philosophy. A similar story emerged in the Redcar parliamentary constituency, which fell largely within the boundaries of Langbaurgh Borough Council. Its Labour MP since 1964, James Tinn, was closely associated with Arthur Seed. In 1983 Tinn's majority was cut from 10,000 to 3,000. His decision not to stand for re-election in 1987 provided another insight into the changing character of politics in this part of Teesside.

In March 1986 Tinn walked out of the annual general meeting of his constituency Labour Party, claiming it was unconstitutional. The following month the South Bank branch passed a motion which stated that 'The branch notes the MP's lack of confidence in the constituency party and calls on Mr Tinn to reconsider his candidature'. Tinn replied that 'if they are trying to make my position untenable', they were 'very unlikely to succeed', adding 'I think I can resist this. We'll see who comes out on top' (*Middlesbrough Evening Gazette*, 3 April 1987). Support quickly came from what seemed an unlikely source: the Conservative group leader on Langbaurgh council, Ron Hall. Speaking at a local Conservative party meeting he deplored the 'underhand way the present rulers of the constituency Labour Party, with the militant Left in control' were trying to unseat James Tinn. Support came also from Langbaurgh's Conservative MP Richard Holt, who condemned the 'excesses of the Loony Left', arguing 'we are seeing manifestations of it in Redcar' (*Middlesbrough Evening Gazette*, 7 April 1986).

Disquiet rumbled on until September 1986, when at a meeting of the South Bank branch Tinn's secretary and agent, Kay O'Neill, moved a vote of no confidence which called for him to stand down. It was passed comfortably, along with another from Cleveland County Councillor Ian Jeffrey which proposed that Tinn be deselected. Tinn reacted that 'he had no intention whatsoever of resigning' and repeated his call for a National Executive Committee inquiry into the local party (*Middlesbrough Evening Gazette*, 25 September 1986).

When the constituency party met in October it gave Tinn ten days to resign, or face a request to the National Executive Committee (NEC) for a new selection timetable. He refused and so the issue went to the NEC. Local Conservatives were keen to present the matter as a 'left-wing takeover' but the constituency party was anxious to emphasise that all attempts at reconciliation with the MP had failed. Kay O'Neill refused to engage in 'public mudslinging' and Tinn would not elaborate on what he described as the 'political dimensions' to the dispute (*Middlesbrough Evening Gazette*, 16 October 1986). Nor would Paul Harford – constituency party chair and prospective parliamentary candidate for Langbaurgh – be drawn. Only Arthur Seed, it seemed, was prepared to comment publicly. 'All the problems', he said, 'have stemmed from the militants and communists who have infiltrated the constituency party'. He went on to add that 'there can be only one possible outcome and that is for these militants to follow the likes of Derek Hatton out of the Labour Party' (*Middlesbrough Evening Gazette*, 18 October 1986).

The NEC set up a full internal investigation into the rift. Before its findings became public, though, Tinn announced in May 1987 that he would not be a candidate in the June General Election. He indicated that 'it would be totally wrong to suggest I attempted to discredit the constituency party or deliberately embarrass it'. There was, he said, 'no deep motive behind this'. Labour leader Neil Kinnock received the news 'with mixed feelings' as the Conservative candidate for the Redcar constituency, Peter Bassett, claimed Tinn had been 'forced out by the left wing'. It also became clear that had Tinn – then aged 64 – remained in Parliament until the age of 65, he would not have received a resettlement allowance of £18,500 (*Middlesbrough Evening Gazette*, 14 May 1987). The constituency party hurriedly selected a new candidate. Its choice, Marjorie Mowlam, won the seat comfortably, increasing the majority to 8,000 and easily held it in 1992.

Events such as these make clear the lengths to which long-established Labour politicians were prepared to go both to preserve their own positions and to try to secure the reproduction of those machine politics and moderate policies that characterised labourism over so much of Teesside. These unholy alliances with local Conservatives were in truth no more than the latest expression of a cross-party consensus that had held sway on Teesside since the 1930s. That 'the enemy' was 'loony leftism' is not surprising either, for in a very real sense radical socialist politics would have posed much more of a threat to traditional labourism on Teesside than did the local brand of conservatism. It points also to the autonomy of politics, and to the role of particular personalities. That Labour recovered much lost ground (Figure 8.2) in the east of Cleveland revealed both growing opposition to the impacts of Conservative policies, and a recognition that the new Labour party (purged to a degree of the old right-wing influences), offered marginally more hope to many people there.

It would be wrong to over-emphasise the extent of political change. In the west of Teesside, the SLD and Conservatives grew in strength in Stockton. This draws attention to the growing socio-spatial polarisation experienced in the area in the 1980s. Equally significant was the way in which Labour local authorities were drawn into a new version of consensus policies centred on the activities of the Teesside Development Corporation. Many of them were unwilling parties to this scheme. However, the realignment of power between central and local government in the 1980s, with an unprecedented centralisation of power within central government, left them scant choice.

3. RECONSTRUCTING CONSENSUS POLITICS: ECONOMIC REGENERATION VIA THE TEESSIDE DEVELOPMENT CORPORATION

Events on Teesside took on a national significance in 1987 because of Mrs Thatcher's historic walk through part of Teesside's industrial wasteland following her third consecutive victory. She reaffirmed the need to 'get those inner cities', and to prioritise central over local government power in urban policy. Under Thatcher local government policies were severely constrained by centrally-imposed expenditure restrictions and legislative limits on local government's room for manœuvre in policy making. For example, between 1981 and 1986, there was an expenditure of £23.7 million on the Middlesbrough Inner Area Programme (IAP). This programme was co-ordinated and managed by the local authorities but funded via central government's Urban Programme. The economic, environmental and social goals of the IAP had, therefore, to be consistent with central government aims and objectives. These included fostering business development via the creation of Enterprise Centres and stimulating private sector investment in inner urban areas (Department of Environment, 1990). This further challenged and constrained the ability of local government on Teesside to pursue its own alternative, autonomous development policies for the area.

Without doubt, the clearest expression of the new order was the designation of large parts of Teesside as an area assigned to an Urban Development Corporation in 1987 (see Figure 8.6). Ironically echoing the concerns of the 1960s and 1970s, its primary task was to oversee the reclamation of thousands of acres of land on both banks of the river, this time not from the sea but rather from the impacts of industrial decline. In this, as in Hailsham's 1963 White Paper, central government chose selectively to endorse the work of local authorities. The conflicting loyalties which this provoked were expressed by John Gillis, Cleveland County Council's chief planner. Parts of his department's work, he said, would

> be handed over to the Urban Development Corporation. That annoys me, it's another occasion when the effort of local government is put into the background and all the credit for the job we've done goes to a central Government quango. On the other hand the job needs doing, and I des-

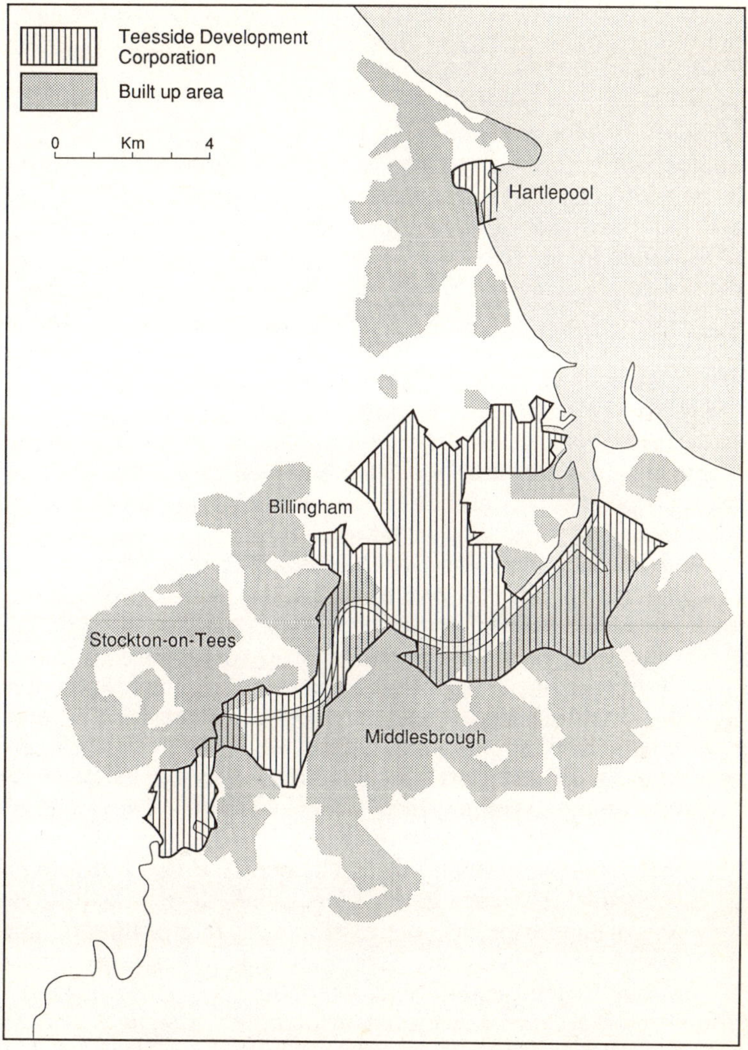

FIGURE 8.6: Boundaries of the Teesside Development Corporation, 1987

perately want it to be done, so if they do it properly I shan't complain too loudly.

Underlying the seemingly simple task of derelict land reclamation was a much more fundamental challenge to the powers and resources of local government – one which was also being experienced elsewhere in the country.

Teesside was one of four 'second-generation' Urban Development Corporations (the 'first generation' being London Docklands and Merseyside established in 1981; the others being at Trafford Park, in the Black Country and on Tyneside). Teesside Development Corporation (TDC) was given a budget of £150–200 million over ten years and, like other UDCs, substantial authority to own and acquire land, invest in infrastructural improvement and build factories. It covered a vast area, which it described – with some justification – as the largest continuous area of deindustrialised land in Europe. Much of this area was the object of a European Community backed 'National Programme of Community Interest' over the period 1984-8, involving a total expenditure on reclamation and infrastructural improvement of £38 million (see Cleveland County Council, 1989b).

Coulson (1989, p. 9) attaches considerable importance to the role of the chairman and/or chief executive of an Urban Development Corporation in defining the character of its approach. This is what he has to say about the TDC:

> In Teesside, the Chairman has a property background and has interpreted his role as getting physical development, bricks and mortar, on the ground as quickly as possible. Its Chief Executive was previously Chief Executive of Corby District Council, has little faith in traditional town planning or structure plans, gives little weight to consultation and involvement of local people, and believes that in most traditional local authority economic development activity 'the fundamental requirements of economic rejuvenation, namely political certainty and decisive decision making to match the requirements of the incoming industry, are irrevocably lost'. The TDC ethos is in that sense the most radical of any of the UDC's, and not dissimilar to that of the London Docklands Development Corporation in its early days.

For local government, the creation of the TDC posed some delicate issues of accountability and consultation, especially given its chief executive's known views about consultation and participation. Coulson (1989, p. 41), for instance, argued that 'the TDC needs to consult more widely and earlier in its process of formulating proposals and plans', whilst Middlesbrough Borough Council was reported as arguing that the TDC operated on a 'need to know' basis (CLES, 1990). These were particularly awkward comments and criticisms as the Development Corporation was not an elected body but a centrally-appointed organisation. Such problems were exacerbated by the tight control on local government finance, in comparison with the TDC's quite substantial budget. The undercurrent of tension was revealed in evidence submitted to the House of Commons Select Committee on Employment in the course of its investigation into UDCs. Duncan Hall, its chief executive, proclaimed that 'the singular reflection of the Development Corporation is the enormous co-operation we have received from the local authorities'. He went on (Employment Committee, 1988, vol. ii, p. 101):

> in the current round we will without doubt be the only Development Corporation that is not using either vesting powers or compulsory purchase powers. There is no coercion involved in the approaches and initiatives of the Corporation, sheer matters of co-operation.

Yet the basis of this co-operation rested on a fair degree of pragmatism on the part of the local authorities, as outlined in a memorandum submitted by the (rate-capped) Middlesbrough Borough Council (ibid., p. 324):

> In terms of developing ideas the TDC has to date concentrated on taking up schemes which have been developed over a period of years by the local authorities ... it can be concluded that its major advantage is that it has funding available to it that is far greater than has been made available to the local authorities and other organisations that have been seeking to carry out these functions in previous years.

Nevertheless, tensions remained. The TDC is clearly happier dealing with business people, developers and consultants than with local authorities, voluntary groups and the wider public on Teesside. On the other hand, the TDC can rightly claim that on occasion it has received conflicting signals, or no clear signals at all, from local authorities there. What is undeniable is the extra public expenditure that flows into the area under the control of the TDC. Given this there can be 'no mileage' for local authorities in outright opposition or criticism since this would only 'alienate the Corporation' and make achieving their own policy objectives more difficult (Coulson, 1989, p. 32). What this demonstrates only too clearly is the importance of power relations within the state in shaping the trajectory of local change.

The creation of the UDCs was generally significant as part of a restructuring of the UK state in the 1980s. The UDC concept was part of a national political strategy in the late 1980s, ostensibly developed as a means of encouraging industrial reclamation and renewal in the inner cities. The focus upon these locations was not coincidental : 'those inner cities' were clear political targets. Nor was the prominence given to Teesside coincidental. Mrs Thatcher's walk had guaranteed that no efforts would be spared to make sure that the TDC succeeded in its mission of transforming the old Labour heartlands of inner Teesside (Figure 8.5). That the UDC concept enabled a Conservative central government to exert strong control over many (largely Labour-controlled) local authorities was therefore very significant in this national political context. But equally, if not more, important was the way in which it embodied the notion of *partnership*, in the sense of co-operation between private capital and the state, on the terms and conditions set by capitalists' requirements for profit. In the process, a new kind of arrangement, drawing on the US experience of urban redevelopment was put into place (see Judd and Parkinson, 1989). In London Docklands, Brindley *et al.* (1989, p. 115) noted the way in which the Development Corporation was closely allied with the private corporate sector, in particular large property development companies. On Teesside (where this kind of accommodative consensus had a long heritage) there were many indications that a similar development was taking place. The ideology of partnership found a marked resonance in these words of the TDC's Duncan Hall (Employment Committee, 1988, vol. II, p. 102):

> there is a singular will and commitment by all of us to make Teesside succeed ... it is that commitment that is built in, and built across the political barriers that could potentially exist in the area, it is that drive for success ... that is making it happen.

In these and other ways, the creation of the TDC encapsulated a continuation of old-established political traditions on Teesside, and within the North-east more generally. Marketing, property-led development and business confidence were to be – on this agenda at least – the new keywords for the 1990s.

This emphasis became clear from an examination of the projects that the TDC was seeking to promote. To some extent, it was involving itself in projects to support 'high-tech' manufacturing, in collaboration with organisations such as the Tees and Hartlepool Port Authority (Teesside Offshore Base), Cleveland County Council (over its existing CADCAM Centre) and ICI and English Estates (Belasis Hall Technology Park). The TDC's support for proposals for a joint venture in higher education by Durham University and Teesside Polytechnic, which came to fruition in 1991 in the form of JUCOT (Joint University College on Teesside) could also be related to the goal of encouraging high-tech activities.

But there is no doubt whatsoever as to where the TDC's main priorities lay: using its resources to encourage speculative commercial and leisure property developments within Teesside. While the main TDC's schemes included some developments of 'high-tech' industry and housing, to help make them more generally acceptable, it is clear that much less priority was attached to housing than in the proposals originally formulated by Coopers and Lybrand in 1987 (see Coulson, 1989, pp. 16–22). The most prominent of the TDC's 'flagship projects' included: Teesside Park, an £80 million scheme on the site of the old Stockton racecourse, consisting mainly of 500,000 square feet of floorspace for retailing, wholesale and leisure projects, with Brookmount as the lead developer; Teesdale Park, on the site of Mrs Thatcher's famous walk, a 250-acre development at Stockton by Murray International that could ultimately involve £500 million of public and private sector investment and an additional 800,000 square feet of office space, 100,000 square feet of speciality retailing floorspace, 750 houses, and the JUCOT development; Wynyard Hall, a £300 million development over ten years by John Hall of Metro-Centre fame; and the Hartlepool Marina, a £150 million project (£51 million as a grant from the TDC) in part of the old coal dock, involving the TDC, the Tees and Hartlepool Port Authority (THPA) and Lovell Partnerships. It has been claimed that these four schemes alone would provide around 20,000 jobs, although considerable uncertainty surrounded this number. The TDC's chief executive had earlier set out his views as to the relationship between investment and new employment: 'I expect £1,000 million to be invested and between 10,000 and 20,000 jobs to be brought into the area' (quoted in *Financial Times*, 7 March, 1989). Clearly at a ratio of (at least) £50,000 per job, a massive influx of investment will be needed to create 20,000 jobs. Whether it *will* arrive in Teesside is another question. And even if it does, and new jobs are created, there are those who have doubts about the quality of such jobs. Councillor David Walsh, chairman of Cleveland County Council's Economic Development and Transport Committee, put it like this (quoted in the *Financial Times*, 12 September 1992): 'I'm not saying that we do not need to diversify our economy. But – I'm not sure that putting up retail warehouses is the best way to create the type of jobs we need'. But whether the projected investment by the private sector and the forecast number of jobs will materialise, and what sort of jobs they would be, all remains to be seen.

Nevertheless, the prospect of creating a 'post-industrial' city, a neomodernist project with a post-modernist architectural veneer, centring on consumption rather than production and generating jobs in these numbers in an area of high unemployment, continues to have attractions to many. As Michael Carr, Labour Leader of Middlesbrough Council, put it (quoted in *Financial Times*, 12 September 1992): 'Although retailing may not be ideal, in an area of high unemployment a job is a job at the end of the day'. This remains the case, even though it is clear that if the TDC's schemes succeed they would have considerable impacts elsewhere in Teesside and not all of this will be positive. Whilst there would be new employment, jobs in similar activities elsewhere in Teesside would be at risk. There is only a limited pool of purchasing power that new commercial, leisure and shopping developments can draw upon. Creating in excess of an additional 500,000 square feet of retailing space would seriously threaten the viability of the existing Middlesbrough and Stockton centres. Building substantial new office blocks in an area which had sufficient vacant office space in the 1980s to cope with forecast demands for the next two decades would simply increase oversupply. Yet in 1990 some 2 million square feet of *additional* office floor space was under construction or planned.

It is difficult, then, to see how such developments would produce 20,000 or so *net* new jobs. Cleveland County Council's own (1990) forecast of net service sector employment growth between 1989 and 2001 is only of an extra 2,500 office jobs: 1,300 in banking and administration; 700 in public administration; and 500 in other services.It is also hard to escape the conclusion that the TDC had become the dominant actor in setting the agenda for 'local' solutions on Teesside into the 1990s and equally hard to escape the conclusion that, despite the significant changes that had occurred, it also represented a strong thread of continuity with past perceptions of appropriate policies for Teesside.

4. CONCLUDING COMMENTS

The political dimension to Teesside's historical evolution has been an important one. The legacy of deferential labour relations and paternalist industrial practices was of great significance to the emergence of a consensus which culminated in the modernisation project of the 1960s. That consensus came under challenge in the 1970s and 1980s in the face of growing unemployment and a concerted environmentalist challenge, generating responses to this in terms of party political change and new policy initiatives during the 1980s. It was no surprise that political parties in the area were drawn towards a new consensus around what is perhaps most appropriately interpreted as a neomodernist project grounded in the property development strategies of the TDC. For a credible alternative to accommodating the needs of private capital, based on a more meaningful collectivism and greater *control* of private sector investment and disinvestment, had no roots on Teesside and it would have been very remarkable had it emerged in the 1980s. In a very real sense, the politics of Teesside were deeply imbued with a political culture that accepted the needs of private capital and the inevitability of waged labour. This was an area in which the new Thatcherite solutions could easily be embraced by some and imposed on others.

CHAPTER NINE

Conclusions, Reflections and Future Directions

1. INTRODUCTION

In this book we have explained the way in which a place called Teesside came into being as a consequence of certain industrial developments associated with private capital. We have followed the development of this place and examined how the fortunes of capital and strategies of the national state have deeply affected the lives of its people. In these conclusions we explore some of the implications of these observations.

2. THE PRODUCTION AND REPRODUCTION OF PLACE: TEESSIDE IN THEORETICAL CONTEXT

Teesside, without doubt, is an area with a long history of consensus politics, of a broad cross-class agreement as to what is 'best for Teesside'. The origins of this can be traced back to its initial creation as a centre for capitalist production, and the specific form that this took. Whilst parts of the contemporary conurbation have a pre-capitalist urban history – for instance, Stockton – the initial formation of most of the area and its subsequent very rapid growth was one expression of the creation of a new pattern of spatially uneven development, an integral part of the process of capitalist industrialisation. Accumulation presupposes profitable production and one hundred and fifty years or so ago profitable production spaces required (*inter-alia*):

1. appropriate natural environmental conditions and access to key raw materials (in Teesside's case, coking coal and iron ore);
2. the construction of new industrial works;
3. new transport systems; and
4. new residential areas to house the flood of in-migrants.

In these ways the capital : labour relation was sedimented into place on Teesside. The new social order of the nineteenth century was based on the clear dominance of capitalist relations of production, and the production of new places (like Teesside) as centres of industrial production.

One consequence of this is that Teesside was built around distinct gender relations and profound class divisions, but these did not necessarily erupt into open conflict because of the way in which social relationships were constituted and understood there. From an early stage, gender relations were moulded into patriarchal forms and class relations into strongly paternalistic ones that extended beyond the workplace and gave form to an emergent local society. Over time, a sense of economic and social cohesion developed as capitalist enterprises became committed to producing profits in and through Teesside. In the process they provided waged employment for members of a working class that had no choice but to sell their labour power somewhere. Over time, too, these people emerged as part of a working class, with its own institutions (social clubs, trades unions, political parties), which in turn developed its own commitments to Teesside. In these ways it became a place in which to live rather than just a space in which to work for a wage.

Certainly, then, the *initial* construction of places such as Teesside, as part of a process of capitalist industrialisation, was very openly dominated by the interests of capital and its need for profitable production spaces. The power of industrial capital was more or less unfettered by a general consideration of the interests of labour. However, with the passage of time there was an increasing representation of non-capitalist interests and, to a degree, social interests not represented through class divisions. In particular, there was a growing representation of the interests of labour (though with a strong gender bias) in trades unionism and within the emergent Labour Party (and its predecessors). More and more, too, the interests of both big capital and organised labour were reflected in and through the activities of the state. The *content* of state policies, especially at local level, became central to the reproduction of a consensus based on place – specific shared interests. The extent to which different social actors could represent *their* interests as dominant in this whilst arguing that in fact they represented the general interests of the place remained a matter of crucial significance. The *implementation* of state policies became central to the attempt to translate this shared vision into practice.

As industrial growth continued on Teesside, the initial constraining effects of the natural environment were increasingly replaced by socially produced ones. As a consequence of commitments made to *this* place initially contingent spatial relations became (to a degree and for a time) causal ones. For the major private sector companies involved in the manufacture of chemicals and iron and steel, and the use of iron and steel in a range of engineering and shipbuilding activities, their growing and massive investments in fixed capital on Teesside provided compelling reasons for a commitment to it (cf. Lapple and van Hoogstraten, 1980). In other ways, too, those companies had invested heavily in creating particular forms of industrial relations, particular types of labour markets, and a local political climate conducive to their profitable operations. These companies provided relatively well-paid and secure employment for their overwhelmingly male workforces. For generations, the main companies had been associated with the idea of a 'job for life' and a level of internal mobility and promotion within the plant or enterprise. Moreover, wages were very largely spent locally, and these in turn circulated to provide a basis for the profitable operations of private capital in retailing and service provision. On the assumption that such paid employment would continue to be available, workers and their families developed a commitment to the place via family ties, networks of friends and the construction of their own institutions within local civil society, albeit one that was sharply divided on gender lines. These shared commitments to place were both reflected in and underpinned by the state, which sought to address the perceived needs of both capital and labour within the context of a political consensus to prioritise the promotion of Teesside's interests. It did this most clearly via the formulation and implementation of 'modernisation' policies.

The commitment to a consensual approach to issues of economic and social development on Teesside is deeply embedded in the consciousness of many of the area's residents as well as being reflected in the practices of its major social actors. Grounded in a shared commitment to place, this consensus cuts across class and other social divisions, producing, as it evolved, a shared view of the local world. This state of affairs has existed on Teesside for much of its recent history. However, it is not one that has equally represented the interests of all the social groups that adhere to it. Furthermore, the form and content of the consensus has changed over time and there have been conflicts, both between and within the major social groupings that have been party to it. None the less, the overwhelming impression is of a persistent (proto) corporatist consensus as to the ways in which economy and society should be either altered or preserved so as to further the interests of Teesside as a place. In this, the area contrasts strongly with other locations where, at different moments in the nineteenth and twentieth centuries, class or ethnic divisions and conflicts have prevented the emergence of such a shared territorial commitment and its translation into specific place-promotional policies.

The consensual approach to tackling Teesside's problems has proved to be remarkably resilient, as events in the 1970s and 1980s revealed. In these years much of the basis on which it had held together over the preceding decades was blown away. In part, this was a consequence of global changes in the pattern of accumulation and the weak position of the UK economy within this international context. This was exacerbated by significant changes in national political responses. In these new circumstances, facilitated by the greatly accelerated turnover time of fixed capital, the loyalties of the major manufacturing companies were sorely tested. They began drastically to re-evaluate their commitment to Teesside. They disinvested at a growing pace and the heart was ripped out of the previous basis of consensus – the promotion of prosperity via the state-sponsored modernisation of key sectors of manufacturing.

The costs of this were largely borne by the working class as unemployment rose, and the living standards of the unemployed and their families fell. Environmental costs continued to be generated both by the companies that remained and by the enormous dereliction associated with plant closure and decline. The proximate cause of all this was the changing investment policy of both the private sector (chemicals, engineering) and nationalised (shipbuilding, steel) manufacturing concerns that had been central to Teesside's growth as an industrial conurbation. Teesside suffered wave upon wave of plant closures, capacity cuts and job losses in these industries. This came on top of the failure of other state policies intended to diversify its employment structure, via increased service sector employment and new forms of manufacturing employment in branch plants and small firms. It might well have been expected that these changes would have broken the old consensus and also destroyed the basis of any form of joint approach to problems of economic and social development there.

In fact, commitment to a new consensus prevailed and a fresh shared definition of what was in Teesside's best interests emerged. This, ironically, centred on a future of consumption and leisure rather than production and work. It reflected the absence of alternatives to shared views defined by the interests of one fraction of capital or another. That this occurred as the area suffered massive industrial decline, rose to the top of the national unemployment league table and continued to suffer the considerable environmental costs of industrial activity is perhaps surprising. It bears powerful testimony to the sense in which politics and society on Teesside had become locked into a view of the world that saw no alternative to 'consensual' policies. The precipitate collapse of the former basis of the local coalition did not lead to a rejection of such an approach to the promotion of the interests of the place. Decline merely led to a search for a new basis for a common ground of interests. The main response (though not the only one) to the ending of one form of accommodation between capital and labour was the creation of a new one. This raises important questions about power relations in Teesside and more generally as they impact upon Teesside.

3. POWER RELATIONS AND THE DETERMINATION OF CHANGE WITHIN TEESSIDE

If the production and reproduction of place is the intended outcome, at least in part, of the conscious strategies of structurally located social actors, then the particular direction and content of change can be seen to reflect the differential powers and resources that those actors possess. There will undoubtedly be circumstances beyond the knowledge and control of even the most powerful social groups, that may compromise their ability to realise their goals. Nevertheless, the differences in the power that social groups can exercise help to ensure that policies which favour the interests of the powerful are implemented. Sometimes, indeed, powerful groups do not actively need to exercise powers that they possess because a tacit promotion of their interests is diffused into 'common sense' (Lukes, 1974). To this extent, their views of the world have become hegemonic. This has often been the case on Teesside. Such differences in covert or overt power can have very important effects in shaping the pattern of stasis or change in a place. In the remainder of this section, we consider some aspects of change on Teesside in the light of these remarks.

First of all, it is clear that on Teesside, as elsewhere, there is a decisive asymmetry in power relations between capital and labour. Historically, the interests of the former have dominated and taken precedence over those of the latter. This was the case from the very beginnings of capitalist industrial production on Teesside. With the passage of time, the interests of labour found a rather fuller expression, especially via the growing involvement of the state in regulating economic and social life. This did lead to improvements in material living and working conditions for many people. Relatively advantageous employment conditions and wage levels were negotiated in the major manufacturing companies, linked to particular forms of trades union organisation and paternalistic capital : labour relations. This did not, however, fundamentally alter the asymmetries in power as between capital and labour: nor, for that matter, did nationalisation.

This became only too clear as public and private employers slashed capacity and employment, and against a background of mounting unemployment joined in a strategy which forced through new 'flexible' conditions of employment and pay. It was not without irony that in this process women became increasingly attractive as a source of labour power. The requirements of employers for part-time and casualised labour were developed in part to fit in more easily with women's continuing commitments to domestic labour. In this sense, the gender composition of the working class on Teesside was reworked, whilst the position of many individual workers worsened. These changes posed major challenges to trades union organisation which had developed through relationships with companies such as ICI and BSC which had once been model progressive employers.

Secondly, it is clear that relations between private capital, labour and the state on Teesside are in many ways more ambiguous than those between capital and labour. There is no doubt, for example, that the dominant chemicals and steel companies relied heavily upon central government regional policy expenditures to restructure their production activities. This was often at the expense of job shedding and to the detriment of those workers who became unemployed. Equally, both central and local governments became deeply involved in supporting the general conditions of production on which these companies depended. Over a long period, too, both central and local government took on a growing share of the costs of the crucial task of reproducing labour power, assuming major responsibility for the provision of education, health and housing – and in the process creating many new jobs, often for women. However, there is also a sense in which both central and local governments were heavily dependent upon the activities of the major chemical and steel companies on Teesside. These industries occupied a critical location in both regional and national sectoral modernisation strategies in the 1960s. In like fashion, speculative property redevelopment was central to the urban regeneration strategies of both the 1960s and 1980s. Given that these were, at best, indicative planning strategies, they were fatally reliant upon private sector investment. This dependence in itself was one reason why the state was prepared to underwrite private sector activities to the extent that it was.

But even here there were tensions, which sometimes erupted in open conflict *between* capitals as well as being reflected in relations between capitals and the state. This became clear, for instance, in the way in which the major employers in the chemicals and steel producing and using industries protected their privileged positions in the labour market. For decades they successfully blocked attempts to introduce alternative sources of male waged employment while offering no resistance to jobs which employed women. Strategies for local employment and industrial diversification were sacrificed in this way, as chemicals and other established industries were favoured. When, as in the case of steel, it became clear that private sector strategies could not guarantee the required restructuring of key manufacturing industries that were seen as vital to the national interest, nationalisation re-emerged as a viable strategy. Within the steel industry, this radically redefined the relationship between central government and the determination of change within Teesside. For a while, it seemed that it offered a route which would secure the future of an expanded, technologically sophisticated, modern steel industry on Teesside. By the mid-1970s it was becoming increasingly apparent that this was not the case. Nationalisation was to be a mechanism for sweeping rationalisation, with massive cuts in capacity and employment. This raised painful questions about both its role as part of national labourist strategy as well as about the coherence of local Teesside modernisation policies and the cross-class consensus on which they were built.

A third dimension of differential powers and resources which decisively affected Teesside was that of relations between central and local government. Over a long period, local authorities had had a growing role in the area within limits set by central government; for example, in terms of educational and housing provision. Especially during the 1960s, when local authorities' activities became central to the implementation of the Hailsham programme proposals for Teesside, there were shared interests and objectives in shaping the pattern of change there. In a sense, the 1960s were the high point of consensus policies and politics on Teesside, not least in terms of relations between central and local government. But by the 1980s a rather different picture had emerged.

One element in this new picture centred on the nationalised steel industry. As the post-1975 policies of BSC made very clear, there was now a sharp difference between central government objectives towards steel production and those of local authorities on Teesside as to the maintenance of jobs and rate income.

Employment in the steel industry continued to fall and local authorities actually began actively to oppose BSC and central government policies. But job losses continued. By the end of the 1980s the by-then privatised BSC was operating a plant which was a fraction of the size of that foreseen in 1973 and with minimal manning levels. Local authorities were ultimately powerless to influence these events. They were not helped by a more general redefinition in relations between central and local governments, which considerably reduced their powers and resources. This was also important in creating space for the establishment of the Teesside Development Corporation in 1987. This agency brought substantial resources from central government to be allocated according to its priorities. Space was also created for the TDC in another way as rampant deindustrialisation left a trail of derelict industrial sites, raising the problem of what to *do* with the vast acreages of land now redundant to the needs of industry and *how* to do it, given the constraints on local authority finance. Local authorities on Teesside saw no alternative to working with this new, central government-appointed body, which became the main state agency defining the agenda for economic change into the 1990s.

What begins to emerge from all this is a complicated set of relationships between capitalist interests, national interests, local interests and the interests of labour. How these are defined, and how they intersect, is a key issue. Clearly, definition of both 'national' and 'local' interests implies a territorially defined sharing of commitments that cuts across other differences such as class and gender. For much of the last sixty years there has been a powerful projection of such a shared territorial interest, arguing the case for Teesside in competition with other areas. Here the assumption has been of a common cause uniting otherwise different or competitive social groups. But the definition of 'local interests' is one that has been substantially (and covertly) shaped by private sector companies and central governments. During periods of rapid economic growth when living standards and conditions improved, the subjugation of the interests of labour and 'local' interests (which overlap but by no means are synonymous) could be effectively disguised or presented in forms that were acceptable to many working-class people. This was assisted by the purchase that working-class organisations had upon local government, and by the fact that Teesside had enjoyed relatively high (male) wages and more or less 'full employment' for several decades. But once the long boom came crashing to an end it became apparent that the interests of capital were very forcibly being imposed on labour, through redundancies and changes in the labour contract. In a similar manner central government imposed its will on the local authorities through cuts in public housing and welfare programmes. In this process of reworking economic and political relationships, the interests of labour and 'local' interests were simultaneously redefined and marginalised within the political agenda on Teesside. This was made clear in the growing emphasis within local policy on the form and content of speculative property development. This emerged as the new motor of local change, as a new political consensus replaced the old. In coming into being this new approach raises critical questions about the representation of 'local' interests and those of labour in the politics of the 1990s.

4. POLITICAL CHOICES AND THE FUTURE OF TEESSIDE

During the 1980s Teesside continued to be characterised by high unemployment rates. Within the conurbation there were very sharp variations in these rates, both between areas and social groups. As a result, Teesside was marked by deep socio-spatial divisions. Old working-class residential areas, blighted by industrial collapse suffered acutely, as did some of the peripheral housing estates. In both cases these were areas of predominantly local authority housing, with very high registered unemployment rates, poor living conditions and poverty. Many households lacked any wage earner, remaining reliant upon working informally or in the 'black' economy and upon various forms of state transfer payment. Some found work abroad or elsewhere in the UK, as international migrant workers or long-distance 'weekly' commuters, but this could never be a generalised solution to the problems of unemployment on Teesside. At the other extreme were areas of owner-occupied housing in the suburbs or in the small towns in the rural periphery, often with two or more wage earners within formal employment and enjoying substantially higher material living standards and conditions. This polarisation contrasts powerfully with the 1960s projections of generalised affluence arising from the successful implementation of modernisation policies.

If Teesside was experiencing high unemployment and associated problems of poverty, it was not through a lack of investment or the flight of branch plants. For much of the post-war period, Teesside had been the location of very considerable fixed capital investment in manufacturing. When industrial collapse did occur, it was overwhelmingly as a result of major established companies restructuring *in situ* rather than as a result of runaway branch plants. In this sense, Teesside may have been in the North-east but it certainly did not fit the popular stereotypes of the causes of deindustrialisation and unemployment there. But, precisely because this was the case, it posed a much greater challenge to the politics and policies of labourism, locally and nationally. Teesside was uniquely positioned at the intersection of national sectoral and regional modernisation policies in the 1960s. Its post-war history epitomises a belief in planning, in state-influenced industrial modernisation as the route to full employment and social progress. But 'planning' in this context meant at best a weak form of 'indicative planning' – a mixture of carrot and stick, through which the state attempted to persuade or bribe private capital to behave in certain ways. There were only limited controls on private capital, and certainly no powers to make private capital do anything other than what it perceived to be in its best interests. Where there was formal state control, via nationalisation, things were little better and expansionist plans very soon became translated into uncoordinated plant closures, job cuts and crisis management.

We have argued that ideas of place-specific coalitions and policies are deeply imbued into the consciousness of key decision makers and social actors on Teesside and beyond. In this we have seen politics and political organisations having an important degree of autonomy. The pattern of politics on Teesside, and continuity within it, was very important in explaining how, when the basis of one consensus was eroded a new one emerged. This new coalition has a degree of stability in spite of the fact that its policies stand in marked contrast to the plans and hopes of the 1960s. Significantly, however, the new consensus is much more authoritarian in character, with the interests of labour given at best token representation.

Nevertheless, the spectacular failure of 1960s modernisation policies was not without its effect. One expression of this was deep unrest within formal Labour Party policies within Teesside and one symptom of this was the prominence of Teesside Members of Parliament and politicians in the birth of the Social Democratic Party. At the same time, this helped in opening up space for alternative issues to be put on the local political agenda. For some time, questions had been raised about the environmental impacts resulting from prioritising industrial interests, especially those of the chemicals and steel companies. As long as the promise of jobs (for the boys) and prosperity was still present, such questions were pushed aside. But as unemployment began to rise and the intended employment effects of modernisation policies failed to materialise, such questions could no longer be so easily dismissed. To the voices of local environmental groups were added those of some local councillors and local authority officers, querying whether the environmental costs of jobless – or worse – industrial growth were worth it. To this was also soon added growing concern over the increasing dereliction resulting from industrial decline. Such environmental opposition continued in the 1980s – for example, over dumping nuclear waste in old ICI anhydride mines – and looks set to continue well into the 1990s. So, too, will unemployment.

Cleveland County Council's Unemployment Strategy emerged in recognition of the growth and persistence of unemployment, and the individual problems and social costs associated with it. It is an attempt to work with and for the unemployed, and in this sense it marks a clear and positive political change. But it is important to keep such policy initiatives in perspective. Not least, they begin from an acknowledgement, and indeed explicitly accept, that large-scale, more or less permanent, unemployment is and will remain endemic. They accept that a proportion of the area's population has become permanently surplus to the requirements of employers. In this sense, such policies seek only to address the symptoms and not the root causes of unemployment. It may be that this is, for the foreseeable future, the only realistic policy response to long-term unemployment and associated poverty. In these circumstances, policies that seek to address the needs of the unemployed are certainly better than no policies at all.

There are those, such as Byrne (1990), who see a greater longer term transformational potential in a combination of such radicalised welfare policies and constitutional reform, decentralising some power to elected regional assemblies. In this way, a progressive labourist political culture could be translated into policies which prioritise working-class interests.

Such changes in themselves would certainly improve the lot of the most disadvantaged and offer the opportunity of more democratic decision making. But the history of Teesside makes it difficult to share Byrne's optimism in the historical record of labourism. But even if such optimism proved to be well founded, a regionalist solution leaves untouched – unasked, let alone answered – a number of crucial questions. Of these, the most fundamental is how a regionalist solution would confront multinational capital – as well as a national and emergent supranational state – in such a way as to reconstruct the area's productive base and progressively to transform its social relations of production and reproduction. This latter has been and remains the pivotal issue (see Beynon and Hudson, 1993).

For Teesside, and places like it, actively addressing the needs of most people living there, but in particular those of its most disadvantaged residents, would necessitate going beyond both radical welfarism and a degree of constitutional reform directly to confront questions of power and control over the production and distribution of goods and services. In this, the relationship between private capital and the institutions of central government and local government would need to be examined, as would their relationship to social groupings which make up places like Teesside. After thirty years in which it looked as if the interests of big capital, the state and a majority of working people and their families could be made to seem compatible on Teesside it became clear that this was an illusion. It would be foolish to try to pretend that the old models have not failed. Corporatist solutions, constructed around perceived shared interests, both nationally and locally, now lack credibility. Attempts to persuade private capital to behave in line with the projections of state indicative plans have been a dismal failure. From many points of view nationalisation has proved just as disastrous for places such as Teesside. This is not to argue that public ownership *per se* should be rejected but rather to acknowledge that the particular form adopted – in particular the nationalised industry – ought to be. Rather than becoming a mechanism for more rational industrial planning advancing the interests of the majority of the population of workers and consumers, nationalised industries as state-controlled companies promoted a savage form of restructuring that paid scant regard to the sensitivities of people in their places. Equally, however, to argue that all economic planning – in the *ex-ante* sense of making decisions about the allocation of output ahead of production – is rendered impossible by the deepening of the social divisions of labour to the point where this takes on causal powers independent, and beyond the reach, of the social relations of production (Sayer and Walker, 1992, pp. 224–30) is overly pessimistic. To dismiss all alternatives to an *ex-post* validation of production via the market simply because of the collapse of the command economies of the USSR and its former Eastern European satellite states is to go too far. History in this sense is not yet at an end. There may well be feasible possibilities for more rational economic planning that are sensitive to the specificities of places such as Teesside. Certainly, discovering and constructing them remains a task to be undertaken but that is a very different matter from an *a priori* ruling of such possibilities from the agenda.

The political strategies of the post-war years prioritised the interests of big capital and central government over those of local communities, local people, workers and their families. If the interests of the latter are to be prioritised, then a very major change in political priorities will be required. At a minimum, prioritising the interests of people in their places would involve a much stronger form of planning, and a radical change in the mode of regulation. The flight of capital from the UK precipitated by the removal of exchange controls in 1979 certainly has not made the imposition of control any easier; nor have the more general changes in information technology which have resulted in more-or-less instantaneous flows of money capital around the world. Maybe it is no longer feasible even to think of national, or even supranational, regulatory regimes which would allow effective planning via control of private capital's (dis)investment decisions, let alone the socialisation of key sectors of the economy. If so, it is better, though painful, to recognise this so that people in areas such as Teesside can better understand the sort of future they face and make their choices accordingly.

Having recognised all this it is nevertheless clear that the collapse of the 1960s modernisation consensus did open up space for issues previously debarred from the local political agenda. No longer could slogans such as 'jobs at any price' or 'people not birds' be used to exclude potentially embarrassing topics. As a result, issues as diverse as environmental pollution, gender relations, illness and health, and political accountability (questions relating to the general quality of life *outside* as well as inside the workplace, and for *all* the people) began increasingly to be voiced. While a new consensus did emerge around the Teesside Development Corporation, it clearly failed to command the breadth of support which the preceding consensus attracted. Partly, this reflects the marginalisation of the interests of organised labour within the new arrangements. It also reflects upon their authoritarian and anti-democratic character; and the fact that their central state agency was unelected and non-accountable. This was all the more so since it was abundantly clear that successful implementation of its strategies would lead to increased social and spatial polarisation within Teesside.

All of this led to a much greater critical awareness of the costs and benefits of the new approach. This questioning then stood in marked contrast to the acceptance of the previous modernisation project, predicated upon an assumption that 'they know best'. It also points to the way in which a political machine which could once control dissent was losing its former powers. While there are clear political continuities, in the attitudes and values of the political elites, the political institutions are operating in new circumstances and are beginning, of necessity, to alter their approach to the local population accordingly.

Of course, questions relating to the capacity of the national state to regulate the national economy, to influence the investment decisions of key international companies – decisions of profound significance to Teesside's future – remain. So, too, do those of how people can get by in Teesside – whether via state transfer payments or wages earned through various forms of formal or informal employment. But the re-emergence, albeit as yet tentative, of a local politics no longer strictly circumscribed by the interests of big capital and the self reproduction of the old political machine, offers hope for Teesside's future. It creates a space in which the aspirations and fears of a much wider spectrum of its population can find public expression in political debate.

The old working-class labourist culture was grounded in a politics of production and it is clear that the material basis of this has been increasingly eroded. As yet, however, it is not at all clear what the bases of a new working-class politics would be – nor of how the relationship between a 'working class' and a 'non-working, working class' will compose itself. Equally, questions of how relationships between men and women, between old and young people, will be dealt with remain unanswered. However these relationships are dynamic processes of great importance.

In summary, much is changing, and rapidly, and we need to know more about the rules which govern the process of cultural transformation out of which Teesside is being reconstructed as a place. Locality studies offer one perspective on this process of change, and would be important for this reason alone. They have an important role to play in helping to reveal how people understand and cope with a world which is rapidly changing around them. Knowledge about this – about the ways in which people attend to these problems in their daily lives – is necessary before we can talk easily and prescriptively about politics and strategy. As the pace of change accelerates, as capital moves globally with an increasing rapidity, so too will there be a greater need for locality studies. These accounts of places can provide a basis for understanding how processes of 'globalisation' are made real in everyday life. Such an understanding is a necessary prelude to discussion of how 'localities' can develop better strategies for survival in a global age.

Bibliography

Adcroft, A., Cutler, T., Hasham, C., Williams, J. and Williams, K., 1991, 'Hanson and ICI: The consequences of financial engineering', *Occasional Papers on Business, Economy and Society* No. 2, University of East London.

Allen, J., 1988, 'Geographies of service', in D. Massey and J. Allen, (eds), *Uneven Re-development: Cities and Regions in Transition*, Hodder and Stoughton, London, pp. 124–41

Atkinson, J., 1985, *Flexibility, Uncertainty and Management*, IMS Report No. 89, Institute of Manpower Studies, University of Sussex.

Bank, J. and Jones, K., 1977, *Worker Directors Speak*, Gower, Farnborough.

Bell, F., 1985, *At the Works*, Virago, London (original edn 1907).

Beynon, H., 1984, *Working for Ford*, (2nd edn) Penguin, Harmondsworth.

Beynon, H. (ed.), 1985, *Digging Deeper: Issues in the Miners' Strike*, Verso, London.

Beynon, H. and Austrin, T., 1993a, *Masters and Servants: Class and Patronage in the Making of a Labour Organisation*, Rivers Oram, London.

Beynon, H. and Austrin, T., 1993b, *The Masters Now: The State and the Reconstruction of a Labour Movement*, Rivers Oram, London.

Beynon, H. and Hudson R., 1991, 'Defending Europe's vulnerable cities and regions: some lessons for the 1990s, based on reflections on the localities debates of the 1980s', paper presented to the Conference on Undefended Cities and Regions Facing the New European Order, Lemnos.

Beynon, H. and Hudson, R., 1993, 'Place and space in contemporary Europe: some lessons and reflections', *Antipode* (forthcoming).

Beynon, H., Hudson, R., Lewis, J. R. Sadler, D. and Townsend, A. R., 1985, 'Middlesbrough: contradictions in economic and cultural change', *Middlesbrough Locality Study Working Paper No. 1*, University of Durham, Department of Geography.

Beynon, H., Hudson, R., Lewis, J. R., Sadler, D. and Townsend, A. R., 1989, '"It's all falling apart here": coming to terms with the future in Teesside', in P. Cooke (ed.), *Localities*, Unwin Hyman, London, pp. 267–95.

Beynon, H., Hudson, R. and Sadler, D., 1986a, 'The growth and internationalization of Teesside's chemicals industry', *Middlesbrough Locality Study Working Paper No. 3*, University of Durham, Department of Geography.
Beynon, H., Hudson, R. and Sadler, D., 1986b, 'Nationalised industry policies and the destruction of communities: some evidence from north-east England', *Capital and Class*, 29, 27–57.
Beynon, H., Hudson, R. and Sadler, D., 1991, *A Tale of Two Industries: The Contraction of Coal and Steel in the North East of England*, Open University Press, Milton Keynes.
Beynon, H., and McMylor, P., 1985, 'Decisive power: the new Tory state against the miners', *Digging Deeper*, Verso, London, pp. 29–45.
Bluestone, B. and Harrison, B., 1982, *The Deindustrialisation of America*, Basic Books, New York.
Boulding, P., 1988, *'Re-industrialisation strategies in steel closure areas in the UK'*, unpublished PH.D. thesis, Durham University.
Bowen, P., 1976, *Social Control in Industrial Organisations: A Strategic and Occupational Study of British Steelmaking*, Routledge, London.
Brannen, P., Batstone, E., Fatchett, D. and White, P., 1976, *The Worker Directors*, Hutchinson, London.
Briggs, A., 1963, *Victorian Cities*, Penguin, Harmondsworth.
Brindley, T., Rydin, Y. and Stoker, G., 1989, *Remaking Planning: The Politics of Urban Change in the Thatcher Years*, Allen and Unwin, Hemel Hempstead.
Bulmer, M. (ed)., 1978, *Mining and Social Change*, Croom Helm, London.
Byrne, D., 1990, *Beyond the Inner City*, Open University Press, Milton Keynes.
Centre for Environmental Studies, 1976, *Public Participation in Structure Planning: The Teesside Experience*, London.
Centre for Environmental Studies, 1985, 'Outer Estates in Britain: East Middlesbrough Case Study', *CES Paper No. 26*, London.
Centre for Local Economic Strategies (CLES), 1990, *Urban Regeneration: A Critical Review of Urban Development Corporations*, Manchester.
Chapman, K., 1986, *Chemicals and the Cleveland Economy*, Cleveland County Council.
Clarke, I. M., 1983, 'The changing international division of labour within ICI' in M. J. Taylor, and N. Thrift (eds), *The Geography of Multinationals*, Croom Helm, London, pp. 90–116.
Cleveland County Council, 1975, *The Economic Impact of North Sea Oil in Cleveland*, Middlesbrough.
Cleveland County Council, 1979, *County Structure Plan Re-assessment Programme, Discussion Paper 1: Employment*, Middlesbrough.
Cleveland County Council Planning Department, 1982, *Manufacturing Change in Cleveland since 1965*, Report No. 22, Middlesbrough.
Cleveland County Council Research and Intelligence Unit, 1982, *Areas of Deprivation in Cleveland*, Information Note (July), Middlesbrough.
Cleveland County Council, 1983a, *Why Cleveland is Different: Its Needs and Expenditure*, Middlesbrough.

Cleveland County Council, 1983b, *The Economic and Social Importance of the British Steel Corporation to Cleveland*, Middlesbrough.
Cleveland County Council, 1985a, *Crisis in Cleveland: From Dream to Nightmare*, Middlesbrough.
Cleveland County Council, 1985b, *Manufacturing Employment Change in Cleveland, 1976–81*, Middlesbrough.
Cleveland County Council, 1985c, *Cleveland Structure Plan: Issues Report*, Middlesbrough.
Cleveland County Council, 1987, *Unemployment Strategy*, Middlesbrough.
Cleveland County Council, 1988a, *Gross Domestic Product: A County Analysis 1977–84*, Middlesbrough.
Cleveland County Council, 1988b, *Regional Development Grant Payments in Cleveland 1978–87*, Middlesbrough.
Cleveland County Council, 1989a, *Cleveland Clothing Training Initiative: Final Report*, Middlesbrough.
Cleveland County Council, 1989b, *Findings of an Evaluation of the Tees Corridor Programme*, Middlesbrough.
Coffield, F., Borrill, C., and Marshall, S., 1986, *Growing Up at the Margins: Young Adults in the North East*, Open University Press, Milton Keynes.
Cohen, A., 1982, *Belonging: Identity and Social Organisation in British Rural Cultures*, Manchester University Press, Manchester.
Cooke, P. (ed)., 1989, *Localities: The Changing Face of Urban Britain*, Unwin Hyman, London.
Coulson, A., 1989, *Strategy and Impact of the Teesside Development Corporation*, Cleveland County Council.
Crossman, R., 1977, *The Diaries of a Cabinet Minister, Volume 3*, Book Club Associates, London.
Department of the Environment, 1990, *Enterprise Zone Information* 1987–8, HMSO, London.
Edwards, B., 1946, *Chemicals: Servant or Master? Life or Death?* National Labour Press, London.
Employment Committee, 1988, *The Employment Effects of Urban Development Corporations*, House of Commons Paper 327 (2 vols), 1987/8.
Fayad, M. and Motamen, H., 1986, *The Economics of the Petrochemical Industry*, Frances Pinter, London.
Foord, J., Robinson, F. and Sadler, D., 1985, *The Quiet Revolution: Social and Economic Change on Teesside, 1965–85*, BBC (NE), Newcastle upon Tyne.
Foord, J., Robinson, F. and Sadler, D., 1987, 'Living with economic decline: Teesside in crisis', *Northern Economic Review*, 14, 33–48.
Gertler, M., 1992, 'Flexibility revisited: districts, nation states, and the forces of production', *Transactions, Institute of British Geographers*, ns, 17, 3, 259–79.
Gill, C., Morris, R. and Eaton, J., 1978, *Industrial Relations in the Chemical Industry*, Saxon House, Farnborough.

Gladstone, F., 1976, *The Politics of Planning*, Temple Smith, London.
Glass, R. (ed.), 1948, *The Social Background of a Plan: A Study of Middlesbrough*, Routledge and Kegan Paul, London.
Gleave, J. T., 1938, 'The Teesside iron and steel industry', *Geographical Journal*, 91, 454–67.
Gregory, R., 1975, 'The Cow Green Reservoir', in P. J. Smith (ed.), *The Politics of Physical Resources*, Penguin, Harmondsworth, pp. 144–201.
Hales, M., 1980, *Living Think Work: Where do Labour Processes Come From?* Conference of Social Economists, London.
Hamer, M., 1974, *Wheels within Wheels: A Study of the Road Lobby*, Friends of the Earth, London.
Harvey, D., 1989, *The Condition of Postmodernity*, Blackwell, Oxford.
HMSO, 1963, *The North East: A Programme for Regional Development and Growth*, Cmnd. 2206, London.
HMSO, 1965, *National Plan*, London.
HMSO, 1969, *Teesside Survey and Plan*, London.
HMSO, 1973, *British Steel Corporation: Ten Year Development Strategy*, Cmnd. 5226, London.
HMSO, 1978, *British Steel Corporation: The Road to Viability*, Cmnd. 7149, London.
House, J. W. and Fullerton, B., 1960, *Teesside at Mid-Century*, Macmillan, London.
Hudson, R., 1986, 'Formulating and implementing Local Authority modernisation policies in Teesside since 1964', *Middlesbrough Locality Study Working Paper No. 7*, University of Durham, Department of Geography.
Hudson, R., 1989a, *Wrecking a Region*, Pion, London.
Hudson, R., 1989b, 'Labour market changes and new forms of work in old industrial regions: maybe flexibility for some but not flexible accumulation', *Society and Space*, 7, 5–30.
Hudson, R., 1990a, 'Re-thinking regions: some preliminary considerations on regions and social change', in R. J. Johnston, J. Hauer, and G. A. Hoekveld, (eds), *Regional Geography: Current Developments and Future Prospects*, Routledge, London, pp. 67–84.
Hudson, R., 1990b, 'Trying to revive an infant Hercules: the rise and fall of local authority modernization policies on Teesside', in M. Harloe, C. Pickvance, and J. Urry (eds), *Place, Policy and Politics*, Unwin Hyman, London, pp. 62–86.
Hudson, R., 1992, 'The Japanese, the United Kingdom automobile industry and the automobile industry in the United Kingdom', *Change in the International Automobile Industry: An International Comparison, Discussion Paper No. 9*, University of Durham, Department of Geography.
Hudson, R. and Sadler, D., 1984, *British Steel Builds the New Teesside? The Implications of BSC Policy for Cleveland*, Cleveland County Council, Middlesbrough.
Hudson, R. and Sadler, D., 1985, 'The development of Middlesbrough's

iron and steel industry 1841–1985', *Middlesbrough Locality Study Working Paper No. 2,* University of Durham, Department of Geography.
Hudson, R. and Sadler, D., 1987, *The Uncertain Future of Special Steels,* Sheffield City Council.
Hudson, R. and Sadler D., 1989, *The International Steel Industry: Restructuring State Policies and Localities,* Routledge, London.
Hudson, R. and Williams, A., 1989, *Divided Britain,* Belhaven, London.
Independent on Sunday, 'Voices from another England', 23 August 1992.
Industry and Trade Committee, 1983, *The British Steel Corporation's Prospects,* House of Commons Paper 212, session 1982–83.
Judd, D. and Parkinson, M. (eds), *Leadership and Urban Regeneration,* Sage, London.
Labour Research Department, 1939, *Coal Combines in Durham,* Farleigh, London.
Lapple, D. and van Hoogstraten, P., 1980, 'Remarks on the spatial structure of capitalist development: the case of the Netherlands', in J. Carney, R. Hudson and J. Lewis (eds), *Regions in Crisis,* Croom Helm, London, pp. 117–66.
Leyshon, A. and Thrift, N., 1989, 'South goes north? The rise of the British provincial financial centre', in J. Lewis and A. R. Townsend, (eds), *The North–South Divide: Regional Change in Britain in the 1980s,* Paul Chapman, London, pp. 114–56.
Linn, I., 1986, *Single Union Deals: A Case Study of the Norsk Hydro Plant at Immingham, Humberside,* Northern College, Barnsley.
Lock, M., 1945, *A Plan for Middlesbrough: The Proposals in Outline,* Text of an Address to Middlesbrough County Borough Council.
Lock, M., 1946, *The County Borough of Middlesbrough: Survey and Plan,* Middlesbrough.
Lukes, S., 1974, *Power: a radical view,* Macmillan, London.
Lumb, R., 1976, 'Planning and participatory democracy: a case study of Yarm', *Working Papers in Social Anthropology, No. 2,* University of Durham, pp. 70–133.
Lynch, D., 1976, 'Planning and participation: democracy in a district of Middlesbrough', *Working Papers in Social Anthropology No. 2,* University of Durham, pp. 6–69.
MacDonald, R., 1991, 'Runners, fallers and plodders: youth and the enterprise culture', Paper Presented to the 1991 National Small Firms Conference, Blackpool.
Marriott, O., 1967, *The Property Boom,* Pan, London.
Massey, D., 1991, 'The political place of locality studies', *Environment and Planning A,* 23, 267–81.
Massey, D., 1984, *Spatial Divisions of Labour: Social Structures and the Geography of Production,* Macmillan, London.
McEachern, D., 1979, 'Party government and the class interest of capital: conflict over the steel industry 1945–70', *Capital and Class,* 8, 125–43.
McEachern, D., 1980, *A Class Against Itself: Power and the Nationalisation of the British Steel Industry,* Cambridge University Press, Cambridge.

Monopolies and Mergers Commission, 1991, *Kemira Oy and Imperial Chemical Industries PLC: A Report on the Proposed Merger*, Cmnd. 1406, London.

Morris, L. 1986, 'The changing social structure of Hartlepool', in P. Cooke (ed.), *Global Restructuring, Local Response*, Economic and Social Research Council, London, pp. 147–57.

Nicholas, K., 1986, *The Social Effects of Unemployment in Teesside, 1919–39*, Manchester University Press, Manchester.

Nichols, T. and Beynon, H. 1977, *Living with Capitalism: Class Relations and the Modern Factory*, Routledge and Kegan Paul, London.

North, G. A., 1975, *Teesside's Economic Heritage*, Cleveland County Council, Middlesbrough.

North of England Development Council, 1975, *Barclaycard on the Move*, Newcastle upon Tyne.

Northern Economic Planning Council (NEPC), 1969 *Regional Ports Survey*, NEPC, Newcastle Upon Tyne.

OECD, 1985, *Petrochemical Industry: Energy Aspects of Structural Change*, OECD, Paris.

Pearson, M., 1992, 'Health', in P. Cloke, (ed.), *Policy and Change in Thatcher's Britain*, Pergamon, Oxford, pp. 215–46.

Pepler, G. and MacFarlane, P. W., 1949, *North East Development Area Outline Plan*, Ministry of Town and Country Planning: Interim Confidential Edition.

Peppin, T., 1990, *'Restructuring of the Demand for Labour: A Study of Labour Market Adjustment Mechanisms in Stockton-on-Tees'*, unpublished PH.D. thesis, Durham University.

Pettigrew, A., 1985, *The Awakening Giant: Continuity and Change in ICI*, Blackwell, Oxford.

Phillimore, P. R. and Morris, D., 1991, 'Discrepant legacies: premature mortality in two industrial towns', *Social Science and Medicine*, 33, 2, 139–52.

Priestley, J. B., 1934, *English Journey*, Heinemann, London.

Reader, W. J., 1970, 1975, *Imperial Chemical Industries: A History* (2 vols), Oxford University Press, London.

Robinson, F. and Storey, D., 1981, 'Employment change in manufacturing industry in Cleveland, 1965–76', *Regional Studies*, 15, 161–72.

Roeber, J., 1975, *Social Change at Work: the ICI Weekly Staff Agreement*, Duckworth, London.

Ross, G. W., 1965, *The Nationalisation of Steel: One Step Forward, Two Steps Back?*, Macgibbon and Kee, London.

Sadler, D., 1986, 'The impacts of offshore fabrication in Teesside', *Middlesbrough Locality Study Working Paper No. 5*, University of Durham, Department of Geography.

Sadler, D., 1990a, 'Privatising British Steel: the politics of production and place', *Area*, 22, 47–55.

Sadler, D., 1990b, 'The social foundations of planning and the power of capital: Teesside in historical context', *Environment and Planning D:*

Society and Space 8, 323–38.
Sadler, D., 1992, *The Global Region*, Pergamon, Oxford.
Sayer, A. and Walker, R., 1992, *The New Social Economy*, Blackwell, Oxford.
Semmens, P., 1970, 'Chemicals', in J. C. Dewdney (ed.), *Durham City and County with Teesside*, British Association for the Advancement of Science, Durham, pp. 330–40.
Stacey, M. 1969, 'The myth of community studies', *British Journal of Sociology*, 20, (2), 134–47.
Storper, M. and Scott, A. J., 1989, 'The geographical foundation and social regulation of flexible production complexes', in J. Wolch, and M. Dear, (eds), *The Power of Geography*, Unwin Hyman, London, pp. 21–40.
Teesside County Borough Council, 1972, *Teesside Structure Plan: Report of Survey*, Middlesbrough.
Teesside County Borough Council, 1973, *Teesside Structure Plan: Draft Document for Participation and Consultation*, Middlesbrough.
Teesside Industrial Development Board, 1948, *Report on the Progress of Industrial Development in Teesside and Cleveland*, Middlesbrough.
Teesside Industrial Development Board, 1949, *Housing Survey*, Middlesbrough.
Tooley, M. J. and Jelgersma, S., 'The future of the European coastal lowlands', in M. J. Tooley and S. Jelgersma, (eds), *The Impacts of Sea-Level Rise on European Coastal Lowlands*, Blackwell, Oxford, pp. 218–50.
Townsend, A. R., 1987, 'Rationalization and change in South Teesside's health service', *Middlesbrough Locality Study Working Paper No. 4*, University of Durham, Department of Geography.
Townsend, P., Phillimore, P. and Beattie, A., 1988, *Health and Deprivation: Inequality and the North*, Croom Helm, Beckenham.
Warren, K., 1980, *Chemical Foundations: The Alkali Industry in Britain to 1926*, Clarendon, Oxford.
Wood, A. H., 1983, 1987, 1992, *The Times Guide to the House of Commons*, Times Books, London.

Index